SMART

WOMEN

FINISH

RICH

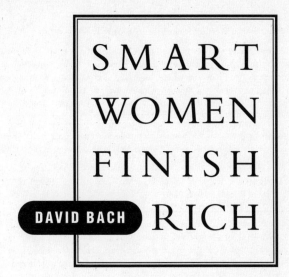

SMART WOMEN FINISH RICH

DAVID BACH

7 STEPS TO ACHIEVING FINANCIAL SECURITY

AND FUNDING YOUR DREAMS

BROADWAY BOOKS   NEW YORK

BROADWAY

A hardcover edition of this book was published in 1999 by Broadway Books.

First trade paperback edition published 1999.

Designed by Songhee Kim

The Library of Congress has cataloged the hardcover edition as:
Bach, David.
  Smart women finish rich: 7 steps to achieving financial security and funding your dreams / by David Bach.
    p.   cm.
  Includes index.
  ISBN 0-7679-0242-4 (hardcover)
  1. Women—Finance, Personal.   2. Investments.   3. Financial security.   I. Title.
HG179.B24   1999
332.024′042—dc21   98-26769
                                                                      CIP

The diagram on page 173 is reprinted with the permission of Successful Money Management Seminars, Inc.

ISBN 0-7679-0243-2 (paperback)

01   02   03   20   19   18

To my beloved grandmother Rose Bach,
who taught me the importance of living life to its fullest.
You will forever be with me in thought and spirit.
I miss you.

Contents

Acknowledgments

My Grandmother Bach once told me that the key to having a fulfilling life was to understand that life's greatest fruit was always at the end of the branch and that you had to be willing to fall out of the tree to get it. The key, I was told, was to have people around you who could catch you should you fall. I have been blessed to have an incredible group of people around me as I go about taking risks to grab the fruit of life. Only because of these people who have supported me am I where I am today.

First and foremost, I owe an incredible amount of thanks to my superstar agent, Jan Miller. You are without question a "Go-to gal," and I am forever grateful for our new friendship and your belief in me and my vision. You make things happen, and I love it! To Jan's support team—Joy Donsky, Lisa Rich, and Shannon Miser-Marven—thank you for all your help with this book; we could not have done it without you.

To Allan Mayer, my collaborator on this project—thank you, thank you, thank you for making this book what it is. You have been from the beginning to the end a true professional and a delight to work with. Thanks for keeping me grounded and sane as we neared the deadline.

To Vicki St. George, thank you for being the angel who tapped me on the shoulder at "Date with Destiny" and told me you could help me make my dream come true. It is because of your help on my book proposal that I was able to have my pick of agents. I will be forever grateful to you and your partner, Karen Risch, at Just Write for being the first experts to believe in and see my vision.

To my incredible team at Broadway Books, I loved you guys from the minute I met you. To my editor, Suzanne Oaks, you are absolutely amazing. Your insight and ideas on this book have been invaluable. I only hope this is the first of many projects that we work on together. To your assistant, Ann Campbell, thank you for keeping me on track and on time; you are great. To Trigg Robinson and David Drake, thank you for the book tour of all book tours. To Bill Shinker, thank you for building such a powerhouse team at Broadway. I am grateful for your interest and belief in me and this book.

Thank you goes to my world class support team back in the office at The Bach Group. To Adam Ezrilov, Kathy Price, Emilie Paisley, Carla Johnson, Carrie Farina, Judy Taggart, Lindsey Noss and Brian Lewis, Emily Bach, and my father, Marty Bach—thank you for keeping the office running so smoothly and our clients happy. Thank you also for understanding my stress and mood changes as I worked on this project and tried to cram six-day work weeks into three days. You are the finest team players a guy could ask for, and I am thankful for your support, friendship, and daily commitment to being the best.

To my many mentors, I owe both thanks and recognition. To my teacher and mentor Anthony Robbins, your friendship, teaching, and seminars have shaped my life since 1990, and for that I am eternally grateful. To Bill Bachrach, your book *Values-Based Financial Planning,* your TAC program, and your friendship have changed my life forever. Thank you for teaching me how to help others tap into their values about money. To Dan Sullivan, your "Strategic Coach" program already has had a major impact on both my life and my teachings. Thank you for showing me the power of focus and simplicity.

To my publicity team at the Ford Group—Arielle Ford, you are the best, and I can't wait to celebrate our future successes together.

To my good friend Jeff Odiorne, who suggested over dinner, "Why don't you just take a day off work each week and write your book?" God, that was obvious. Thanks for coming up with it! To my close friends who have both listened to me talk about this book and supported me emotionally throughout the process, I thank you for your love and friendship. To Guy Sengstock, my personal trainer: No one listened to me talk about this book more than you. Thank you for keeping me in shape and upbeat.

To my many clients and students with whom I have grown and from whom I have learned along the way, thank you for allowing me to make a wonderful living doing something I love.

Thank you to all of the people that provided me with valuable insight and feedback on this book. In particular, special thanks goes out to Eric Peterson of Hicks Pension Services, Sue Varenchik of GE Capital Assurance, and Shela Camenisch, attorney-at-law.

To my incredible mother, Bobbi Bach, thank you for raising me to believe I could accomplish anything. You gave me the greatest gift a mother could give, the gift of love, security, and confidence.

To my successful sister, Emily Bach, you epitomize today's Smart Woman who is living smart and finishing rich. I am very proud of you.

To my father, Marty Bach, I never realized how much work it took to get to the level of success you have achieved. Now I do. You always have been there for me, and I love you for it. Thank you for brainwashing me into the investment business and supporting me in everything I've done. This book would not have been possible without your support.

And finally to my new wife, Michelle: You are without question the most wonderful woman I have ever met. Thank you for your fantastic input on this book, for always bringing a smile to my face, and for being my safe island in the storm. The value you add to my life is immeasurable.

I love you all with all my heart.

David Louis Bach
San Francisco, California, 1998

WHY SMART WOMEN ARE TAKING CONTROL OF THEIR FINANCIAL FUTURES

I'll never forget the moment I asked my mom, "What really makes the world go round—money or love?" I was only about five at the time. She looked me straight in the eyes and said, "David, love is what makes life special . . . but without money you are in deep trouble!"

Actually, "deep trouble" are my words. What my mom really said can't be repeated. I had never heard my mom use an "adult" swear word before, so even at age five I knew then and there that not having money could be really painful. The obvious next question that came to my five-year-old mind was "Are we rich, Mom?" That question took a little longer for her to answer (I think she eventually made me go play with my toys), but the thought of money has stayed with me ever since. If not having money is so bad, why don't more people figure out how to get and keep it? It can't be that hard. Or can it?

More than 25 years later, I'm privileged to make my living teaching thousands of people—mostly women—how to invest and manage their money. And I'm happy to report that when you strip away all the baloney, learning how to handle your own finances turns out to be relatively easy. Indeed, through my "Smart Women Finish Rich!" seminars, I've already helped thousands of women travel the same road to financial independence you are going to take in this book. They have learned—as you will—the three keys to smart money management

that enable a woman to gain control over her own financial destiny
. . . and, yes, finish rich:

- How to use both your head and your heart in making
  financial decisions.
- How what I call "the latté factor" can transform even the
  most modest wage earner into a significant investor.
- How my "three-basket" approach to financial planning
  can assure you not only long-term security but the ability
  to realize your lifelong dreams.

As you will discover, my approach to personal money management
involves some powerful and exciting techniques. And all of them are
pretty easy to master. Before we get started, however, it might be a
good idea for me to address a question that often comes up at this
point—namely . . .

WHO AM I TO HELP YOU FINISH RICH?

One way to answer this question is to tell you that I am a Senior Vice
President and financial advisor for a major New York Stock Exchange-
based firm, and work in Orinda, California, where I am a partner of
The Bach Group, which manages over half a billion dollars of people's
money. Most of my hundreds of clients are women who have come to
me after attending one of my investment seminars or through referrals
from other women.

But what you probably really want to know is why a man (and yes,
I admit it—I can't hide the fact that I am a man) is so driven to teach
and empower women to take control of their finances.

Well, the answer has mainly to do with my grandmother. Her name
was Rose Bach, and she was unlike any other grandmother I ever met.

My Grandma, the Investor

The head buyer for wigs at Gimbel's (back when Gimbel's was one of
America's leading department stores), Grandma Bach was a working

woman at a time when most women weren't. Now, my grandparents were never wealthy; in fact, they never even owned their own home. Nonetheless, my grandmother decided at a very early age that she wanted to be an investor. Acting on her own, she took her earnings and put as much as she could afford into stocks and bonds. Over time, and without any advice from her husband, she built up a high-quality portfolio. When she passed away recently, at the age of 86, her investments were worth close to $1 million—this, from a woman whose first job paid only $10 a week!

There were many things my Grandma Bach taught me, but for our purposes, there's one lesson that deserves to be singled out:

You don't have to be rich to be an investor!

Of course, by becoming an investor, if you do it wisely like my Grandma Bach, you will almost certainly get rich!

It was Grandma Bach who helped me make my first stock purchase. I was seven years old, and my favorite restaurant in the world was McDonald's. So whenever I spent time with my grandmother, she would take me there for lunch. One day, at her prompting, instead of asking for catsup for my fries when I marched up to the counter, I looked at the woman on the other side and asked, "Is this company public?"

The counter lady looked back at me as if I were nuts, then called over the manager. Yes, he told me, McDonald's was a publicly traded company. After a little persuasion from Grandma Bach (and a lot of vacuuming and dishwashing), I saved my allowance for three months and managed to accumulate enough money to buy three shares of McDonald's Inc.

That was 23 years ago. Since then McDonald's stock has gone up in value and split so many times that those original three shares of mine have multiplied into close to 200 shares. If I'd had enough money to purchase 100 shares of the company back then (an investment of around $10,000 at the time), my McDonald's holdings would today be worth close to $500,000! (I often give my parents a hard time for not having loaned me the additional money.) And all I had done was go out to lunch with my grandmother when I was a little kid and put my allowance into a company whose hamburgers I liked.

Every Woman Can Be Wealthy

Because Grandma Bach was my biggest inspiration as a child, I grew up thinking every woman was like her—aware of the importance of investing and pretty darn good at it too. So it came as something of a shock to me, when I followed my father into the investment business, to discover that, if anything, the opposite was true. Most women never receive even a basic education in finance until it's too late—which is to say, after they get divorced or widowed and suddenly find themselves forced to deal with everything at the worst possible moment. The result, all too often, is financial devastation.

I wanted to help. I wanted every woman to have the information, the education, and the tools to take care of herself financially no matter what the circumstances. So I designed an investment seminar called "Smart Women Finish Rich!" in which I did two important things. One, I addressed the heart as well as the head, recognizing that financial planning is as much an emotional issue as it is an intellectual one. And two, I laid out a simple but effective pathway that any woman could follow to achieve financial security and freedom.

The response was immediate and incredible. First dozens, then hundreds of women signed up for my classes, and over the last few years I've conducted this seminar for thousands of women throughout the country. Why the huge response? In a word, necessity. As one student told me, "Growing up, no one taught me about money, not my father, not my mother, not my school—so I realized it was time to teach myself." Explained another student: "Nobody is going to take care of me. I have to take the responsibility myself." Added a third: "We'd be in deep trouble if we left everything up to our husbands. We need to know about our finances so we can be independent and take care of ourselves."

Though my students come from all walks of life—rich, poor, old, young, married, single—virtually all of them believe in the empowering importance of education. As a working mother of two from Walnut Creek, California, put it after taking my course, "Understanding your own finances is as important as knowing about your health. You can't make financial decisions if you're not educated."

What *I've* learned from my seminars is that women *want* to be responsible for their financial futures. The problem is, most of them just don't know how to get started. Or if they've taken steps in certain areas, they've neglected others. I can't tell you how gratifying it's been for me to see the thousands of women who've been through my seminars taking control of their financial destiny, making better decisions about their financial future, and feeling great about their financial well-being as a result.

WELCOME TO THE CLUB!

And now you are going to join their ranks.

Congratulations are in order, for you've just taken a very important step to achieving financial security and independence. The fact that you've picked up this book shows that you've decided to take control of your financial future. You may not believe it, but in making that decision and acting on it, you've just completed the hardest part of the process.

Congratulations too because your timing couldn't have been better. The fact is, there's never been a better time in the entire history of the planet for women to be taking control of their financial futures. These days not only are women pursuing successful careers, but in many cases it's the woman's paycheck that supports the family. (Indeed, seven out of every ten personal checks written in America are signed by women.) In all, working women currently earn more than $1 trillion a year and account for upwards of 52 percent of all earned household income in this country. There are currently nearly 8 million female-owned businesses in America, generating more than $2.3 *trillion* in annual revenues. What's more, according to the National Foundation for Women Business Owners, women are starting new companies at *twice* the rate of men. Women employ more people than the 500 largest industrial firms in America combined, and within the next few years they will own a majority of the nation's small businesses.

Something Men May Not Want to Hear . . .

Having worked as a financial planner and advisor with literally thousands of women over the past few years, there's something else I can tell you about women and money: As a rule, women make better investors than men. When women become investors, they generally devise a plan, and then they stick to it. In a word, they "commit." Men, on the other hand . . . well, we've all heard that dreaded phrase "fear of commitment," haven't we? Rather than stay with a great, solid investment, men often get bored and start looking around for the next "hot thing."

My experience is that women simply do not do this. As a rule, women who invest tend to be wary of so-called hot tips. Not many men. Time after time I have had male clients phone me with orders to buy 1,000 shares of stock merely because they heard a "hot tip" at the gym or on the golf course. Often these requests to make a stock purchase involve no research, just brazen bravado.

And this is not just my opinion. The statistics bear me out. In 1996 women's investment clubs outperformed their male counterparts by a wide margin, earning an average return of more than 21 percent, vs. just 15 percent for the men. Just a fluke, you say? Well, according to National Association of Investors Corporation, women's investment clubs have outperformed men's in *9 out of the last 12 years*!

Do you find that surprising? Many of us do. That's because we've unthinkingly accepted the stereotype that money management is a man's "game"—one that women simply aren't suited to play. Why? It may have something to do with the fact that most of us grew up watching our fathers manage the family money. Certainly, many women have told me that was the reason it never dawned on them to take an active role in shaping their own financial futures. Whatever the cause, however, far too many women decide early on that when it comes to money, they'd prefer to stay on the sidelines. They say things like "Well, I'm not good with money," or "I'm not driven by money," or "I'm not materialistic," or "Money doesn't make you happy," or "Why bother—the more you make, the more the government will take," and on and on, trying to justify their fear of dealing with their financial situation.

A "Game" You Can't Sit Out

I think that is a mistake. As a woman today, you've got to stop watching and start participating. Even more important, you've got to start calling the shots for yourself. There's no getting around it: This so-called money game (a misnomer if ever there was one) has very real, very serious consequences for all of us. People who say they've decided not to play the money game are only fooling themselves. After all, how we handle our money colors every aspect of our lives—the education of our children, the sort of home we provide our families, the type of contribution we make to our communities (not to mention all those mundane things like the kind of food we eat, the clothing we wear, and the vacations we take).

The fact is, none of us really has a choice: We are all playing the money game whether we want to or not. The only question is: Are we winning?

Most people, unfortunately, are not. Why? Because no one ever taught them the rules. Think about it. How could you possibly ever win a game—or even do well at it—if you didn't know the rules? You couldn't. Maybe every once in a while you'd luck out—but that's all it would be: luck. You couldn't depend on it; you certainly wouldn't want to risk your bank account, your retirement income, or your dream of a brand-new house on it.

So what we need in order to take control of our financial destiny is a copy of the rules. An instruction manual. A road map.

More Good News for Women

That's what this book is: It's a financial road map that will show you how to get from where you are right now to where you want to be. The good news here is that women tend to be pretty good about using road maps. Certainly they're better than most men. Men generally prefer to drive around aimlessly, hoping to spot a familiar landmark, rather than admit they're lost and ask someone for directions. You know what I'm talking about. I'm sure you were once out on a date, or maybe you were in the car with your husband or your father, and suddenly you realized you had been driving for what seemed like an awfully long time with no sign of the Wayne's Kountry Kitchen you were looking for. The conversation probably went something like this.

YOU: Honey, I think we're lost. Maybe we should stop in a gas station or something . . .

> HIM: No, we're fine. I know exactly where we are.
> YOU: But . . .
> HIM: I *said* we're fine. It's just a ways up here—I'm sure of it.

Of course, what each of you was thinking at the time was something else again.

> YOU: He doesn't have a clue where we are. If he'd just pull over and get some directions, we could figure this out and get there!
> HIM: I can't believe we're lost! I thought I knew the way. Jeez, where *are* we? I probably should stop and ask for directions, but if I do that, she'll know I don't know where we are, and so will some stranger. How much of a loser would *that* make me!

The same thing tends to happen with our money. As a rule, men feel they are supposed to know what they're doing when it comes to personal finance, so even when they don't, they often pretend that they do and resist asking for help. As a result, many men wind up making wrong turns onto bumpy back roads that wind up stranding them (and you) 100 miles from Wayne's Kountry Kitchen.

Women, on the other hand, have relatively few hangups about admitting it when they don't know something. That's why they can make better investors than men. It's because they don't have any trouble with the idea that they have to have an education in order to be successful. Women are comfortable not only learning and studying but also asking questions—and by asking questions, of course, they learn more. I see this in my investment seminars all the time. When women take the classes, they study, read, and ask questions. Their goal is to become educated—to learn the techniques of managing their own finances. It's not to prove to everyone else in the class that they're smarter than the instructor. (That role invariably goes to some guy sitting in the back of the room who thinks he has all the answers—but whose money is still sitting in a savings account earning a measly 2 percent interest.)

IT'S TIME FOR YOU TO TAKE CHARGE

The basic premise of this book is simple. I believe in my heart and soul that no matter what your age, status, or situation—whether you're in your 20s or your 80s; whether you're single, married, divorced, or widowed; whether you're a career woman or a homemaker—you as a woman are more than capable of taking charge of your finances and your financial future. All that's required is that you be given the right tools—which is where this book comes in.

A Journey That Will Change Your Life

In the pages that follow, what we are going to do is embark on a journey—a seven-step journey that begins with education and ends with your taking action. By the time it's done, you will have learned the fundamental principles of personal financial management—principles you can use to turn your dreams of freedom, security, and independence into concrete realities.

As you will see, the seven steps that make up our journey to financial security and independence cover a considerable amount of ground. At the same time, however, they are individually quite easy. They are so easy, in fact, that not only will you be able to use them to change your life, you also will be in a position to teach them to the people you care about so they can achieve the same kind of success you have.

Specifically, our seven steps consists of a series of easy-to-understand, practical strategies for taking control of your financial future—specific strategies you can begin implementing before you've even finished reading. As you make your way through them, you'll learn not only what your options are, but which options might be best for you—and how to design a customized course of action tailored to your own particular situation.

In the first leg of our journey, you'll find out what you don't know—but should—about your own personal and family financial situation. After that, you'll learn how to identify your own deep-seated attitudes toward money, how to define the personal values those attitudes reflect, and how to create realistic financial goals based on those values. Once you know where you want to go, you'll be shown exactly what you need to do to get organized and how you can start building a nest egg on even the most modest income (just like my Grandma Bach did). This last point is especially important, since so many women seem to think that investing and financial planning make sense only for people with high incomes and lots of money. As you'll see by the time we're finished, it's not how much you make that counts, it's how much you keep!

Finally, our program will lay out a series of simple yet powerful strategies designed to provide you with: (1) an effective plan for long-term security, (2) financial protection against the unexpected, and (3) the ability to build the kind of life you've always dreamed about. Along the way, it will explain everything you need to know about tax planning, wills, insurance, the stock market (including the nine big mistakes most investors make), retirement planning, how to buy a house, and how to hire a financial advisor.

In the end, whether you earn $25,000 a year or $25,000 a month, our seven-step journey will dramatically change the way you think about money—and by doing that, it will change your life.

Become One of the Financial Elite

Individually, each of the seven steps in our journey is as powerful as it is simple. Indeed, as I suggest to the women who attend my seminars, if you manage to learn and apply just two or three of the seven steps, I am confident you will wind up in better financial shape than 90 percent of the people in the country. If you do four or five of the steps, I believe you will find yourself in the top 5 percent of the population—financially better off than 95 percent of Americans. And if you do all seven of the steps, I believe you can elevate yourself to the nation's financial elite—the top 1 percent of the population. What's more, you'll be able to bring your family and loved ones along with you.

And as you acquire the tools you'll need to control your economic destiny, our seven-step program also will help you learn to become comfortable with the idea of taking financial responsibility for yourself. This is a key point, for the psychological and emotional aspects of financial planning are enormously important. Yet, for some reason, most approaches to the subject ignore them.

The fact is, of course, that nothing brings out emotion like the topic of money. (According to marriage counselors, it is the leading cause of divorce.) Needless to say, everyone attaches different emotions to the issues of saving and investing. Some people save to create security and provide for their families; others spend to feel free or experience adventure. Whatever the case may be, the emotions we attach to money often determine whether we will live our lives in comfort or poverty. Yet people rarely know what is truly driving them emotionally when it comes to money.

The Bag-Lady Syndrome

Among women, the impact of emotion on their financial lives shows up clearly in what experts call "the bag-lady syndrome," in which women who are materially well off still find themselves living in daily fear of going broke and being forced to live on the street. I can't tell you the number of female clients of mine with investment portfolios worth literally millions of dollars who have sat in my office and asked me, "David, if the market goes down, will I be a bag lady?"

This sort of worry may be baseless, but it is real, and it can't just be dismissed. By showing you how to understand the emotional and psychological needs that affect the way we all think about money, the program in this book will teach you how to overcome the fears that often lead to financial paralysis and, worse, shortsighted decision making. Equally important, you'll learn how to create a meaningful agenda from which you can design a long-term financial plan that will truly reflect what you are really looking for in life.

HOW BEST TO USE THIS BOOK

Before we begin in earnest, I want to give you some tips on how to read this book. First, please think of this book as a tool. As I put it earlier, it's a kind of road map—your personal road map to a successful financial future. At the same time, I'd like you to think of me as your "money coach," a new friend who can offer some helpful advice on how you can get to where you want to go.

You also should understand that each of the seven steps that make up this book can be followed separately or in conjunction with the others. My recommendation is that you go through them in order, reading each chapter at least twice before you move on to the next one. Why? Because repetition is the secret of all skill, and when we read something for the first time, we don't always catch it all or retain as much as we may like.

Another suggestion: As we progress on our journey together, and as you learn lots of new things about handling money, don't get bogged down by all the stuff you suddenly feel you should have done years ago but didn't. If I bring up something you didn't know or wish you had known sooner, don't get down about it. What you are *not* doing right now is not the issue. The issue is what you *will* be doing with your newfound knowledge once you finish reading this book.

With that in mind, I'd like to share a quick story with you about a young woman who attended one of my seminars.

It's Never Too Late . . . or Too Early!

Lauren stood up in the class looking a little depressed. "David," she said, "I think I'm the youngest woman here and I'm not sure I belong here, but I know I need to get started planning for retirement and I don't know what to do."

As I scanned the class, I realized Lauren was right about one thing. She probably was the youngest of 100 or so women in the room. I smiled at her, then turned to her classmates and asked, "How many of you ladies here wish now that you had taken a class like this 20 years ago?"

Every hand in the room went up. I looked back at Lauren. "It looks to me," I said, "like you're in the right room at the right time."

A few weeks later Lauren came into my office. It turned out she was 28, college-educated, and was pursuing a career in management consulting. Like many women her age, however, Lauren was not taking advantage of her retirement plan. In fact, even though she was earning more than $50,000 a year, she was living paycheck to paycheck.

Employing the same techniques that I will show you in this book, I showed Lauren how she could get her spending under control immediately and start "maxing out" her contributions to her retirement plan. As a result, less than three years later, Lauren now has more than $20,000 in her retirement account, and at the rate she is saving, she could easily have $2 million to her name by the time she reaches her late 50s! Even more exciting, by using the tools you will learn in this book, Lauren got herself a new job and has doubled her income! Today, at age 31, she is totally in charge of her money and has a brilliant new career that pays her what she is worth.

Now, I'm not going to take credit for all of this. Lauren deserves most of the credit. She attended the class, took the advice, and (most important) acted on it.

And you can too!

Remember, this book is about moving forward and taking control of your life, not giving yourself a hard time for what you didn't know before you picked it up.

Finally, this book is meant to be fun. Enjoy yourself. You are about to embark on an exciting journey to the new "you"—a woman in control of her destiny who has learned how to take charge of her own financial future.

Let's get started!

LEARN THE FACTS—AND MYTHS—ABOUT YOUR MONEY

Wendy sat in my office, perched on the edge of her chair, alert, inquisitive, and a little bit embarrassed. An experienced and highly successful real-estate agent, she had come to me for a financial consultation—and the facts of her situation were hardly reassuring. Although she earned well over $250,000 a year and was able to put two kids through private school at an annual cost of $15,000 each, her personal finances were a mess. A self-employed single parent, she had less than $25,000 saved for retirement, no life or disability insurance, and never bothered to write a will.

In short, this intelligent, ambitious businesswoman was completely unprotected from the unexpected and utterly unprepared for the future. When I asked Wendy why she had never done any financial planning, she shrugged and offered a response I'd heard countless times before: "I've always been too busy working to focus on what to do with the money I make."

Looking across the restaurant table, I could see the sadness in my mother's eyes. A good friend of hers had just gone through a bitter divorce. Suddenly, after more than three decades of marriage to a wealthy surgeon, the friend now found herself living in a tiny apartment, struggling to make ends meet as a $25,000-a-year secretary. Like many formerly well-off women, she had never paid much attention to her family's finances, and as a result her estranged husband was able to run rings around her in the settlement talks. It was a terrible thing—all the more so because it could have been prevented so easily—and it made me *wonder if my mother was similarly in the dark. So I asked her. "Mom," I said, "do you know where the family money is?"*

I thought it would be an easy question. After all, my father was a successful financial consultant and stockbroker who taught investment classes three nights a week. My mother had to be up to speed on the family finances.

At first, however, she didn't reply. Then she squirmed slightly in her chair. "Of course I know where our money is," she finally said. "Your father manages it."

"But where is it? Do you know where he's got it invested?"

"Well, no, I don't. Your father handles all that."

"But don't you have your own accounts, your own line of credit?"

My mother laughed. "David," she said, "what do I need a line of credit for? I have the best bank in the world—your father."

The reason I've started our journey with these two stories is that I know you are a very special woman—the kind of woman who believes in herself. Specifically, you believe that you possess the abilities and the intelligence to have the kind of life you feel you deserve. (If you didn't, you would have never picked up this book in the first place.) You also believe—correctly—that money is important and that you need to learn more about accumulating and protecting it. Finally, I know that you are someone who recognizes that it takes more than a single burst of enthusiasm to improve yourself and develop new skills; it also takes commitment and education.

That is why the first step of our journey is all about getting motivated to educate yourself now and on an ongoing basis about your money and the role it plays in your life. I believe that no matter what your current situation is—whether you are already wealthy or living paycheck to paycheck—a little education combined with motivated action can go a long, long way.

I also know from working with thousands of women that, sadly, neither Wendy the real-estate agent nor my mother are at all unusual. Yes, women have long owned nearly half of the financial assets in this country. Yes, most women work and nearly half of them are their family's main income earner. Yes, the statistics about divorce and widowhood are appalling. Yet, despite all this, the sad fact is that shockingly few women know even a fraction of what they should about the state of their own personal and family finances.

By the same token, very few people know all of the fundamental principles about money that you are about to learn. And most important, even when they think they do, they rarely follow the principles on a consistent basis. This last point is a key one, for as you will discover in the course of our journey, it is not what we learn that makes a difference in our lives but what we do with what we learn.

THE FACTS AND MYTHS
ABOUT YOU AND YOUR MONEY

What we're going to do in this chapter is familiarize you with what I call the financial facts of life. By the time you have taken in all the facts, you will understand fully why it's essential that you take charge of your own financial future. Moreover, you will be totally motivated to get started learning how to do it.

The first fact of financial life to understand is that while planning ahead is important for everyone, it's more important for women. Indeed, though in many ways we live in an age of equality, there is no question that . . .

Fair or not, women need to do more financial planning than men.

As I said in the introduction, compared to previous eras, this is a great time for you to be a woman. In terms of opportunities and resources, you couldn't have picked a better time to begin a journey to a secure financial future. And it's more than just a matter of economics. Because of advances in both technology and public attitudes, women are not only living longer than ever before, they are active longer. In my seminars, I often joke that today's 80-year-old women are drinking "green juice" and doing aerobics every morning. I know my Grandma Bach was like that. Up to the age of 86, she hiked five miles a day and went dancing three nights a week! In her mid-80s, my grandmother enjoyed a life that was more active, socially and physically, than mine was at 30!

But if the good news is that we live in an age in which the barriers that held women back for so long seem finally to be falling, the bad news is that there are still many obstacles to be overcome. For one thing . . .

Women still typically earn 25 percent less than men.

For another, women are less likely to have a steady income stream over the course of their lifetimes. In some cases, that's due to discrimination, but it's also due to the fact that responsibilities such as child rearing and caring for elderly parents cause women to move in and out of the workforce a lot more than men do. In all, over their working lifetimes, women spend a total of $11^1/_2$ years off the job on average, versus only 16 months for men.

What's more, according to a recent study by the U.S. Department of Labor . . .

Women are the ones hurt most by corporate downsizing.

That's because it takes women longer to find new work, and the replacement jobs women get are often part-time posts that offer less pay and fewer benefits.

As a result of all this, your accumulated pension benefits probably are going to be lower than those of your male counterparts—that is, if you have a pension at all. While half of all men get one . . .

Only about one woman in five over the age of 65 receives a pension.

But it's not simply that as a woman you'll have fewer benefits to look forward to. It's also that, as a woman, you'll have to make them go further. Specifically, you probably are going to live longer than most of your male counterparts (by an average of about seven years, according to the National Center for Health), which means that you are going to need even more retirement resources than they will. And not just for yourself. Because of your longer life expectancy, chances are that the financial burden of caring for elderly parents will fall on your shoulders.

What All This Adds Up to Is One Big Ouch!

This, in a nutshell, is why long-term financial planning is more important for women. Compared to men, you've got to be more farsighted, start saving earlier, and stick to your plans with more discipline. Fortunately, doing all this is not only possible, it's actually relatively easy. The trick is simply recognizing that it needs to be done—which leads us to the other basic fact of financial life: Ignorance is *not* bliss. Quite the contrary . . .

It's what you don't know that can hurt you!

A wise woman once said, "It's not what you know that can hurt you but rather what you don't know." I'd like to extend that thought a bit and suggest that what generally causes the most suffering and pain is *what you don't know that you don't know.*

Think about that for a minute. In our everyday lives, there are really only a few categories of knowledge.

- What you know you know (e.g., how much money you earn each month)
- What you know you don't know (e.g., what the stock market will do next year)
- What you know you should know (e.g., how much it will take for you to be able to retire comfortably)
- What you don't know you don't know (e.g., that in 1997 the government made 824 amendments to the tax code, many of which could directly affect how much you will be able to afford to spend on child care, college tuitions, medical expenses, and your own retirement)

It's this last category, by the way, that causes the most problems in our lives. Think about it. When you find yourself in a real jam, doesn't it always seem to be the result of something you didn't know that you didn't know? (Consider the "prime" Florida real estate you bought that actually was in the middle of an alligator swamp.) That's the way life is—especially when it comes to money. Indeed, the reason most people fail financially—and, as a result, never have the kind of life they want—is almost always because of stuff they didn't know that they didn't know.

This concept is incredibly simple, but it's also tremendously powerful. Among other things, it means that if we can reduce what you don't know that you don't know about money, your chances of becoming financially successful—and, most important, staying financially successful—can be significantly increased. (It also means that the more you realize you don't know as you read this book, the happier you should be, because it shows you are already proactively learning!)

So how do we apply this concept? Well, I think the best way to reduce what you don't know that you don't know about money is to learn what you need to unlearn. That is, you need to discover what you may have come to believe about money that isn't really true. Or, as I like to put it . . .

Don't fall for the most common myths about money.

Whenever I conduct one of my "Smart Women Finish Rich!" seminars, I generally begin the class by suggesting that the reason most people—not just women—fail financially is that they have fallen for a bunch of money myths that are simply not true. As we're learning the facts, I think it's important to spend a little time exploring these myths and learning to recognize them for what they are. The reason is simple: By doing this, you lessen the chances that you'll ever be taken in by them.

> ## MYTH NO. 1:
> MAKE MORE MONEY AND YOU'LL BE RICH!

The most commonly held myth about personal finances is that the most important factor in determining whether you will ever be rich is how much money you make. To put it another way, ask most women what it takes to be well off, and they will invariably say "More money."

It seems logical, right? Make more money and you'll be rich. Now, you may be thinking "What's wrong with that? How can it be a myth?"

Well, to me, the phrase "Make more money and you'll be rich" brings to mind certain late-night TV infomercials, with their enthusiastic pitchmen and slick get-rich-quick schemes. My current favorite is the one in which a guy wearing a gold necklace smiles into the camera and says you can earn a fortune while lying on the sofa watching television. Without getting into the question of whether his particular scheme makes any business sense, let me suggest to you that the basic premise of his pitch—namely, that the key to wealth is finding some quick and easy way to boost your income—is simply not true. In fact, what determines your wealth is not how much you make but how much you keep of what you make.

I'll take that even further. I believe that most Americans who think they have an income problem actually don't. You may not believe that.

It's possible you feel you have an income problem yourself. Perhaps you're thinking right now "David, I'm sorry. I don't care what you say—with my bills and expenses, I'm telling you I have an income problem."

Well, I'm not saying that you might not be facing some financial challenges. But I would be willing to bet that if we were to take a good look at your situation, we'd find that the problem really isn't the size of your income. Indeed, if you're at all typical, over the course of your working life you will likely earn a phenomenal amount of money. If you find that hard to believe, take a look at the Earnings Outlook chart.

EARNINGS OUTLOOK

How much money will pass through your hands during your lifetime and what will you do with it?

Monthly Income	10 Years	20 Years	30 Years	40 Years
$1,000	$120,000	$240,000	$360,000	$480,000
$1,500	180,000	360,000	540,000	720,000
$2,000	240,000	480,000	720,000	960,000
$2,500	300,000	600,000	900,000	1,200,000
$3,000	360,000	720,000	1,080,000	1,440,000
$3,500	420,000	840,000	1,260,000	1,680,000
$4,000	480,000	960,000	1,440,000	1,920,000
$4,500	540,000	1,080,000	1,620,000	2,160,000
$5,000	600,000	1,200,000	1,800,000	2,400,000
$5,500	660,000	1,320,000	1,980,000	2,640,000
$6,000	720,000	1,440,000	2,160,000	2,880,000
$6,500	780,000	1,560,000	2,340,000	3,120,000
$7,000	840,000	1,680,000	2,520,000	3,360,000
$7,500	900,000	1,800,000	2,700,000	3,600,000
$8,000	960,000	1,920,000	2,880,000	3,840,000
$8,500	1,020,000	2,040,000	3,060,000	4,080,000
$9,000	1,080,000	2,160,000	3,240,000	4,320,000
$9,500	1,140,000	2,280,000	3,420,000	4,560,000
$10,000	1,200,000	2,400,000	3,600,000	4,800,000

Source: *The Super Saver: Fundamental Strategies for Building Wealth* by Janet Lowe (Longman Financial Services Publishing: United States, 1990)

The numbers don't lie. Over the course of their lifetimes, most Americans will earn between $1 million and $3 million!

Based on your monthly income, how much money does it look like you will earn in your lifetime? It's well into seven figures, isn't it? Don't you think you deserve to keep some of that money? I do—and I bet you do too! Unfortunately, most of us don't keep *any*. In fact, the average American works a total of some 90,000 hours in his or her life—and has nothing to show for it at the end! The typical 50-year-old in this country has less than $10,000 in savings!

How do we explain that? It's simple, really.

The problem is not our income, it's what we spend!

We'll go into detail on this concept in Step Four. For now, just trust me on this one. It's not the size of your income that will determine your financial well-being over the next 20 or 30 years, it's how you *handle* the money you earn.

I know that sounds hard to believe, but it's true. Consider the findings in a recent book that I recommend highly to my students. It's called *The Millionaire Next Door,* and it was written by a man named Tom Stanley, who interviewed hundreds of millionaires and came up with some findings that surprised me and probably will surprise you.

There's a phrase Texans use to describe someone who is all show and no substance: "Big hat, no cattle." What Stanley found was that most millionaires are just the opposite. In other words . . .

SMALL HAT, LOTS OF CATTLE

Here are some of Stanley's findings.

- The average net worth of a millionaire is $3.7 million.
- The average millionaire lives in a house that cost $320,000.
- The average millionaire's taxable income is $131,000 a year.
- For the most part, millionaires describe themselves as "tightwads" who believe that charity begins at home.
- Most millionaires drive older, American-made cars. Only a minority drive new cars or ever lease their cars.

- Fully half of the millionaires Stanley surveyed never paid more than $399 for a suit.
- Millionaires are dedicated investors—on average, investing nearly 20 percent of their total household income each year.

What amazes me about these facts is that a family with a net worth of nearly $4 million (the average net worth that Stanley surveyed) is, by most people's standards, very wealthy. I certainly feel $4 million is a rather comfortable amount to have accumulated, and I'd be willing to guess that you do too. Yet the income these people earn (an average of $131,000 a year) is really not all that high. It's certainly above average, but it is definitely not of the extraordinary magnitude we tend to associate with people who have amassed great wealth.

The fact is, what has allowed most of these people to become millionaires is not how much they've made but how little (relatively speaking) they've spent. To use a sports metaphor, while their offense was probably pretty good, the defense they've played with their money has been nothing short of brilliant.

Unfortunately, most people handle their finances in the opposite way. They are great on offense and lousy on defense. As a financial advisor, I've personally met in my office with many people who make over $100,000 a year and feel wealthy and live wealthy but in fact are not wealthy.

Here's a case in point.

BIG HAT, NO CATTLE

Nora first came to see me after attending a retirement-planning course I taught at the University of California–Berkeley Extension. The moment she entered my office it was clear I was dealing with a very successful woman. Her clothes were the current year's top of the line, she was wearing a gold Rolex watch worth at least $10,000, and I had seen her drive up in a brand-new $82,000 Mercedes-Benz (which, it turned out, she leased).

A fit and attractive 48-year-old, Nora owned and ran a company that employed ten people and grossed more than $5 million a year. But though her personal income was more than $200,000 a year and she had been pulling down a six-figure income for well over a decade, her net worth was almost zero! Nora didn't even have a retirement account started. She did have about $50,000 in equity in her home, but she also had two mortgages on the house, on which she owed a total of $400,000. To make matters worse, Nora had run up more than $35,000 in credit-card debt!

After she filled me in on her situation, I shook my head and said, "Nora, are you planning on working forever?"

She looked at me, confused. "What do you mean?" she asked.

"Well," I said, "were you planning on working for the rest of your life?"

"No," she replied. "I hope to retire by the time I turn 55."

"Really?" I said. "With what?"

Nora blinked at me, not seeing what I was getting at.

"Is your business salable?" I continued.

Nora bit her lip. Her business, she explained, was built mainly on a few good relationships that probably couldn't be transferred to anyone else.

"I see," I said. "Then I suppose you have a wealthy relative who is planning to die in time for you to inherit this money when you turn 55?"

Once again, Nora looked perplexed "No," she said slowly, "I don't have any inheritance coming."

"Then I'm confused," I said. "How are you going to retire? You don't have any savings. You can't sell your business. The equity in your house is minimal."

Nora shrugged. "I make so much money," she said, "that I thought I could play catch-up."

SPEND MORE THAN YOU MAKE, AND YOU'LL HAVE A SERIOUS PROBLEM!

I'd like to tell you there was a quick fix for Nora, but there wasn't. First of all, Nora had some really bad habits—the worst of which was that she simply spent more than she made, all the time! Second, she didn't really believe me when I told her that she needed to change her ways and change them fast.

It took Nora 18 months to get around to opening a retirement account and making her first contribution. That, however, was four years ago, and these days, fortunately, Nora is a completely different person. Every two weeks now, like clockwork, she sends me a check for her retirement fund. Not only is she fully funding her retirement account, but she is putting away even more money in some additional tax-deferred accounts (which we will cover in Step Five). So far Nora has managed to save close to $90,000, and by slightly increasing her monthly mortgage payments, she will have her house fully paid off in 15 years instead of 30, which will save her close to $285,000! (You'll learn how you can do this for yourself in Step Six.) Equally important, she has stopped leasing brand-new luxury cars (instead, she bought a used one), and she has paid off all her credit-card debt.

Nora isn't bringing home any more money than she was before. Yet now, for the first time, she is building real wealth. What changed? The answer is her spending habits—and, most important of all, her investment habits. That's the key. Like Tom Stanley's millionaires, she saw through the income myth and learned that it's not how much you make, it's how much you keep.

One important advantage Nora did have going for her was that she realized early on that she had to take care of herself, which is one reason why she started her own business. Instinctively, she understood that one of the most fundamental principles of smart money management is self-reliance—or, as I like to tell my clients . . .

Don't ever put your entire financial fate in someone else's hands.

This brings us to the second biggest myth I see women falling prey to—what I call the Cinderella myth, otherwise known as the "My husband will take of me" myth (or, even worse, the "Find and marry a wealthy man and everything will be fine" myth).

MYTH NO. 2:
MY HUSBAND (OR SOME OTHER MAN) WILL TAKE CARE OF ME.

Now, before I go into detail on this subject, let me say that I know it is entirely possible that you are happily married or that you have chosen to be happily single. Nonetheless, I have found from experience that this myth is worth spending a little time on, for some version of it affects nearly every woman. Indeed, over the years, hundreds of women have shared with me their painful personal stories of how their lives were nearly destroyed by the belief that some man—if not a husband, then a father, or an employer, or a financial advisor—would take care of them. And when I started to write this book, many more women implored me not to pass over this issue lightly. So here goes.

> *It's neither safe nor practical to assume that the man in your life can be counted on to take care of your finances.*

Why do I say this? Let's look at the facts. If men generally have been in charge of their families' money for the last century or so, then clearly they have not been doing a very good job. Consider this sobering statistic . . .

> *Only 5 percent of Americans can afford to retire at age 65!*

That's right—only 5 percent of Americans (that's just 1 in 20 of us) have annual incomes in excess of $25,000 a year at age 65. I'm sure I don't have to tell you that in many places $25,000 a year won't cover even basic living expenses. Would it cover yours?

But wait, the bad news gets worse. As I noted earlier, women live longer yet tend to earn fewer pension and other retirement benefits than men do. Thus you are likely to be forced to make do with even less.

What all this adds up to at retirement—or, more accurately, does *not* add up to—is another scary statistic . . .

> *The average income for a woman over 65 is less than $7,000 a year.*

You *can't* live on that—not these days, not in any semblance of comfort. And quite frankly, I wouldn't want you to have to try!

But, you may ask, what about Social Security? That will help, won't it? Maybe—assuming the system is still around by the time you reach retirement age. (And there's no guarantee it will be.) The fact is, Social Security was never intended to be a retirement plan. At most, it was designed to provide an income *supplement.*

Look at the numbers. In 1997, the latest year for which figures are available, the average retired woman's Social Security benefits totaled just over $663 a month, or less than $8,000 a year. As of this writing, the *maximum* benefit any retired person can collect is $1,342 a month—just $16,104 a year. In other words, the most anyone can possibly hope to get from Social Security these days, no matter how much he or she put into the system over a lifetime, is a little over $16,000 a year. That may be okay for walking-around money, but you sure wouldn't want to have to live on it. Unfortunately, millions of people have no choice but to try to do just that. You don't want to be one of them.

That's not to say you should forget about Social Security. It's just that you shouldn't count on it to provide more than a small fraction of your retirement income. How small? For most people, Social Security makes up less than a fifth of their retirement income.

As it happens, there's a very simple way to find out now what your Social Security check ultimately will look like—and I can't emphasize enough the importance of taking advantage of it right away. This is especially crucial for women, since, as I mentioned before, women tend to work less consistently throughout their lifetimes than men—and, as a result, often their Social Security benefits turn out to be much smaller than they had been expecting.

What you want to do in order to avoid any unpleasant surprises down the road is to put in a request for what's called your "Personal Earnings and Benefit Estimate Statement." This document shows your Social Security earnings history and estimates your future benefits. The Social Security Administration will provide you with a benefits statement for absolutely no charge, but you have to ask for it.

This is something you should do immediately. Today. This very minute. It's really quite easy. Just call your local Social Security office (you'll find the number in the front of your local telephone directory under "Federal Government") and tell them you want to order a copy of your estimated benefits statement. You can also request the form online, by visiting the Social Security Administration's Web site at www.ssa.gov.

When it comes to divorce, women still end up with the short end of the stick.

Yes, we all want to believe that we can count on our spouses. Unfortunately, the statistics tell a very different story. Fully 50 percent of all marriages these days end in divorce. What about alimony and child support and community property? The bleak truth is, once her husband is gone, the average divorcée sees her standard of living plummet. According to a simulated study done by the Women's Legal Defense Fund, which was cited in the book *A Women's Guide to Savvy Investing,* custodial parents (typically the women) will see their incomes drop by 25 percent. At the same time, to add insult to injury, the standard of living for noncustodial parents (typically the men) generally rises by more than 35 percent! In California these statistics may be even worse. According to author Ken Dychtwald, who wrote the immensely popular book *Age Wave,* a California study showed that in the first year after a divorce, the standard of living for older women dropped 73 percent, while the standard of living rose for men by 42 percent.

These statistics are hardly news. But despite all the attention they've received in recent years, apparently many women remain convinced that they will be the exception to the rule—and they are shocked when they're not. I can't tell you the number of women who've come to me for advice after being absolutely blindsided by the husbands in whose hands they'd trustingly placed their futures. Unfortunately, by then it's usually too late to do more than try to pick up the pieces.

To be fair, there *are* many good men out there. But even if you're fortunate enough to have wound up with one of them, that's still no guarantee of a happy and secure future. Why? Because no matter how good the man in your life is, sooner or later he is going to die—and whether it's sooner or later, it probably will be before you do. Remember, the average woman lives seven years longer than the average man. Of course, no one likes to think about this. Indeed, it's terrible how many well-intentioned men who sincerely love their wives and families simply refuse to face up to this inescapable truth. The worst thing about this sort of denial is that it leads otherwise good husbands to put off dealing with disagreeable reminders of their mortality such as life insurance and wills. And that's a prescription for disaster. For try as we might to ignore it . . .

The average age of widowhood today is just 56!

Because of our unwillingness to accept this unpleasant reality, we tend to be woefully unprepared to cope with it when it comes to pass. That's why, for a woman, losing a husband is generally as devastating economically as it is emotionally. Indeed, fully 80 percent of all widows living in poverty were not poor before their husbands died. How did they get that way? Inadequate—or, more likely, nonexistent—planning. How else do you explain the fact that one out of every four widows goes through all her husband's death benefits within two months?

When I shared this notion in one of my investment seminars, a woman named Sarah stood up in tears. "David," she told the room, "everything you're saying is true. I'm 57, and my husband was a successful lawyer who owned his own practice. He passed away six months ago and now I'm almost bankrupt."

I asked Sarah how this could have happened. It turned out that though her husband specialized in trusts and wills, he had never bothered to do one for himself!

The entire group was aghast. I could see the question on everyone's face: *You mean a lawyer who wrote wills for a living didn't have a will himself?* But when I asked the class, "How many of *you* have a will?" less than half the people in the room answered in the affirmative. And when I asked further, "How many of you have reviewed your will in the last five years?" less than 10 percent of them raised their hands. So maybe Sarah's story shouldn't have been surprising after all.

Then I asked Sarah, "If your husband was so successful, why are you almost broke?" She replied that when her husband died she discovered that the $2-million home in which they lived carried a $1.5-million mortgage. With her husband gone and no income of her own, the massive mortgage payments were now way beyond her means. As a result, Sarah found herself forced to put the house up for sale. Unfortunately, this was at a time when the California real-estate market was badly depressed, and she couldn't find a buyer. To make matters worse, not only had her husband neglected to make a will, he had never taken out life insurance. And as if that wasn't bad enough, he had used their home as collateral on loans for his law practice—which was now defunct, because his former partners had elected to start a new firm without the obligation of her husband's debts! Sarah was in big trouble, all because she had assumed her husband would take care of her, and *he* had not prepared for the unforeseen.

Sarah's case was extreme, but it was by no means unusual. In any case, there is an important lesson to be learned from her experience: Don't ever let the "some man will take care of you" myth become your reality. It's a recipe for disaster.

There's one more myth I want to share with you.

MYTH NO. 3:
THE GOVERNMENT FINALLY HAS GOTTEN INFLATION UNDER CONTROL.

There seems to be an increasingly widespread notion that we no longer need to worry about inflation. This is a particularly dangerous myth not simply because it's untrue, but because it breeds complacency. Indeed, I can't think of anything more financially self-destructive than the idea that we don't need to worry so much about the future because the government finally has gotten inflation under control.

It certainly would be nice if that were true. Unfortunately, it's not. To the contrary . . .

Inflation is still Public Enemy Number One.

Sometimes when I teach a class, someone will raise a hand and actually try to debate this issue. "But, David," she will say, "it sure looks as if the government has control over inflation. After all, I don't see things costing a lot more today than they used to."

Well, that's not what the statistics say. What the numbers tell us is that over the last 20 years, the annual increase in the cost of living has averaged about 5 percent; over the last 10 years, it's averaged about 3.5 percent. Based on that, it's probably a safe bet to figure that inflation will run at about 4 percent a year for the foreseeable future.

Now, that may not sound like very much, but it is. After all, when most people retire, they do so on a fixed income. Unfortunately, if you retire on a fixed income and inflation continues at 4 percent a year, you are going to be in deep trouble. Why? Because, at that rate, your purchasing power will be cut nearly in half within 15 years. In other words, the dollar sitting in your purse today will be worth only about 50 cents a decade and a half from now. In 20 years, it will be worth only about 40 cents.

There's nothing new about this phenomenon. When I talk about inflation in my seminars, one of biggest laughs I always get is when I ask "How many of you drove here tonight in a car that cost more than your first home?" What's amazing is that usually a third of the people in the class raise their hand. That's the power of inflation. Here's another example: The car I drive today cost more than twice what my parents paid for their first home in Oakland, California, and it was a nice five-bedroom house with three bathrooms. If you think I'm exaggerating, take a look at this chart.

CONSUMER PRICES: STICKER SHOCK SINCE 1970

Typical Prices	1970	1980	Today	Projected in 20 Years
House	$25,600	$64,000	$135,150 *	$463,508
Automobile	3,400	6,910	22,321 ***	89,965
Gasoline (10 Gal.)	3.48	9.68	12.18 *	30.81
Stamp	.06	.15	.32 **	1.11
Day in Hospital	47	134	390 *	1,872

Sources:

* American Chamber of Commerce Researchers Association (ACCRA) Cost of Living Index—2nd quarter 1997
** United States Post Office
*** National Association of Auto Dealers—October 1997 year to date

There is no denying the lesson these numbers teach us.

The future is going to be expensive.

That's why, despite all the recent talk about how inflation is no longer a problem, I still consider it to be Public Enemy Number One. The good news here is that learning how to keep your nest egg growing faster than inflation isn't all that hard. But if you don't recognize inflation as a problem in the first place, chances are you won't bother to try to do anything about it—and if you don't try to do anything about it, you are going to find yourself in a world of hurt one day. So don't believe the myth about inflation being under control.

Show Me the Money

Now that we have exposed these money myths for what they are and looked at the external realities of what we can expect in our financial futures, let's examine the facts. The place to begin is close to home, with information about your own personal financial situation. Why here? By way of explanation, let me share a personal story with you.

When I was younger, I once asked my father why so many women seemed to be so devastated financially after a divorce or the death of a husband. "David," he said, "women are not typically involved with the family finances. So when it comes time to split up the pie, they don't know how much pie there is to split up, or even where to find it."

That's it? I thought. *Women don't know where the money is?* Could it really be that basic? I doubted it.

Out of curiosity, I took my mother to lunch to see if she agreed with my dad's assessment. What followed was the scene I described at the beginning of this chapter. As I mentioned, a good friend of my mom's had just gone through a brutal and costly divorce. Quite understandably, my mother was very upset about it—not least because her friend was now in financial trouble so serious that she had been forced to take a secretarial job and move to a tiny apartment.

"But, Mom," I said, "they were living in a million-dollar house. Where did all the money go?"

"It turned out her husband had used all the equity in their house to build up his medical practice," my mother explained with a sigh. "And now, with the HMO situation, his practice isn't doing so well."

As much as I hated to admit it, it looked as if my dad was right. The terrible outcome was a result of the woman's lack of knowledge about her family's finances. She had signed papers allowing her husband to take out a second mortgage without knowing or even asking about what she was signing. The result was, for her, a financial disaster. It was scary.

With that in mind, I asked my mom the test question: "Do you know where *our* family's money is?"

As I said, though I thought this would be an easy one for her to answer, it turned out that she had no idea. All she could tell me about our money was that my dad took care of it. And when I pressed her about her ignorance, she simply laughed at me.

I couldn't believe it. This, from a woman who was president of a million-dollar nonprofit theater group, involved in numerous charity boards, and published two professional newsletters. This brilliant, beautiful woman was the same person who, when personal computers first appeared on the market, convinced the family that we needed one—and then singlehanded taught herself to master its intricacies so completely that she was able to computerize my father's entire business! Yet she hadn't a clue as to where our money was invested.

I was horrified. If a woman as sharp and successful as my mom could be so in the dark about money, what was happening to the millions of other women in this country who weren't married to men who managed money for a living? In the years since then, of course,

I've seen firsthand how widespread this sort of ignorance is and how much damage it can do. So with that in mind, I ask you now the same question I asked my mother . . .

Do you know what's going on with your money and your family's money?

To help you answer this important question. I've prepared a short quiz. Take a few moments to complete it, answering true or false for each statement. The results should give you a good idea of how knowledgeable you are (or aren't) about your personal finances.

THE "SMART WOMEN FINISH RICH" FINANCIAL KNOWLEDGE QUIZ

True or False:

[ ] [ ] I know the current value of my home, including the size of the mortgage and the amount of equity I've built.

[ ] [ ] I know the length of the mortgage-payment schedule and how much extra it would cost each month to pay down the mortgage in half the time. I also know the interest rate we are paying on the mortgage and if it is competitive in today's market.

[ ] [ ] I know how much life insurance I [and my spouse, if applicable] carry. I know how much cash value there is in the policy, and I know the rate of return my cash value is earning.

[ ] [ ] I know the details (including amount of coverage, cost, monthly or yearly payment, etc.) of all other insurance policies carried by myself [and my spouse, if applicable]. This includes health, disability, term life, and so on.

[ ] [ ] I have reviewed my life-insurance policy in the last 12 to 24 months to see if the price I am paying for it is still competitive in today's marketplace.

[ ] [ ] If I own my own home, I know what kind of homeowner's coverage I have and what the deductibles are. If I rent, I know the amount of renter's insurance I have and what its deductible is. In either case, in the event of a fire or other catastrophic loss, I know whether my insurance will reimburse me for the actual cash value of

True or False:

             my property or the cost of replacing it at *today's* current values.

[ ]   [ ] I have attempted to protect my family's nest egg from lawsuits by carrying an "umbrella" insurance policy that includes liability coverage.

[ ]   [ ] I either prepared my own tax return this year or reviewed my tax situation with the person who prepared my return.

[ ]   [ ] I know the location and amounts of all my or my family's investments, including

- cash in savings or money-market accounts:
- CDs or savings bonds
- stocks and bonds
- real-estate investments (deeds, mortgages, rental agreements, etc.)
- collectibles (valuation and where items are)

[ ]   [ ] I know the annualized return generated by each of the above investments.

[ ]   [ ] If I or my family owns a business, I know the current valuation of the business, including how much debt it currently carries and the value of its liquid assets.

[ ]   [ ] I know the value, location, and performance of all my retirement accounts [and those of my spouse, if applicable], including IRAs, SEP-IRAs, Keoghs, and company pension plans.

[ ]   [ ] I know the percentage of income I am putting away for retirement and what it's being invested in [and, if applicable, how much my spouse is putting away and what he is investing in].

[ ]   [ ] I know if I (and my spouse, if applicable) am making the maximum allowable contribution to my retirement plan at work, whether my employer is making matching contributions, and what the vesting schedule is.

[ ]   [ ] I know how much money I [and my spouse, if applicable] will be getting from Social Security and what my [and, if applicable, his] pension benefits will be.

[ ]   [ ] I know whether my [and my spouse's, if applicable] income is protected should I [or my spouse] become disabled.

True or False:

> Because I own disability insurance. In addition, I know what the exact coverage is, when the benefits would start, and whether the benefits would be taxable.

[ ]   [ ]   I [or my family] maintain a safety deposit box, know how to gain access to it, and have reviewed its contents within the last 12 months. If I have the only key, other family members know where to find it if something should happen to me.

Scoring:

Give yourself 1 point for every time you answered "true" and 0 for every time you answered "false."

14 to 17 points: Excellent! You have a good grasp of where your money is.

9 to 13 points: You're not totally in the dark, but there are some areas in which your knowledge is less than adequate.

Under 9 points: Your chances of being hurt financially because of insufficient knowledge are enormous. You need to learn how to protect yourself from future financial disaster.

If you scored well on this test, congratulations! But don't go out and start celebrating just yet. Even among knowledgeable money managers, it's rare to find anyone, male or female, who has a handle on *every* aspect of their own finances and what they could and should be doing to assure themselves a secure future. So even if you scored 12 or above, I guarantee you'll discover many secrets and ideas that will be of enormous value to you in the pages that follow.

WHAT IF I DIDN'T SCORE WELL?

If you didn't score so well, take heart—by the time you've finished this book, you'll know *exactly* what you need to take immediate charge of your financial health and invest wisely for your family's future security.

If you're like most people, you probably knew some of the answers but not all of them—and some of the questions may have struck you as awfully complicated. Trust me, none of it is really that difficult.

Before long you'll be surprised by just how easy understanding your finances can be. Indeed, you'll probably wonder why you ever thought any of it was confusing. In the meantime, don't panic because you've just discovered there is all this information about your family finances that you don't know. We'll take care of it all soon enough.

At this point, what's important is simply that you realize that there's a lot you don't know—and, even more important, a lot that you now *want* to know. If that's how you feel, pat yourself on the back—you've completed Step One. You are motivated to educate yourself about how to take control of your financial future—which is what the "Smart Women Finish Rich!" journey is all about.

ENOUGH WITH THE BAD NEWS . . . LET'S GET TO THE GOOD STUFF!

It's possible that some of the myths about money that I've presented to you in this first step has struck you as being overly negative. If so, I apologize. As a rule, I make it a policy to avoid negative people, those dream stealers, as I call them, who seem to enjoy raining on other people's parades. But I started our journey this way for a reason: because I know you purchased this book in order to make a positive change in your life, and sometimes change can be difficult. In fact, many people live their lives going nowhere and doing nothing, not because they like where they are but simply because they are afraid of change. Overcoming this fear takes real motivation. It has to hurt so much that finally you can't take it anymore and you say, "Enough is enough! I want my life to be different!"

It's in this spirit that I've offered some cautionary tales and depressing statistics. I simply want you to come to grips with the fact that if you don't take care of your financial future, no one—not the government, not your employer, not your spouse—is going to do it for you. And it definitely won't take care of itself.

But don't let the negativity get you down. Remember: Those gloomy facts and figures don't have to be your reality!

I often repeat to clients what my Grandmother Bach used to tell me. "You know, David," she would say, "when I was growing up, going to work, starting my career, many people asked me why was I worrying about retirement plans. 'You'll have Social Security,' they'd say. 'You'll have a pension from your company.' But even at a young age, I didn't think it was a good idea to depend on someone else to take care

of me—not my employer, not the government, not even your grandfather."

That's why, unlike most of her friends, my grandmother always
made a point each time she got a paycheck of putting some money
aside and buying some high-quality stocks or bonds. It's also why,
unlike most of her friends, when she reached retirement age, she was
able to enjoy herself in worry-free comfort.

I hope now that you've accomplished Step One, you're motivated
to take control of your financial future by getting educated about your
money.

Now it's time to begin Step Two, in which we take a look at what's
important to you about money.

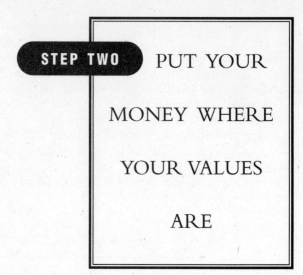

PUT YOUR MONEY WHERE YOUR VALUES ARE

As a financial advisor I specialize in doing what we call values-based financial planning. What this means is that I help my clients discover (often for the first time) what their true values about money actually are.

Initially at least, talking about personal values often throws people for a loop. It's not the sort of thing most of us expect to be discussing with a financial professional. Most people assume that when they meet with a financial advisor, the conversation will focus on investments, on assets and liabilities, on taxes and how many years they have to go before retirement. Well, all that does need to be talked about, but it's not where I believe the conversation should begin. What needs to be discussed first is what is really driving you when it comes to money.

Think about it. Your attitudes about money are what define everything that matters about your personal financial situation: how much money you need, how hard you are willing to work for it, how you will feel when you finally get it. That's why I can say with total confidence that once you understand what money really means to you, you will be unstoppable. Indeed, the process I am about to share with you is probably the single most effective tool I know to help people create a life plan that will lead them to the ultimate financial security they want.

A "SMART WOMEN FINISH RICH!"

SEMINAR IN ACTION

I gave a seminar recently in my hometown of San Francisco, but it could have been anywhere. As usual, the room was filled with women, of all ages and types—old, young, rich, poor, single, married, you name it. Also as usual, I began with an announcement and a question. "My name is David Bach," I said, "and I'm here to show Smart Women how to finish rich. Would that be okay with any of you?"

Virtually in unison, every woman in the room shouted out, "Yes!"

That's generally the answer I get. I grinned at the crowd and continued. "Well, here's my next question, and it's the most important one I will ask you tonight. But don't worry—it's also the easiest." I looked out at them intently. "When you stop and think about it, what's really important about money to you?"

The room was totally silent. "Come on," I said. "This is easy. Think."

Still, nobody said anything.

"The reason you came here tonight is because you recognize that money is important," I persisted. "But what is really important about it? Most important, what is important about money to *you*?"

Finally, someone broke the silence. "No more student loans!" a young woman called out.

I turned to the big pad that had been placed on an easel behind me. Pulling out a marker pen, I wrote down what the young woman had said. "Okay," I repeated, "what's important about money to you is 'no more student loans.' What else? Who else wants to tell me what's important about money to them?"

A 60ish woman sitting a few rows behind the "student loan" woman was the next to answer. "Security," she said. "I want to know that if something should happen to my husband, I won't need to worry."

I nodded and wrote "security" on the pad.

Then another woman spoke up. "Freedom," she said. "What's important about money to me is freedom."

I turned to face this woman. "That's great," I said. "But freedom means different things to different people. What's important about having freedom to you?"

The woman stood up and looked around the room. "I just want to know I can do what I want to do when I want to do it."

Before she could go any further, another woman jumped to her feet. "I've got one," she shouted. "I want to know that my husband can't control what I do. What's important to me is knowing I have choices."

She was joined by yet another woman who said what was important about money to her was "feeling like I can do what the Lord meant for me to do with my life, which is to help others."

Within about ten minutes, I had filled two entire sheets with different reasons why money was important to one or another of my students. It was incredible. Money clearly meant something different to each and every woman in the room.

Then I started circling some of the words and phrases I had written down. First I circled "security," then "freedom," then "ability to have choices," "happiness," "live a life of meaning," "able to do what God wants me to do," "more time with family," "help others," "feel satisfied," and "feel happy." By the time I was done, about 80 percent of the reasons I had written down were circled. That first answer—"pay off student loans"—wasn't among them, though. Neither was "pay off credit-card debt," or "pay off mortgage," or "travel to Hawaii."

Leaving the class to wonder about this for a moment, I looked out at them and shook my head. "Once again," I said, "a group of women has proven to me how much more in touch with yourselves you are than men." I paused for a moment. "Have you noticed what almost all of you did?" I asked. "Take a close look. Every reason I circled has one thing in common."

The sea of faces staring back at me seemed stumped.

"Look closely," I repeated. "Almost all of the reasons you listed were *values.* Notice how only a few of the reasons I wrote down are goals, like 'pay off school loans' or 'get the mortgage paid off.' Almost everything here is an idea like security, freedom, and happiness. These are values—*your* values—the most important things in life. They're the stuff you will do just about anything in the world to achieve—because ultimately they are truly who you are!"

Slowly, first on just a few faces, then on more and more of them, I could see a light dawning.

"Guess what, ladies?" I continued. "What you just did was the most important part of taking control of your financial future, and you did it almost effortlessly. You see, as women you have a tremendous advantage over men: You are already in touch with your feelings and your values. For the most part, men don't get this stuff. It takes them way more time." I grinned at the class. "Pretend you're a man right now," I instructed. "What would you say if I asked you what's important about money to you?"

The room erupted. "Cars!" someone shouted. "A big house!" someone else said. "A boat!" "Football!" "Beer!" "Women!" The class couldn't stop. It was hilarious.

I laughed along with them. "Exactly," I shouted over the hubbub. "It's all goals, all stuff. No values."

Then I got serious again. "Without values, goals rarely get accomplished," I said. "Show me someone who is not reaching their full potential, and I'll show you someone who missed the importance of designing his or her life around their values. Values are the key. When you understand them correctly, they will pull you toward to your dreams—which is a lot better than having to push yourself!"

WHAT'S IMPORTANT ABOUT MONEY
TO YOU?

What I've just described is the way I usually start my "Smart Women Finish Rich!" seminars. In the pages that follow, I'm going to take you on the same personal journey that this group of women—and thousands of women like them—have taken in my classes and in my office. That is, we're going to discover what is important about money to you and in turn discover your values.

The process of understanding "what's important about money to you" is absolutely essential. Asking yourself what money means to you, after all, quickly forces you to evaluate what it is you are looking for in life. And understanding what you are looking for in life is the foundation on which all smart financial planning is based.

Think about it. How could you possibly put together an empowering financial plan unless you know what it is you really care about? Let's say what's important about money to you is the security it can provide, but your current state of financial affairs has you living from paycheck to paycheck. Well, then, something is wrong, isn't it? Clearly, your financial behavior is out of whack with your deepest values. Similarly, let's say what's important about money to you is the freedom it can bring you, but in actuality you are tied to a job working 60 hours a week to pay a mortgage on a large home—wishing all the while that you were traveling more. Once again, your financial life is in conflict with what you are really all about.

Money is not an end in itself. It is merely a tool to help us achieve some particular goal. If the way we handle our money conflicts with our personal values, we are not going to wind up living happy and fulfilled lives.

So how do you figure out what you are looking for in life and how to use money as a tool to get it? Well, fortunately, you don't have to go to Tibet and meet with a guru on a mountaintop. All you need to do is get clear about what your values are. Once you've done that, it will be easy to develop your financial goals (which we will do in Step Three).

What's great about this process is that it is one of the most powerful legs of your journey to financial security as well as one of the least complicated. What makes it so simple is the fact that you already know what your values are. They are not something you have to study for years to learn. The fact is, most of us have a pretty good sense of who we are and what's important about money to us. These things may not be immediately apparent, but with just a little bit of digging some amazing realizations will pop to the surface.

So now let's eavesdrop right now on some values conversations I've had over the years. By listening in, you should begin to see how the process works. Specifically, what you are about to learn is how to put your values down on paper and build what I call a **values ladder.**[*] This simple but highly effective tool will help you clarify what's pulling you toward (or keeping you from) taking control over your own financial situation. Once you understand how the process works, we can apply it to your situation and life and make sure that from this day forward, your values are clear so that you are pulled only toward your financial goals.

ONE WOMAN'S VALUES EXERCISE

Here's an example of a conversation that worked really well and helped a client of mine greatly. Jessica was a successful 33-year-old computer salesperson who met with me in my office after taking one

---

[*] The values conversation and values ladder are concepts derived from Bill Bachrach/Bachrach & Associates, Inc. and have been included here with permission.

of my investment classes. She was married (to her college sweetheart) and had an 8-year-old daughter and a dog named Teddy.

Jessica seemed very focused the day she came to see me, and we got right down to business. Having already attended my seminar, she knew exactly what I was trying to get at when I asked her to tell me what was most important to her about money.

"Well, David," she said, "I guess when I think about money what's really important to me is security."

"That's great," I said. "Of course, security means different things to different people. Help me to understand what's important about security to you."

Jessica didn't hesitate. "Having security lets me feel that I'm free to do what I want, when I want," she replied.

"And what does that feeling of being able to do what you want mean to you?" I asked.

"I guess it means having a sense of freedom. Not feeling constrained by the duties of life."

"I see. So what would not having these constraints in your life and having this freedom mean to you?"

Jessica thought for a moment. "It would mean that I'd have more time to be with my daughter, who is growing up so fast that she's going to be in college before I know it," she said. "And I could spend more time with my husband and my friends, who I rarely see now because I'm always so busy."

"Okay," I nodded. "Let's assume for a moment that you have security, and that as a result you have the freedom to spend more time with your daughter and your husband and your friends. What's important about being in that position to you?"

"Well, I guess it would make me feel calmer and happier," Jessica responded. "Definitely happier. Right now I feel burned out all the time. I'd like to not be tired for a change."

"And what's important to you about that?" I asked her.

Jessica smiled wearily. "I just spend so much time rushing around now trying to do everything—working, being a wife and a mother, keeping the house and bills in order—that I don't feel like I have a life. Some days I don't even remember what it feels like to not be exhausted."

"So it's important for you to not rush around and to feel you have a life again," I said.

Once again Jessica did not hesitate. "Yes, definitely," she said firmly. "I want my life back."

When I asked Jessica what she would do if she had her life back, she said she'd start taking better care of herself, exercising and eating better. When I pressed her on why she wanted to do that, she said her aim was to live longer and be a better example to her daughter.

"Okay," I continued, "so now that you are going to live longer and be an example to your daughter, what else would you do with your life?"

Jessica frowned for a moment, lost in thought. "That's a tough one to answer," she said finally. "I'm not sure."

I wasn't about to let her off the hook. "I know you're not sure," I persisted, "but if you *were* sure, what do you think you would say?"

"Well," she said slowly, "I guess if I really had my life together the way I wanted it, I would focus on getting more involved with charity groups in my community."

In response to my follow-up questions, Jessica explained that "making a difference and giving something back" was really important to her.

"Is there anything more important to you than making a difference and helping others?" I asked.

Jessica looked me in the eye. "I just want to know that when I go, I'll have lived a full life, loved, been a good example to my daughter and my family, and really made a difference." She blushed self-consciously. "That's all," she said.

That, of course, was a lot—a lot to think about, and a lot to remember when it came time to construct a financial plan. Fortunately, as Jessica and I talked, we kept a record of the values that were important to her, in the order that she had come up with them. On the next page, you'll see Jessica's values ladder. As you can see, at the bottom of the ladder is Jessica's **first value**, security. Above it, each successive rung contains the next value that Jessica told me was important to her.

Take a moment and reread the conversation. Notice how quickly Jessica and I were able to build her values ladder.

Does Your Financial Behavior Match Your Values?

What Jessica and I learned from our values conversation was that there was nothing more important to her than having more time to devote

Jessica's Values Ladder

making a difference
helping others

WIA | living longer &
example to daughter | TY?

WIA | not rushing/feeling
like I have a life | TY?

WIA | feeling calmer
and happier | TY?

WIA | more time with
daughter/husband | TY?

WIA | freedom/no duty
constraints | TY?

WIA | security | TY?

(ALWAYS START WITH)
"What's important about money to you?"

to her family and community. As things stood, most of her time (and energy) was going to her job. With that in mind, the next thing we did was look at Jessica's financial situation and habits to see how they stacked up against her values ladder.

As a computer salesperson, Jessica earned about $75,000 a year. That's a solid income by any measure, yet for some reason she was still living from paycheck to paycheck. Hence, the pressure she felt to spend so much time at work.

Why was Jessica so strapped for cash? We looked at her spending patterns and found that she was spending a lot of money on what were clearly nonessential items: more than $300 a month on clothes, $100 on a car phone, $350 on restaurants, $150 on dry cleaning, $525 on a leased car, and on and on. In all, she was spending over $2,000 a month—well over half her take-home pay—*on things that had absolutely nothing to do with what was most important to her*: namely, having more time to devote to her family and community.

When I pointed this out to her—that she was spending more than four hours of every eight-hour workday toiling to pay for luxuries that did nothing to give her the life she really wanted—Jessica was shocked. But fortunately, she was also motivated to change her ways. Once she realized how much time and energy she was, in essence, wasting, she worked out a plan under which she was able to start saving money for the first time (and thus stop living from paycheck to paycheck) while slowly cutting back the number of hours she put in at work (thus giving her more time with her family).

The Breakthrough

Jessica got more out of our values conversation than just a new financial plan. She told me later that she also came away with a sense of clarity about her life's purpose that she hadn't really had before. "It made me realize that much of what I was doing with my time had little or nothing to do with my own values about who I am and who I want to be," she said. As a result, she added, "Now when I am doing something, I am much clearer with myself. I always ask myself, 'Is this in line with my values?' If it's not, I try to not do it." Of course, as Jessica acknowledged, there are some things that can't be avoided, but at least she now knows where her focus is supposed to be.

Equally important, the conversation also made Jessica realize that she didn't need nearly as much money as she had thought in order to get what she really wanted out of life. As she told me, "It showed me that while I've been spending so much time trying to increase my income, I've actually been squandering money on things that have nothing to do with the values that are important to me. I realized that a new dress, a fancy car, and a car phone were not worth all the weekends I was spending at the office."

Once that became clear, she said, she found it much easier to cut back on unnecessary expenses. "I immediately felt calmer about who I was and where I was going," she reported. "I hadn't had such a sense of inner peace in a long time. It's hard to believe that a question as simple as 'What's important about money to you?' can lead to such an important breakthrough, but it definitely can."

If It's Not About Returns, What *Is* It About?

Values exercises are not just for younger women. Taking a good look inside yourself can be a worthwhile undertaking no matter what your age—especially in this era of economic boom and record stock prices, when so many of us have become so obsessed with growth figures and rates of return that the point of saving and investing sometimes gets forgotten.

Take Helen, an older client of mine. Helen was very upset when she came into my office. At first glance, it was hard to see why. A fetching 72-year-old, Helen was a "child of the Great Depression" and, as a result, always had watched her spending and savings very carefully. Ever since her husband had passed away six years earlier, she had been living on Social Security and a widow's pension. In addition, she had some $500,000 in bank certificates of deposit that had been paying her 8 percent annual interest (or $40,000 a year). In short, she had more than enough money to live on.

So what was bothering her? Well, it seemed that her bank had informed her that her CDs were about to mature, and if she wished to roll over her savings into new CDs, the best interest rate she could get now was only 5 percent.

"What am I going to do?" Helen asked me. "These rates are so low, yet I can't afford to take any risk with my money."

When I asked Helen how she spent the $40,000 a year she earned from her CDs, she gave me a look and said she put the money into a savings account at the bank. In other words, she didn't need it to live on.

With that in mind, I asked her what was so important about this $40,000 a year in interest that she was earning but not spending. She said it gave her a sense of security. As we continued what quickly became a full-fledged values conversation, she explained that she wanted to know that she would always be independent; for her, being independent meant never having to be a burden on her family. Her grandchildren, she said, meant the world to her. "I just love them so much," Helen added fervently. "I want to be able to give to them and not need to take."

"And what would you like to give them?" I asked.

Helen's eyes lit up. "You know," she said, "I've always thought it would be so special to take the whole family on a cruise to Alaska." As she told me about this dream trip, she glowed. Her smile disappeared, however, when I asked her why she didn't just do it.

"Oh, David," she said, "it would cost at least $10,000."

"So?" I replied. "You've been earning more than four times that on your CDs every year." I shook my head. "Helen," I said, "you have your health, you have all these assets, and you have this wonderful dream of taking your family on a trip—and what are you doing? You're sitting in my office worrying about whether your CDs are going to pay you 8 percent or 5 percent. What does it matter what the interest rate is if you're not going to use your money to make your life the way you want it to be?" I then asked Helen the final question on the values ladder: Was there anything more important to her than her family?

As it turned out, there wasn't.

Within a week of our meeting, Helen visited a travel agent and booked the cruise we had discussed. The trip cost her about $12,500. It was the most money she had ever spent on a luxury in her entire life. What was important, however, was not what she spent but what she got—which was the joy of sharing a wonderful experience with her children and grandchildren.

Take a look at Helen's values ladder, and note how quickly we were able to use that simple question about the importance of money to help her build a future that was exciting for both her and her family.

The point of this story is that values-based financial planning helped Helen use her money the way money is supposed to be used—to make life better. If your money is not helping you make your life better, then something is wrong. Chances are you're not making a connection between your values and the role money plays in your life. The importance of making that connection is the point of this story and the point of this chapter.

Helen's Values Ladder

(ALWAYS START WITH)
"What's important about money to you?"

CREATE YOUR OWN VALUES LADDER

Pretend you are arriving at my office in Orinda, California. You're going to meet with me, one on one, to create your own personal values ladder to the new you—a woman totally in control of her own financial situation.

You enter my office. In the middle of a round table at which you and I will sit is a piece of paper containing a blank values ladder just like the one that follows. We're going to use it to help you figure out what's important about money to you.

1. Start by relaxing. Take a minute to collect your thoughts. Our objective is for you to give answers that reflect how you really feel—not how you think someone else thinks you should feel. Remember, whatever your values are, they are the right ones for you.

2. Ready? Let's start with the single most important question: Ask yourself: *What's important about money to me?*

3. Write your answer on the bottom rung of the ladder. Remember that we're looking for values (basic aspirations such as *freedom, happiness, security,* and so on) and not goals (which generally involve specific amounts of money or particular acquisitions). If you've just gone through the jolt of a divorce and find yourself on your own with two kids to take care of, for example, your value might be "security." Or maybe you're a single entrepreneur who dreams of traveling around the world, in which case your initial value may be "freedom."

4. Now we need a little more perspective on the values you're listing, because the value you choose means different things to different people. Ask yourself: *What's important about _____ [your value] to me?* Write your answer on the next rung up the ladder.

5. Let's assume for a moment that _____ [your second value] has become a reality for you. Ask yourself: *What's important about _____ [your second value] to me?* Write your answer on the third rung of the ladder.

6. Continue climbing the ladder, filling in your answers as you go up. Don't cheat yourself. The biggest mistake people make when they conduct a values conversation on their own (and even sometimes in my office) is not taking the process deep enough.

Your Values Ladder

(Always start with)
"What's important about money to you?"

It's important to keep digging, because only rarely will the values you hold most important be among the first ones you list. Just keep asking yourself: *What's important about* _____ [the last value you gave] *to me?* You'll know you're done when you can't think of anything more important than the last value you mentioned.

Tapping into Your Values

For those of you who may be having trouble figuring out what is a value vs. what is a goal—and many people do—I've listed some examples in the boxes that follow. By studying the lists, you'll get a better idea of the difference between the two. Don't cheat, though, and borrow some values from my list just because they sound good and you're having trouble filling out your ladder. If the values you write down don't truly reflect what you feel in your heart, then they won't work to motivate you.

SOME EXAMPLES OF VALUES

Freedom	Connection with others
Security	Independence
Happiness	Fulfillment
Peace of mind	Confidence
Power	Being the best
Helping others	Making a difference
Helping family	Fun
Realizing my true potential (self-actualization)	Growing
Greater spirituality	Adventure

What follows are examples of goals that people come up with when they do the values-ladder exercise. Remember, we are not looking for goals. We are looking for values. (We'll get to goals in Step Three.)

SOME EXAMPLES OF GOALS

Pay down debt
Have $1 million
Not run out of money
Pay for college
Buy a house
Travel (*Travel is a goal; what traveling does for you is the value. I bring this up because travel is mentioned quite often in values conversations.*)
Get a new car
Redecorate
Retire rich
Donate money
Tithing (*As with travel, the reason you give to charity is a value; what or how much you give is the goal.*)
Put money in my retirement account
Not work
Start my own business
Put my child through college
Get divorced
Get married
Stay married (*Money affects marriages—no question about it. But contrary to what many people believe, it's not how much money you have that matters. It's how you communicate and make decisions about your money that determines whether financial issues will bring you together as a family or drive you apart.*)

What If I Can't Come Up with Enough Values?

This almost never happens. Everyone has lots of values—more than you might think at first. Give yourself some time for them to occur to you. But don't turn it into a marathon. The whole exercise should not take more than 15 minutes! In my office, the average values conversation lasts less than 10.

Also, there are no right or wrong answers here. The only mistake you can make is to be less than honest. In my classes, I always jokingly tell the audience, "Don't look at your neighbor's paper. Those are her values, not yours."

Go All the Way!

The reason our values ladder is designed to elicit at least six personal values is that we are trying to get you to look deep within yourself— so deep that you will come away with a really intense awareness of what is most important to you. Understanding this, you should be able to stop wasting your time, energy, and money on things that don't really matter to you—and begin focusing your resources on the things that do!

As should be clear by now, although we are focusing on the question of money, what we really are getting at in our values conversation is the essence of what matters to you about life in general. That's what makes the technique so powerful. It enables you not only to lay out your values but to define who you are and what direction you want to take your life.

Don't Think You Can Skip This Step

Don't be like some students who take my classes and try to skip this step in the mistaken belief that the values-based approach is nothing more than "New Age feel-good stuff." There's nothing New Age about getting in touch with your values. The Greek philosopher Socrates was talking about that sort of thing back in 400 B.C. The key to human advancement, he taught, could be expressed in two simple words: "Know thyself." So don't get sidetracked.

As you will see as we continue through our journey, the seven-step approach builds on itself. If you don't complete this step, you'll find the next one much harder than it needs to be. That's because doing Step Two gives you a certain momentum that makes Step Three really easy.

Congratulations! You Have Completed Step Two!

The thing to remember about this step is that we had you look closely at your values for a very practical reason: Knowing "what's important about money to you" not only makes it possible to plan your future intelligently, it also makes it easier to stick to your plan. Once they know what their values are, people will do more to protect them than just about anything else in the world. Values are not tasks or resolutions, like "eat less," "save more," or "keep the house clean." Values are not things we get bored with. Values are what we believe in, they are what motivate and shape us.

Now that you have constructed your own values ladder, keep it handy. We're going to use it in Step Three when we start defining your specific financial goals. But there's one more thing you've got to do before you're ready to design that road map to your financial future. *You need to figure out where you stand today financially.*

FIGURE OUT WHERE YOU STAND FINANCIALLY ... AND WHERE YOU WANT TO GO

Imagine that after working late seven consecutive nights, your boss tells you that as a reward for your extra effort he's decided to send you to Paris for a week, all expenses paid. The only catch is, you must be there by the end of the day tomorrow and you must make the arrangements yourself.

No problem, you say, and immediately call up a travel agent. It's after hours, so you get the answering machine. "I need a flight to Paris," you tell the machine, "arriving no later than tomorrow evening." Then you leave your name and phone number and hang up.

The next morning you get a frantic call from the travel agent. "We couldn't book your flight," she tells you.

"Oh, no!" you complain. "Now I'm not going to get to go!" You begin to yell at the travel agent, questioning her competence, but she quickly cuts you off. It's not her fault she couldn't book the flight, she says, it's yours.

"My fault?" you say indignantly. "How is it my fault?"

"You told us where you wanted to go," the travel agent replies, "but you didn't tell us where you are now. How can we get you a flight if we don't know where you're leaving from?"

When it comes to planning a trip, chances are you'd never make a mistake that elementary. But you'd be surprised how many people slip up in precisely the same way when it comes to planning their finances. They plunge into all sorts of detail about what they want to accomplish, what investment they should buy, and where they want to be, without first making sure they know where they stand now.

DO YOU KNOW WHERE YOUR MONEY IS?

If I asked you about your current financial status, could you, right now, list on a blank piece of paper all your assets and liabilities, including your investments, bank accounts, mortgages, and credit-card debts? Do you have an organized filing system in which all your financial documents can be found easily? Or have you left all that stuff to your husband or your accountant? If you're working, do you know how the money in your company pension plan is invested?

You might want to turn back to Step One at this point and take a look at how you did on that quiz about your family's money. If you're like most people, you probably scored lower than you'd like. That's okay. This is where we start to fix the problems you found back there.

Knowing Where Your Money Is Sounds Obvious, But Trust Me—Most People Don't Have a Clue

Having been a financial coach for hundreds of clients, I can tell you from firsthand experience that most people really don't know where they spend their money and where their money is invested. I've had clients come into my office with shopping bags filled with mutual fund statements, bank statements, 401(k) printouts, you name it. Take

Karen and Tom, a successful couple in their 50s. They came into my office one day, dumped the contents of a bulging department-store shopping bag onto my desk, and announced ruefully, "David, we're the people you talk about in your seminars!" We started going through their statements together, and you know what? Even though Karen and Tom had been organized enough to save the statements they'd been sent, most of the envelopes had never been opened! They hadn't looked at their accounts for months.

Now I'm sure that *you*'re not like this, but I'll bet many of your friends are.

Six IRAs, Five Bank Accounts, Four Insurance Plans . . .

After two hours of going through Karen and Tom's stuff, we managed to figure out where all their money was: It was stashed in 12 separate mutual funds, 6 different IRA accounts, 5 bank accounts, 2 old and 2 new 401(k) plans, and 4 separate insurance policies.

Unbelievable, right? Wrong. Karen and Tom are typical of many successful people. As Karen explained it, somewhat defensively, "Tom puts all the responsibility of managing the money in my hands, but with a career and three kids I don't have time to keep track of it all. I really don't know how others find the time."

"You're right, Karen," I said, "No one has the time to monitor what they have, unless they are professional money managers. And I know a lot of professionals who don't take care of their own money because they're so busy taking care of other people's!"

Make Getting Your Financial House in Order Now a Priority!

Old or young, rich or poor, married or single, it doesn't matter—one of the first things we do at The Bach Group after discussing our clients' values is to figure out their current financial condition.

To accomplish this, I have my clients fill out what we call a "Financial Inventory Worksheet." You'll find a copy in Appendix 2.

NOTE: *Don't complete the worksheet until after you've finished reading this book! Why? Sad but true, most people never get past the first few chapters of books like this one if they have to stop reading and fill out a form. So wait until you've gotten through the whole book before you start in on the worksheet.*

If you are like most people, you probably already have all your financial information totally organized. In fact, I'm sure that all of your financial documents are right now sitting in an easy-to-use filing system with brightly colored folders and neatly typed labels. And because all your financial documents are so well organized and easy for you to review, completing the worksheet in the back of the book shouldn't take you more than 30 minutes, right?

Obviously, I'm being a bit facetious here. Usually when I discuss filling out the inventory worksheet in my investment classes, I call this project a "homework assignment." And when I get to the part about most people having all their financial information in color-coded files, the women in the room either laugh or groan. At that point, I say, "For those of you who use the shopping-bag approach to filing, it may take a little longer."

To be honest, I have had some clients who've told me that this "homework" took them only about 15 minutes (usually because they had everything on a financial software program like Quicken or Microsoft Money). But for most people, it generally takes at least an hour or two.

And don't worry if it takes you even longer than that. Some people find the assignment requires an entire weekend. If you're one of them, don't be daunted. It simply means that you really need to do it!

Getting Organized Is One of the Keys to Financial Security

Admittedly, getting organized sometimes can be a painful experience. I've had some clients who thought they were financially secure, only to discover, after listing all their assets and liabilities, that they weren't doing as well as they had imagined. Then again, I've had plenty of others who completed the worksheet and found they were much closer to financial independence than they realized. Either way, they were much better off knowing the truth about their financial situation.

Take Betsy and Victor, two clients of mine who got a lot out of the process. Their story is quite typical, and I hope it will inspire you to emulate their example.

BETSY'S STORY: LEARNING WHERE YOU STAND

"When I first took David's investment class, I got really excited about the opportunity to become involved in my family's finances. I have to admit, however, that the homework assignment of 'getting my financial house in order' did seem a bit intimidating.

"The thing I liked best about the Financial Inventory Worksheet was that it was something that produced immediate results. I knew my family's financial documents were totally disorganized. I also knew that my husband, Victor, probably didn't know what our net worth was.

"The other thing I really liked about this step was that it gave me an easy way to approach my husband about getting involved with our finances. I basically came home from the class and said, 'Victor, I've got a huge homework assignment and I know I'm going to need your help. Do you think we could work together on it this weekend, because I'm not sure I can do it without you?'

"That approach really worked with Victor, since it wasn't like I was accusing him of anything or trying to take control of the finances. And when I showed him what the assignment was, he readily admitted it was something that we should have done years ago. As Victor put it, he had always wanted to get our financial documents organized, but it was a lot like cleaning out the garage—easy to put off.

"In the end, it wound up taking us almost the entire day to do—a lot longer than the 30 minutes David had promised. But as David said, the fact that it took so much longer meant we really needed to do it.

"When we were through, I could really see for the first time just where our family stood financially. I realized for the first time that we were actually doing a pretty good job of saving money. We had very little debt and our retirement accounts were really starting to add up. Seeing this all on paper got me excited about looking at what else I could do to improve our financial situation."

VICTOR'S STORY: A WEIGHT OFF HIS SHOULDERS

"When Betsy came home with this homework assignment to get our financial house in order, quite frankly I was embarrassed. I knew I had taken on the responsibility of managing the family's money, and I felt I had been doing an okay job—but I also knew there was a lot of stuff all over the place, not well organized.

"I have to admit it really felt good when we finished filling out the inventory worksheet that weekend. For the first time in years, Betsy and I really discussed where our financial life was. By getting all of our assets and liabilities down on paper, we were finally able to see in black and white where we actually stood and how much our family was worth. While I always sort of had a running total in my head, filling out the inventory worksheet made it clearer and easier to deal with. I have to say—it's quite a weight off my shoulders to have Betsy involved with our money now. It takes some of the pressure off of me."

FROM MY POINT OF VIEW . . .

When I met with Betsy and Victor in my office after their weekend "housecleaning" session, we had a great time. They really had enjoyed getting their finances organized and were excited to talk about where they stood.

Because they had done such a thorough job filling out the worksheet, my job actually was quite easy. One of the first things I noticed was that they had both been opening individual retirement accounts (IRAs) at different banks each year for nearly eight years. They had done this because they thought that's how you get the best return on your money—and also because they had heard that "diversifying" was important, and they believed that going to a lot of different banks was how you diversified.

Actually, what they really were doing was letting their retirement dollars lay dormant at a measly 5 percent annual rate, which didn't even keep up with inflation. I was able to help them consolidate all their accounts into one custodial IRA and then reposition the money they had invested into more appropriate growth investments. I will explain how we did this—and how you can too—in Step Five, when we discuss your "retirement basket." For now, what matters is that by getting organized, Betsy and Victor were able to see where they stood and what they needed to do to achieve their goals.

DO YOUR HOMEWORK

The way we work at my office is simple. We send prospective clients the Financial Inventory Worksheet and ask them to fill it out completely before they come in. Nonetheless, some clients show up without having filled out their sheets. Often I'll kid them and ask if they were the kind of students who never did their homework on time. Joking aside, however, there's no getting around the fundamental reality: Until you get your finances organized, you can't get started creating financial security—and ultimately your financial dreams.

So no excuses. When you finish this book, you must fill out the Financial Inventory Worksheet in Appendix 2. It's the best way to start getting organized and involved in your finances and, most important, determine your net worth. (This is key, since if you don't know what you are worth, you won't know where you are starting from.) By the time you are done, you will have a better grasp of your financial situation than the vast majority of Americans. You will know not only your personal net worth but also where you spend your money and how your newfound wealth is going to be built. You—not someone else—will be in charge of your financial destiny.

Your First Job: Find Your Stuff

Completing the Financial Inventory Worksheet is probably the most crucial homework assignment you'll get in the course of this book. But don't start working on it yet. At this point, all I want you to do is begin finding your "stuff." Doing this now will make it much easier to fill out your worksheet later. So let's get going.

1. Find your tax returns from last year and put them in a file labeled "Tax Returns." If you've got copies of older returns, include them too. Ideally, you should keep copies of your returns for at least seven years.
2. Get all the statements you have from all of your retirement accounts (including all work-related family retirement accounts) and put them in a file labeled "Retirement Accounts."
3. Get all your checking-account and savings-account statements together and put them in a file labeled "Checking and Savings."

4. Get all your statements from any nonqualified investment accounts you may have (basically, that means any investments you own outside of your retirement accounts) and put them in a file labeled "Nonretirement Accounts."
5. Get all your credit-card statements and put them in a file labeled "Credit-Card Debt."
6. Get your home-mortgage statements and put them in a file labeled "Home Mortgage."
7. Get the records concerning your other major liabilities (such as car and boat loans or leases, second-mortgage statements, etc.) and put them in a file labeled "Liabilities."
8. Get all your insurance documents (including your home or renter's policies, disability coverage, and health plans) and put them in a file labeled "Insurance."
9. If you have children, get the statements for any savings or investment accounts you've set up for them and put it all in a file labeled "Kids' Accounts."
10. Get any information you may have on your future Social Security benefits and put it in a file labeled "Social Security."
11. Get your will and other trust documents and put them in a file labeled "Family Will or Trust."

As you dig into this assignment, the first thing you probably will notice is that you don't have all of these documents. In some cases, you may have lost them or thrown them away. In others, you may never have had them in the first place. For example, chances are you've never bothered to order your Personal Earnings and Benefit Estimate Statement from the Social Security Administration. Or maybe you don't have disability insurance. Whatever the case, it does not matter at this point. All I want you to do now is create the above-mentioned files, whether you have anything to put in them or not. It shouldn't take very long. After all, there are only 11 of them.

Once you're done, put the folders in a file cabinet and feel good about yourself. You are already more organized than you were when you first picked up this book and are better prepared to complete the inventory worksheet.

If You're Part of a Couple . . .

If you are married (or are in some similarly committed relationship), you definitely should try to get your significant other involved in this project. But be diplomatic. After all, while you've been getting excited about getting organized, your mate has been innocently going about his day with no idea that you are planning to "clean house" financially. A word of advice: Don't suddenly start jumping all over your partner for being disorganized. Remember—he hasn't read this book. (At least not yet.)

As I tell the women who take my seminars, it's probably not a good idea to run home and tell your husband, "Honey, there's this financial advisor named David Bach and he says that as a man you are more than likely doing a really terrible job managing our finances, so from now on I'm going to be in charge of our money. Now, show me where it is!" Nor should you announce, "I just learned that you probably will die before me. And if you don't drop dead soon, I'll still need to protect myself in case you meet some bimbo and decide to divorce me. So show me where all the money is!"

Now, obviously, I'm exaggerating a little bit. I doubt you would ever be so blatant. But I also know that it is very easy to get excited by a set of new ideas.

And I do want you to get excited. That's the whole point of this book—to get you excited enough to make drastic changes in your life. Still, I don't want a bunch of angry men out there looking for my head. More important, I don't want you to be met with an immediate wall of defensiveness and negative feedback.

My grandmother taught me that you can accomplish anything in life if your approach is right. In this case, the right approach involves recognizing that if you are part of a couple (and this goes for same-sex relationships as well), money issues should be handled jointly. Chances are, at this point yours are not.

That's one of the great things about this financial housecleaning process. Not only does it show you where you stand financially, it's also, as Betsy pointed out, a very proactive way for couples to start working on their finances together. In filling out the worksheet, nobody is judging or criticizing anyone. All you are doing is getting your stuff organized. If your husband or significant other says, "It's taken care of, honey—don't worry about it," you simply reply, "Great. Show me how it's taken care of and let's discuss it together." If he continues to balk, explain to him how important it is to you to get involved with the family's finances and that knowing where everything is simply a fundamental part of the process.

What If the Man in Your Life Won't Cooperate?

For most of you, this process of discussing your finances with your husband or significant other is not going to be a big deal. My experience is that most men really do want their mates to be involved with the family's finances. I can't tell you how many men have said to me over the years, "I'm so glad my wife is taking an interest in this stuff. She never seemed to care before, and I always worried about how she would cope if something were to happen to me. Having her involved is a real relief."

The point is, someone who really loves you should not be threatened by your wanting to know where the family money is. The key is how you present it. Some men have fragile egos. What can I say? We like to think we are in charge and that we know what we are doing. Of course, for the most part you know that we are not in charge and that you are. That's fine—just don't let us know that you know it.

In the event your family already has someone who helps to manage your money (a financial advisor or an attorney or an accountant), then I strongly suggest that you make an appointment to meet with that person. Most likely, he or she does not know exactly where you stand, and completing the Financial Inventory Worksheet really will help the person to better help you. The initial phone call can be as simple as this: "I'm making an effort to get involved in handling the family's financial decisions. I understand you have been working with my husband [or whomever] and I would like to meet with you to discuss where we stand financially."

When you make the appointment, I strongly suggest that you and your significant other go to this meeting—and all future meetings—together. I can't stress this enough: Financial planning should involve both of you equally. The biggest mistake I see couples make is not handling it together. In our office, if a man calls to make an appointment and tells us that his wife does not need to come with him because he's "in charge of the money," we won't take the meeting. That's how strongly we feel about the importance of doing financial planning as a couple.

HEADING IN THE RIGHT DIRECTION

Microsoft, which in my opinion is one of the smartest companies in the world today, recently ran what I thought was one of the world's smartest advertising campaigns. The campaign wasn't about software but rather about our lives and where they might be headed. Their television commercials, which I'm sure you saw, asked the question straight out: "Where do you want to go today?" (with the idea obviously being that Microsoft could get you there).

As a Smart Woman, the challenge you face now is to answer that question for yourself—to take the foundational work we have just done (including looking at your values and getting your family finances organized) and use it to create a compelling future that inspires and excites you.

So where do you start? Well, here's a hint . . .

Success leaves clues.

Have you ever noticed that some people seem to have it all? Their lives always seem to be going in the direction that they want. They always seem to be moving forward, never pushed off course by life's daily demands and challenges. No matter what happens to them, they come out on top.

Don't you just hate those people?

I threw that in just to see if you were paying attention. Of course, you don't really hate them. But doesn't it make you wonder? Why is it that some people can be so successful, have so much fun, and make it seem so easy?

The answer, I believe, lies in the fact that for the most part successful people have specific goals. In the book *The Eleven Commandments of Wildly Successful Women,* author Pamela Gilberd interviewed 125 women who achieved extraordinary success in both their work and their personal lives. What she found was that most of these women had one thing in common: They all knew where they wanted to go. They had goals. They created their own plans and they focused on making them happen.

The master motivator Napoleon Hill, who wrote the renowned book *Think and Grow Rich,* phrased it differently, but it amounted to the same thing. According to Hill, to achieve your dreams you have to focus on what you want your life to be about. He called this developing "Definiteness of Purpose." After studying the most successful people of his time, Hill concluded that individuals who had this "definiteness of purpose" found it easier to prioritize their time, effort, and money—and, ultimately, to reach their dreams.

Now, "developing definiteness of purpose" is nothing more than a fancy way of saying "setting yourself specific goals." And what Hill teaches us is that successful people do just that. When you ask them, they can tell you where it is they want their life to end up and what they are doing to make sure they get there.

Getting Beyond "Shoulda, Coulda, Woulda"

It's been said many times that if you want to be successful, you should do what successful people do. I wholeheartedly subscribe to this belief. (This is what I was getting at before when I said that success leaves clues.) In other words, if successful people set specific goals for themselves, maybe that's something you should be doing too.

With that in mind, let's spend a moment talking about what a goal is . . . and what it is not. The dictionary defines a goal as the purpose toward which an endeavor is directed. That's clear enough, but it's only part of the story. The fact is, not just any purpose will do. In order to empower us, a goal must be specific. Otherwise, we will treat it as nothing more than a wish—what I call the "shoulda, coulda, woulda" phenomenon.

You know what I'm talking about. It's possible that at times you have succumbed to this phenomenon yourself. I certainly have. As you will learn in Step Four, I used to be a raging shopper. I'd get home from a shopping spree and think, "I really should have left those credit cards home" or "I should have bought less stuff." My point here is that back when I was shopping too much, spending less was for me a wish, not a goal. Spending less didn't become a real goal for me until I took a piece of paper and a pen and wrote down the words: "I will not buy anything with my credit cards anymore. I will use only cash."

Achieving Your Goals Isn't Something That Just Happens

If goals were easy to achieve, then the entire world would be successful. But that's okay. You didn't buy this book because you expect life to be easy. Rather, you are a woman who knows that to make things happen in life, you have to get involved. But let me ask you something: Do you have written goals right now? Is there a piece of paper somewhere in your home or office on which you have written down what it is you are striving for?

More than likely the answer is no. In fact, studies show that less than 1 percent of Americans write down specific goals for themselves each year. That's a shame, because writing down your goals is powerful.

In a study done at Harvard University more than 40 years ago, researchers polled the graduating class of 1953 to find out how many students actually had clearly written, specific goals and a plan for achieving them. This being a class of highly intelligent people at one of the world's most renowned universities, you'd expect the answer to be most of them, right?

Not even close. In fact, only 3 percent of the class had taken the time to write down their goals.

Now here comes the really interesting part. Some 20 years later, researchers polled this same group of graduates to see how they had fared in life. It turned out that the 3 percent who had written down their goals had accumulated more wealth than the other 97 percent of their class combined! Researchers reported that these people also seemed to be healthier and happier than their classmates.

I was in college when I first heard about this study, and I wondered if achieving your goals could really be that easy. "Put in writing what you want and focus on it daily"? Well, it may not be easy, but over the years I definitely have seen it work.

Writing a $10-Million Check . . . to Yourself!

One of my favorite stories about the power of writing down your goals involves someone we both know. Actually, we may not know him personally, but it definitely feels like we do because these days it seems like he's everywhere. I'm talking about Jim Carrey, the star of such hit movies as *The Mask, Batman Forever,* and *Liar, Liar.*

Just a few years ago, in the late 1980s, Carrey's career was starting to stall. He had managed to get a few small TV jobs but seemed nowhere near to realizing his dreams of major stardom. It was at this point in his life, when he was struggling to the top, that he went for a drive in the Hollywood Hills and visualized what it would be like to be rich and famous. Carrey did more than just dream, however. He parked his car, pulled out his checkbook, and wrote himself a check for $10 million. He dated it: "Thanksgiving Day, 1995."

For the next several years, Carrey kept that check in his wallet. When times got tough, he would take it out and stare at it, thinking about what his life would someday be like when his talents and efforts finally were rewarded.

The rest, of course, is history. Carrey got noticed on the TV series *In Living Color,* and his first two movies, *Ace Ventura* and *The Mask,* were huge hits. Late in November 1995, he was offered $10 million to star in *Mask 2.* The following year, with *The Cable Guy,* his price went up to $20 million a picture!

Now, you can be a skeptic like many people and say, "Oh, that was just dumb luck." Or you can focus on the fact that Jim Carrey had Napoleon Hill's "Definiteness of Purpose." He didn't "shoulda, coulda, woulda" his goals into wishes that fade away. He put them in writing, and by making them specific, he was able to make them happen.

See, Hear, Feel, and Smell Your Way to Your Dreams

In my seminars, when we get to talking about creating goals, I often tell a story about two women. One is named Jill and the other is named Jane. Jill and Jane both want to have successful financial futures, and both believe in keeping a written list of their financial goals. As it happens, they have at least one goal in common: They both want to own a vacation home. But while Jill writes down her goal as "Buy vacation home," Jane is a lot more specific. "I will own a vacation home by January 1, 2000," she writes. "It will be a three-bedroom house with two baths located on the west side of Lake Tahoe. The mortgage will range between $350,000 and $400,000. I will take out a 30-year mortgage but make extra payments to pay it off in 18 years. I will save $65,000 over the next 36 months to make my down payment."

Now let me ask you the question I ask the students who attend my seminars: Which of these two women do you think is more likely to reach her goal of owning a second home?

The answer, obviously, is Jane. The reason: Jane has been incredibly specific about what she wants and how she intends to get it. Indeed, she has been so specific that she practically can see, hear, feel, and smell that lakeside home. And that's the key. Specificity transforms a vague dream into a concrete, achievable goal. If you can practically see, hear, feel, and smell a goal, the chances are excellent that you'll not only know what's required to make it real, you'll actually *do* what's required to make it real.

The challenge facing you is to create goals that are equally specific and empowering.

THE "SMART WOMEN FINISH RICH"
QUANTUM LEAP SYSTEM

Let's say for a moment that you buy what I'm saying. Let's say you accept that you should have goals and that you believe they should be in writing and you want to make them as specific as possible. Now I want to show you a way to formulate a series of goals that will allow you to take a quantum leap toward your dreams in the years ahead. I promise you—if you follow the rules I'm going to lay out, your life just 12 months from now will both surprise and delight you.

> **RULE NO. 1**
> UNTIL IT'S WRITTEN DOWN, IT'S NOT A GOAL—
> IT'S JUST A SLOGAN.

If you don't put what you want in writing, then you might as well not even waste your time thinking about it. You are kidding yourself. Your goals *must* be written down. Think about it. How many times have you had a "great idea" that you thought could make you a fortune, only to forget what it was a week later? Why? Because you didn't write it down.

If your goals are worth focusing your effort and time on, then they must be worth recording—and if *you* don't record them, who will?

In a nutshell, writing down your goals makes them real and easy to focus on. So from now on, you must commit yourself to recording all your goals on paper. *No excuses.*

RULE NO. 2

GOALS MUST BE SPECIFIC, MEASURABLE, AND PROVABLE.

Even if it's in writing, if you are not specific about what it is you want to attain—or if you've written down something that really can't be measured or proven—then once again, what you've got isn't a goal, it's a wish.

For instance, there is no point in writing down "I want to be wealthy in the year 2000." That is useless. What you should be writing down is something much more specific—something like "I will put aside 10 percent of my gross income every month for the next 36 months, at which time I will have a minimum of $48,000 in a pretax retirement account." (I'll explain what a pretax retirement account is in Step Five.) Similarly, you shouldn't write down, "I will be debt free." Rather, you should write something like "I will pay off my VISA bill over the next 12 months. I will pay cash for all purchases until my credit-card debt is completely gone, and I will never spend over $100 on an item without leaving the store and giving myself 48 hours to consider whether I really need that item."

The point is that a goal is very difficult to attain if it's vague. You have to be able to show someone (the most important someone being yourself) exactly where the finish line is. After all, if you don't know precisely what your goal is, how will you be able to tell whether you've attained it or not?

RULE NO. 3

TAKE SOME IMMEDIATE ACTION WITHIN THE NEXT 48 HOURS TO START MOVING TOWARD YOUR GOAL.

Let's say that, like Jill and Jane, your goal is to be able to purchase a vacation home on Lake Tahoe. Now, that's a long-term goal; realistically, you don't expect to accomplish it for at least five years. But that doesn't mean there isn't anything you can do right now, in the next 48 hours, to move toward that goal. You could, for example, call the Tahoe Chamber of Commerce and ask for a list of reputable real-estate agents. You could then telephone some of those agencies and ask for information about available houses that fit your price range and interest. You could take out a subscription to the local Tahoe newspaper in order to keep abreast of what is happening in the community.

There are many things you could do. The key is to *do something*. Take an action—any action—that will make the goal you have written down feel more real and specific!

> ### RULE NO. 4
> ONCE YOU HAVE WRITTEN DOWN YOUR GOALS, PUT THEM SOMEPLACE WHERE YOU CAN SEE THEM EVERY DAY.

I keep mine in my Day-Timer. Some people I know post theirs on the mirror in their bathroom. The point is that you should read your goals every day. By seeing your goals each day (preferably in the morning when you first wake up), you reaffirm to yourself what you are focusing your life on. As a result, you will find yourself subconsciously seeking out information and contacts that can help you attain your goals. In addition, reviewing your goals every day helps to make them clear and, ultimately, very personal and real to you.

> ### RULE NO. 5
> SHARE YOUR GOALS WITH SOMEONE YOU LOVE AND TRUST.

I have heard it said time and time again that you should keep your goals and dreams to yourself, because "other people will try to talk you out of them or squash them." Well, that's total nonsense!

I can't tell you how mad it makes me to think of all the years I wasted keeping my goals and dreams to myself because of bad advice like that. The fact is, the best way to reach your goals is to get help. But if you don't share them with anyone, how are your friends or coworkers going to be able to offer you support and assistance?

I first learned the power of this rule at one of Tony Robbins's "Date with Destiny" seminars. Tony was doing a session on goal setting, and he told the group, "If you keep your goals inside you, you are missing out on the world that wants to help you." Well, I didn't really believe that the world wanted to help me. Then again, this was Tony Robbins, one of the greatest motivational experts in the world, so I figured, "What the heck, it can't hurt to try."

At that point, Tony broke us up into groups and told us to share our biggest dream or goal for the year. Once my group formed up, I hesitatingly announced, "I want to write a book for women on investing called *Smart Women Finish Rich*." Everyone nodded and said that sounded great. Ten minutes later, after the group had dispersed, an incredible woman named Vicki St. George tapped me on the shoulder. "I heard you want to write an investment book for women," she said. "I've worked with Tony for ten years and now I run my own writing company called Just Write. I'd love to work with you to help you make your book a reality."

I ended up hiring Vicki about three months later, and the book proposal she helped me create was instrumental in getting me one of the top literary agents in the country.

ONLY YOU KNOW WHAT YOU CAN DO

If you share your goal with someone you love and he or she says "Oh, you can't do that" or "No, that won't work," remember—that person really doesn't know what you can or cannot do. He or she knows only what *he* or *she* can or cannot do. Many well-intentioned people will tell you that you can't do something simply because it's beyond their own capabilities. Ignore these people; their negative beliefs are their problems, not yours. Keep sharing your goals until you find someone who will support you.

And here is something else to think about: If your friends really don't support you and your goals, maybe you need a new set of friends. I consider myself very fortunate because I am surrounded by incredible friends. When I originally told them I wanted to write a book, each and every one of them said, "That's great, go for it, I can't wait to read it." And periodically after that, they would ask me how my book was coming along. This inspired me even more. It also put a little pressure on me to keep focusing on my goal. Both the support and the pressure really helped me get the job done.

The key point here is that few things affect how successful you will be as much as the people with whom you surround yourself. If becoming financially independent is really important to you right now but you don't have any close friends to whom you feel you can turn for support, then go out and make some new friends. Join a women's investment club in your area. Take some evening classes on retirement planning. Do something that forces you to get out of your immediate comfort zone and meet some new people. There are many organizations you can join to get help and learn new skills. Take advantage of them.

RULE NO. 6
DEVELOP GOALS THAT FIT IN WITH YOUR VALUES.

In Step Two, we went through a process specifically designed to help you get in touch with your values about money. Use what you discovered about yourself and what you are looking for in life to create goals that will make your dreams a reality.

For instance, if the phrase at the top of your values ladder is "spend more time with my family," then write that down on your goal list. But remember, you must make the goal measurable and specific. So be sure to indicate *how* you want to spend time with your family—what you want to do and when you will do it. And involve your family; enlist their ideas and opinions. Tell them, "I've determined that one of my most important values is to spend more quality time with you, and I'd like to plan some special family time together." Get them to suggest specifics, and then, together, write them all down on paper.

If you do this, not only will your goals be written and specific, but your family will be your support team because you've gotten them involved in your newfound spirit.

RULE NO. 7
REVIEW YOUR GOALS AT LEAST ONCE EVERY 12 MONTHS.

At an absolute minimum, you should review your goals and redo this process once each year. Ideally, I recommend you carry out this review process the last week in December so you can start the new year with total passion and renewed enthusiasm. I go through this process each December myself. In addition, every three months I spend an entire day reviewing both how I am doing and where I want to go. In this way, I am forced to recommit emotionally to my written goals, which in turn helps me refocus my efforts to make them become a reality. If I find I can't recommit to all my goals, that's a major sign it's time to rethink—and probably rewrite—what's on my list.

Remember, this is your list and your life. You should be in charge of what is and what is not important to you. And don't consider a change of heart to be a failure on your part. Your goal list is not a "to do" list. It is much more important. It is your life-planning process!

LET'S GET STARTED!

Both in my office and in my class, I always ask my clients and students the same question to elicit their goals.

"In a perfect world, if you and I were sitting together three years from today, what would have to happen for you to feel you have made not just good, but GREAT financial progress with your life?"

The point of this question is quite simple. Before you get into investment strategies, what you need to do to become financially secure is be clear about exactly what it is that you want and feel you need.

Think back to Step Two, in which you worked out what was important to you about money. The point of writing down your values then was to make it easier for you now to articulate a series of goals that can help you put your values into practice.

So based on what you said in Step Two, and how you feel now, what is it that you would like to see happen in your life over the next three years that will require money? Do you want to see yourself get out of credit-card debt? Do you want to own a home? Is your goal to be able to afford to retire in three years? Maybe you would like to move to Paris and study art. Or start your own business. Or expand a business that you already own. Whatever the case may be, use the values you came up with in Step Two and write down, on the chart that follows, what would have to happen for you to feel three years from now that you have made successful progress.

Do it now.

GOALS
Designing a Proactive Life!

THERE ARE TWO PARTS TO THIS EXERCISE:

- Ten blanks for writing down your goals between now and three years
- A form in which you specify your five most important goals over the next three years

STEPS:

- On this page, below, fill in the ten blanks with as many goals as possible that you want to accomplish during the next three years.
- On the next page, specify:
    1. Five Most Important Goals
    2. Make Specific, Measurable, and Provable
       (i.e.: How much will it cost?)
    3. Immediate Action in the Next 48 Hours
    4. Who Will You Share Your Goals With
    5. What Values Does It Help You Accomplish
    6. What Challenges Will You Face
    7. Strategies to Overcome Anticipated Challenges

1.   6.
2.   7.
3.   8.
4.   9.
5.   10.

TOP 5 GOALS	MAKE SPECIFIC, MEASURABLE, AND PROVABLE	IMMEDIATE ACTION IN THE NEXT 48 HOURS	WHO WILL YOU SHARE YOUR GOALS WITH	WHAT VALUES DOES IT HELP YOU ACCOMPLISH	WHAT CHALLENGES WILL YOU FACE	STRATEGIES TO OVERCOME ANTICIPATED CHALLENGES
1						
2						
3						
4						
5						

Figuring Out Where You Want to Be

Many people call what we have just done together goal setting. I call it *Designing a Proactive Life!* However you label it, one thing is inarguable: If you can't figure out where you want to be in 3 years, how are you ever going to be able to plan out your life 10 to 20 years from now? Equally important, how will you know how much money you are going to need to reach your goals? The answer is, you won't and you can't.

Why three years? Three years is a very useful amount of time to work with. You can accomplish a tremendous amount in three years. In fact, you can change your life.

Consider the story of Lucy, a woman who used this question to make massive changes in her life. Lucy took my "Smart Women Finish Rich!" seminar a few years ago, but unlike many of my students, she didn't come to my office to review her finances when the class was over. In fact, I didn't hear from her almost an entire year.

When we finally sat down together, my first question to Lucy was why she had waited so long to come see me.

"Well, David," she began, "when you asked us in class where we wanted our lives to be in three years, I realized that I had some serious decisions to make."

Indeed, it turned out that my question had led Lucy to transform her life totally.

LUCY'S STORY: TURNING OFF THE AUTOMATIC PILOT

"What I realized after thinking about that question of David's was that after 32 years of marriage, I was not happy. I was living a loveless life. I also realized that more money was not going to make my marriage any better—not then or in three years. So for me the question was: Do I have enough money to get divorced? If I don't want to be married, can I afford to be single?

"The more I thought about this, the more I realized it wasn't simply an issue of money. I truly did not want to go on with my life the way it was. My kids were grown, I was just starting 'the fun phase' of my life, as David had put it in the class, and I realized that the time was now to make a decision. So I made one.

"On the worksheet I had received in class, I wrote down, 'Get separated and independent of Sam within three years.'

"Once I had written that down, I got to thinking. Why should this take three years? I realized it shouldn't. I also realized that I had probably wasted the last ten years of my life with Sam, because I had never really stopped to ask myself where it was I wanted my life to head. Looking back, I see now that I had let my life get on 'automatic pilot.' Unfortunately, as a result of being on automatic pilot, I had ended up at a destination that did not work for me.

"Now, however, thanks to the three-year question and the technique of writing down your goals, my life has been dramatically changed for the better."

FROM MY POINT OF VIEW . . .

I find Lucy's story incredibly empowering. Less than three years after she took stock of her values and goals, she is a new person. First and foremost, she is divorced. And while I am not an advocate of divorce, in Lucy's case it happened to be necessary. Was it hard for her? You bet it was. But, in fact, both of her children supported her decision. (Indeed, they wanted to know why she had waited so long.)

Second, as a result of the divorce settlement, Lucy has been able to pay off her home mortgage completely, and we have positioned her additional assets to grow for her retirement. With a well-defined plan in place, Lucy can look forward to retiring in ten years without having to worry about money.

Third, she has upgraded her career from a position in retail sales to office management at a law firm, and she is increasing her job skills on a daily basis.

Finally, and most important of all, Lucy is happier than she has been in years.

IS YOUR LIFE ON AUTOMATIC PILOT?

Letting your life go on automatic pilot has a tendency to lead to disaster. Yet we do it all the time, usually without noticing it.

The best and quickest way I know to protect yourself from this syndrome is to stop, think, and put in writing what it is you specifically want out of life. In addition to formulating these wants in terms of three-year goals, I suggest you also write out intermediate and long-term goals. If you haven't already done so, remember to use the "Designing a Proactive Life" worksheet on pages 76–77.

Remember to use the seven rules of goal setting I listed earlier. Most important, remember that this is your opportunity to create the future you want. Have fun with this. If you create a really compelling future for yourself, you will find yourself jumping out of bed every morning, knowing you are facing not just another day but a day full of promise that will bring you closer to the future that you want!

Don't Let Challenges Get You Down!

Guess what? It's possible that you could do this entire exercise and still not stay on track and reach your desired goals. Why? Because life is filled with "challenges," both financial and personal, and unless you prepare for them, you could get stopped dead in your tracks.

So here is what I want you to do. After you write down your goals, I want you to list *in detail* all the potential challenges that could derail you from attaining them. Notice I don't call them "problems." I want you to wipe that word out of your vocabulary. Short of death (which is the only permanent problem I know of), there *are* no problems. There are only challenges.

Now, with that in mind, I want you to put down on paper everything you can think of that possibly could prevent you from achieving your goals. You may be thinking that I'm being pessimistic, but trust me on this—I'm not being pessimistic, I'm being realistic. By highlighting all the potential challenges on paper, you are acknowledging two very important realities: that there are challenges, and that you can come up with ways to overcome them.

In fact, that is the next step. Once you've listed all the challenges you can come up with (and I'll bet that right now without realizing it you are thinking subconsciously of all the reasons why you might not be able to make your goal a reality), I want you to write down a specific "solution" for each of them. And don't despair—all challenges have solutions.

I call this process drafting your "Personal Plan for Success." An example of a Personal Plan for Success that I used with a client when discussing retirement planning follows. Take a look at it and then create one for yourself and your number-one goal.

A Personal Plan for Success
Designing a Specific Plan to Overcome Your Challenges

STARTING LINE

SPECIFIC GOAL

Date: 1998

Barbara's number-one goal is to retire at age 58 with $1 million.

Current retirement assets are $250,000.

CHALLENGES YOU MAY FACE	SPECIFIC STRATEGIES TO OVERCOME CHALLENGES
Not saving enough money	Maximize contributions starting tomorrow in company-sponsored 401(k) plan
Spending too much money	Spend cash only
Too much credit-card debt	Cut up credit cards; stop using them
Too much credit-card debt	Make goal to pay off credit cards, starting with smallest debt first
Not making enough money	Look for specific ways at work to "add more value"; meet with boss, discuss strategy to get a raise
Family spends too much money	Discuss specific financial goals and get their input on ways we can work as a team
College costs	Explain financial goals and challenges of retirement to son, Tom, and explain the importance of Tom's getting a job now to help with college costs
Not enough time to get everything done	Wake up an hour early each day and focus on goals and plans.

VICTORY

DESIRED OUTCOME

Desired Date: 2007

Barbara wants to live a worry-free retirement that includes travel and lots of fun.

Based on her expenses, $1 million will provide her with an income she cannot outlive.

A Personal Plan for Success
Designing a Specific Plan to Overcome Your Challenges

STARTING LINE

SPECIFIC
GOAL

CHALLENGES YOU MAY FACE

SPECIFIC STRATEGIES TO OVERCOME CHALLENGES

VICTORY

DESIRED
OUTCOME

Challenges Are Your Building Blocks to the Future You Want!

As you finish Step Three, I want you to think about the following question: When was the last time you did something perfectly the first time you tried it?

The answer is probably never.

Imagine if when you were a toddler, crawling around on all fours, your parents had berated you for not being born a "walker." Imagine if instead of encouraging you, they criticized and yelled, saying things like "I can't believe you can't walk—you'll never be able to walk." It would have been not only cruel but dumb. The fact is, sensible adults do the exact opposite with their kids. We not only encourage them when they start trying to walk, we run out and buy all sorts of high-tech video equipment to record it all. We take rolls and rolls of film to capture the moment when the child finally takes his or her first step.

So why is it that we start criticizing ourselves for not "walking" the first time we try to take a step? If this is the first time you have ever put down in writing what you want your life to be about, what your goals for the future are, you should be congratulating yourself—not feeling badly if your initial attempt doesn't turn out perfectly!

Remember, your first attempt to record your goals is not supposed to be perfect. Each time you do this exercise, it will become easier, and you will become better at designing your life. The exciting thing you should realize is that by making the effort to write down your goals, you are saying to yourself "I am responsible for my future." Nothing could make you more powerful.

By itself, the single act of writing down your goals makes you special. Don't believe me. Test it. Do this entire step, put everything down in writing that I have suggested, then ask your friends and family if they have written goals. Not "ideas" about where they want their life to go, but actual written goals. Most likely, you will find that you are now a unique woman. In fact, my guess is that when they learn you have put your goals down in writing, your friends and family will begin to hold you in higher esteem. You also may find them deciding that they too should have written goals. So share this chapter with them. You may become the inspiration that your friends and family need to make their lives even better.

Congratulations! You Have Finished Step Three

Now let's take the goals and dreams you have written down and learn about a powerful system that will enable you to achieve them without having suddenly to start earning a lot of money. This system employs something I call "the Latté Factor," and it is the most powerful and easy way I know of to transform a woman's financial goals and dreams into reality.

USE THE POWER OF THE LATTÉ FACTOR . . . HOW TO CREATE MASSIVE WEALTH ON JUST A FEW DOLLARS A WEEK!

Have you ever heard someone say, "If I could only make more money, then I could really start to become a saver, or maybe even an investor"? Perhaps you've even said something like that yourself.

If so, you may have been mistaken. Making more money won't necessarily make you a better saver or investor. Look at the newspapers—virtually every day someone famous, someone you or I might reasonably regard as a huge money earner, declares bankruptcy. Take M. C. Hammer, the hip-hop star. In the early 1990s, Hammer was one of the world's highest-paid performers, earning a reported $35 million in one year. Almost overnight, he had gone from being a bat boy for the Oakland Athletics to a millionaire many times over. I remember thinking how incredible it must have felt to become so wealthy so quickly. Then one day I saw Hammer on television taking a reporter through the extravagant house he was building in Fremont, California. The place was huge. Though it was only half finished, it was rumored to have cost him more than $10 million already.

When I saw how out of control his spending was, I told friends that M. C. Hammer would be bankrupt in five years. I was wrong. It was only about three years later that he declared bankruptcy. Unfortunately for M. C. Hammer, being rich and famous did not lead to financial security. But M. C. Hammer is not alone . . .

DO YOU RECOGNIZE ANY OF THESE PEOPLE?

Larry King, Francis Ford Coppola, Debbie Reynolds, Redd Foxx, Dorothy Hamill, Wayne Newton, Susan Powter, Burt Reynolds. Do you know what they all have in common? Aside from being famous, they have all filed for bankruptcy. So did 1.4 million other Americans in 1997. That represented a nearly 20 percent increase in bankruptcy filings in just one year! What accounts for this epidemic of insolvency? Well, among other things, Americans have become addicted to spending money by using "plastic cash." In 1997 consumer debt hit a record $1.25 trillion! Which leads me to suggest . . .

It's time to keep more . . . and spend less.

As I noted back in Step One, the reason most people fail financially is not because their incomes are too small but because their spending habits are too big. In other words, they spend more money than they make. This may sound awfully basic, but it's true. If you spend more than you make, you always will be in debt, always stressed, rarely happy, and eventually poor or bankrupt.

Controlling your spending, though, isn't all there is to being a Smart Woman and finishing rich. You also must make a point of saving a portion of every dollar you earn. No matter how large your paycheck is, if you don't save, you will never live a life of financial abundance. (Just ask M. C. Hammer.)

Whether you are a highly compensated doctor or lawyer supporting mortgages on two homes or a more modestly paid teacher, office worker, or sales trainee who barely makes the rent each month, the key to financial independence can be summed up in three little words . . .

Pay yourself first.

Why in the world would you work 40 (or 50, or 60, or more!) hours a week, and then pay someone else first? Search me, but most Americans pay *everyone* else before they pay themselves. Most of us pay the IRS first (through our withholding tax), then our mortgage or our rent, then our utilities, then our car payments, then our VISA or American Express bills, and on and on. If by some miracle there is something left over after all those payments—meaning there have been no "Murphy's law" disasters, like the car breaking down or the washing machine dying—then maybe (and I mean just maybe) we might manage to put away a few dollars for our future.

I call this the "Pay Everyone Else First, You Last" system, and it stinks. It's like having "investor dyslexia"; it's all backward. Among other things, it's why the average American has so little in the bank and so much in credit-card debt.

Whatever You Do, Don't Pay Uncle Sam First!

Of all the crazy things people do with their money, the one I really can't fathom is paying their taxes before they pay themselves. Not even the government expects you to do that. If the government did expect to get paid first, it wouldn't have enacted laws to that allow us to put part of our earnings into retirement accounts such as IRAs and 401(k) plans *before* the tax man takes his cut. This is called "pretax" investing, and it is the single smartest thing you can do to build wealth.

Unfortunately, millions of Americans don't take advantage of pretax investing. Instead, they let state and federal tax authorities funnel off as much as 40 percent of each paycheck—that's 40 cents out of every dollar they earn—before they even get to see it. This is a huge mistake. In Step Five, you'll learn all about pretax retirement accounts. Until then, just remember that the government really does want you to have financial security—so much so that it's willing to give you a break on your taxes if you use part of your earnings to fund a retirement account. Whatever you do, don't pass up this break. You've earned it!

THE 12 PERCENT SOLUTION

So what does "pay yourself first" mean? It means that whenever you make any money, no matter how much or how little, before you spend any of it on anything else, you should put some of it aside for your future.

Now, when I say "before you spend any of it on anything else," I mean *anything* else. That includes your rent or mortgage, your credit-card bills, even your payroll withholding tax. Ideally, you should pay 12 percent of the gross—meaning your total earnings *before taxes*—into some sort of retirement account that you will never touch until you actually retire. Of course, it's possible that because of how much you make or the kind of retirement account you have, you may not be eligible to put that much into a pretax retirement account. In that case, you should make up the difference by putting money into an after-tax account.

Why do I suggest putting away 12 percent of your gross income? Well, for years the financial experts have been suggesting that to prepare properly for retirement, everyone should be saving at least 10 percent of what he or she makes. Of course, when they say "everyone," the experts are really talking about men—and in this case, at least, what's good enough for men isn't necessarily good enough for women. After all, women live longer than men—and as a result, they need to put away more money for their retirement. How much more? Well, if women's retirements tend to last 20 percent longer than men's—and that's what the statistics tell us—then women's retirement nest eggs need to be 20 percent larger. In other words, if the experts say that men should be putting away 10 percent of their pretax income, then as a woman you should be putting away 12 percent of yours.

Now, I realize that saving 12 percent of your income may sound like a lot. But believe me, it's not as hard as you might think. The trick is not to let the figure overwhelm you. Rome wasn't built in a day, and neither is a new financial future. If you can't imagine saving 12 percent of your income right now, then start with 6 percent and make it a goal to bump up your savings rate by 1 percent a month for the next six months.

If even 6 percent seems like too much, do what I often suggest to clients of mine who really have a problem with the idea of saving. Start off putting away just 1 percent of your income. (I have never met anyone who could look me in the eye and tell me they couldn't save 1 percent of their income.) Then increase the amount by 1 percent a month for a year. At the end of a year, you will be saving 12 percent of your income and you will barely have noticed the difference.

It's a lot like getting in shape to run a marathon. People who train for a marathon don't say to themselves "Today I think I'll run a marathon" and then go out and run 26 miles. They start off running a block, then 2 blocks, then a mile, then 2 miles . . . until one day they are running 26 miles (and are actually enjoying it). Think about your goal of saving 12 percent of your income the same way. Day by day you are striving to become financially stronger. Before you know it you will be in great financial shape!

What About the Real World?

Paying yourself first is one of those concepts that strike a lot of people as sounding great in principle but having very little application in the real world. And I wouldn't be at all surprised if right now you are thinking *Sure, I'd love to pay myself first. Just tell me where I'm going to get the money.*

Well, I'll let you in on a secret: You already have it.

That's right. No matter how much or how little you earn, you already make enough money to pay yourself first. Your problem—and it's not just *your* problem, it's almost everyone's problem—is not that you don't make enough, but that you spend too much.

Learn to control your spending, and everything else will fall into place.

Spend a Dollar Today and You Lose It Forever

When I was a student at the University of Southern California, my favorite pastime was shopping. Some people get black belts in karate; I had a black belt in shopping. I could go to the mall with my friends and easily spend thousands of dollars in just a few hours. Every week I would come home with bags and bags of clothes. As I often tell my students today, you know you're shopping too much when you can go into your closet and find clothes you don't remember buying. Well, I could. My wardrobe was to die for. Unfortunately, the bills were to die for too—literally! Every month I would close my eyes as I opened my VISA bill.

The truth was that my spending was out of control. It never mattered how much money I made, I always spent more. As soon as my credit-card bills were paid, I'd go off on another spending spree.

My life changed when I packed up everything I owned one summer and put it in a storage unit. (At USC, you couldn't leave your possessions in your campus apartment over the summer.) As I was filling up this $50-a-month storage facility under a freeway in L.A., I started thinking *What if there's an earthquake and this freeway collapses and destroys the warehouse? My clothes would get ruined!*

All of a sudden it hit me: I'm looking at a storage unit with "stuff" in it and worrying. Of all the potential consequences of a devastating earthquake, here I am more concerned about *stuff* than about people. Even worse, I'm paying *money* to store stuff that I haven't even paid for yet because it's still on my credit card!

I started laughing so hard I had to sit down. It dawned on me there was an entire industry of storage units around the country filled with people's "stuff." Think about it! How absurd is it to buy so much stuff that you have to pay someone else to store it because you don't have anywhere to put it yourself! The moral seemed clear.

Buy less stuff and you'll be rich!

That insight changed my life. Suddenly I realized that instead of spending money I didn't really have on things I didn't really need, I should be putting my resources into something that mattered. And what could possibly matter more to me than my future? Forget about things; what I really should be concerning myself with was doing whatever I could to assure myself the kind of life I felt I wanted and deserved. And that's just what I did. From that day on, I stopped wasting my money on ridiculous shopping sprees and started investing in myself.

Trust me—if a world-class, black-belt shopper like me can cut back, you can too. It's not easy, but it can be done, and it will change your life just like it changed mine.

Now, just because you're not buying new clothes every week like I used to doesn't mean you're not spending money you should be saving. You'd be surprised how easy it is to be wastefully extravagant without realizing it. The fact is, often the "little" purchases in life— what I call the Latté Factor—make the difference between being a millionaire and being broke.

Making the Latté Factor Work for You

In my investment classes, I tell my students that any woman can become an investor—and in the process put herself on the road to financial security—simply by putting aside as little as $50 a month. Invariably, someone in the audience will raise her hand at this point and say, "David, I'm living paycheck to paycheck. I'm in debt, and I'm barely making it. I don't have this $50 a month you keep talking about."

One day I challenged just such a young woman on her assertion that she didn't have enough money to invest. Deborah was 23 years old and worked at an advertising agency. She wasn't being paid a whole lot, and she insisted there was no way she possibly could put $50 a month into her retirement plan at work. As she put it, she was "dead broke and destitute." So I asked her to take me through her average day.

"Well," she began, "I go to work and then I research—"

"Do you start your day with coffee?" I interrupted her.

A friend of Deborah's who was sitting next to her started to laugh. "Deborah without coffee in the morning is not a good thing," she said.

Picking up on that, I asked Deborah if she drank the office coffee.

"No way," Deborah replied. "The office coffee is the worst. I go downstairs and buy a latté every morning."

I asked, "Do you buy a single or double latté?"

"I always buy a double nonfat latté."

"Great," I said. "Now, what does this double nonfat latté cost you every morning?

"Oh, about $2.50."

"Do you just get a latté, or do you also get a muffin or a bagel with that?"

"I usually get a biscotti."

"Do you get the biscotti with chocolate on them?"

"Oh, yes," Deborah enthused. "I love the ones with chocolate."

"Great, Deborah. Now, what does the chocolate biscotti cost?"

"I guess about $1.50."

"So you're spending about $4 a day for latté and biscotti. Interesting."

I let Deborah continue taking me through her day. In the process, we found another $10 in miscellaneous costs—a candy bar here, a Power Bar there, a protein shake in the afternoon, and so on.

When she was done, I pointed out that just by cutting out her latté, a couple of Diet Cokes, and a candy bar, Deborah could save about $5 a day—and that $5 a day equaled roughly $150 a month, or almost $2,000 a year. This $2,000 could be put into her retirement plan at work, where it could grow tax-free until she retired. If she put in $2,000 every year, and she invested it all in stocks (which have enjoyed an average growth rate of 11 percent a year over the last 50 years), chances are that by the time she reached 65, she would have more than *$2 million* sitting in her account. In other words, she would be able to retire a multimillionaire!

By the time I had finished, Deborah's eyes were as big as saucers. "That is so amazing," she said. "I never realized my double nonfat lattés were costing me $2 million!"

So I ask you now . . .

Are you latté-ing away your financial future?

I'm not trying to pick on you if you are a coffee lover. I happen to enjoy a great cup of coffee in the morning myself. I just want to point out a simple fact:

Everyone makes enough money to become rich.

What keeps us living paycheck to paycheck is that we spend more than we make on stuff we don't need. Take the $16 you were going to waste over the next few days on junk food (you'll be healthier without it) and the $9 you were going to throw away on two glossy magazines (you can borrow a friend's copies), and you'll have $25 this very week that you can devote to savings. Keep this up and you'll soon be putting away 12 percent of what you earn. Before you know it, your life will begin changing dramatically for the better. Once you see the 12 percent solution at work, you automatically will start looking for ways to save even more. The process creates a new habit—one that will make you feel great!

Getting Your Spending Under Control

The hardest part of any undertaking—whether you're preparing for a marathon or trying to contain your spending—is getting started. With that in mind, here are six exercises that should help you get your spending under control . . . and ultimately make it easy for you to pay yourself first.

EXERCISE NO. 1
KNOW WHAT YOU EARN.

This may seem obvious, but in these days of direct-deposit payroll programs and automatic checking, many of us don't know exactly how much we actually earn, both before and after taxes. Go get your last paycheck. What does it say your monthly gross income is? What's your net? Write down those numbers below.

I currently earn $_____ a month before taxes, and $_____ after taxes.

EXERCISE NO. 2
ESTIMATE WHAT YOU SPEND EACH MONTH.

In Step Three, I asked you to figure out where your money is. Now I want you to figure out where your money *goes*.

Most people do not have a clue about how much they really spend each month and on what. To be financially healthy, however, you need to have a solid grasp of your spending patterns. Only after you've seen the numbers in black and white can you figure out where you can cut back.

In Appendix 1, you'll find a form with the heading "Where Does Your Money *Really* Go?" Use it to estimate how much you spend each month on everything from food and shelter to lipstick and movie tickets. Then add 10 percent for what I call "Murphy's law" expenses—those unexpected bills for car repairs and plumbing problems that always seem to crop up when you least expect (or can afford) them. To make sure your estimate is in the right ballpark, review your last three months' worth of your checks, receipts, and credit-card bills. Once you're satisfied you have a reasonably accurate figure, write it down.

I currently spend $_____ a month.

Now subtract your monthly spending total from your monthly after-tax income. Is your cash flow positive or negative? Your goal, obviously, is to have a positive cash flow. The next four rules should help you do just that.

I earn a month after taxes   _____

I spend a month approximately − _____

Cash flow monthly   = _____

EXERCISE NO. 3
TRACK WHAT YOU *REALLY* SPEND.

For the next seven days, I want you to record every single penny you spend. I call this the "Seven-Day Financial Challenge." Eventually you should do this for a full month, but right now, to get yourself started, I want you to try it for just seven days. Get yourself a 50-cent pad, and over the coming week, write down every purchase you make, no matter how big or small. (This means *everything:* highway tolls, candy bars, late fees on videos you forgot to return—everything.)

This seven-day challenge actually can be fun. The trick is to be yourself. That is, don't change your behavior. Spend money just as you always have. The only thing you should be doing differently is writing everything down. Once you have captured your spending habits on paper, you will quickly see where you are wasting money and you can decide where it makes sense to cut back. (One woman I know found that the simple act of writing down expenditures made her so self-conscious about being extravagant that her excess spending stopped cold. "I just hated the idea of having to write down that I was spending $80 on a sweater I didn't need," she said. "So rather than having to write it down, I didn't buy the sweater.")

EXERCISE NO. 4
START PAYING CASH.

After you have tracked a typical week's expenses and are ready to start changing your ways, the easiest thing you can do to reduce your spending automatically is to start paying for everything with cash. That's right, cash! Remember that green stuff with the pictures of the dead presidents on it? It's time to start using it again.

When you buy things with credit cards or use checks, you don't feel the significance of your spending. I dare you to stick $500 in cash in your wallet and try to spend it frivolously on some impulse purchase like a new sweater or a pair of shoes or a stack of new CDs. You won't be able to do it. That's because cash makes you think more about exactly how much you are spending and for what. (As one client of mine told me, a pair of shoes marked down to $150 doesn't seem like that much of a bargain when buying it means taking eight $20s out of your wallet.)

You'd be surprised what a dramatic change this single action can make. I can't tell you how many of my students have told me that when they went to a cash-only system, their spending dropped by 20 percent in a single month!

EXERCISE NO. 5
GIVE YOURSELF A CREDIT-CARD HAIRCUT.

Here's an idea that I am sure occurs to you every time you get a large credit-card bill: Take a pair of scissors and cut up one of your credit cards. Just one. (I don't expect you to cut them all up—not, at least, on your first attempt.) When you finish reading this chapter, go through all your credit-card bills, pull out the biggest one, and then cut that card into about ten pieces.

The feeling of power you will get from this small token gesture can be tremendous. Just try it. If you think you can handle it, cut up more than one card. Remember, if worse comes to worst, you can always call the credit-card company and order a new one.

> **EXERCISE NO. 6**
> NEVER SPEND MORE THAN $100 ON ANYTHING WITHOUT
> TAKING 48 HOURS TO THINK ABOUT IT.

The idea here is simple. Most Americans spend far too much money on impulse purchases they really don't need to make. It can be a pair of shoes, a new VCR, an expensive dinner. The point is, stores are designed to make sure you get caught up in the excitement of shopping, and before you know what's happened, you've bought something.

So set yourself a ceiling. I suggest $100, but it can be any amount that makes sense to you. Once you've set it, do not permit yourself to buy anything for that amount or more without first leaving the store and giving yourself 48 hours to think about it. By forcing yourself into this "cooling-off" period, you give yourself a chance to decide rationally whether the purchase really is necessary. If you still feel like buying it two days later, great! Chances are the item in question will still be there—maybe even on sale!

I know how effective this exercise can be from personal experience. As I mentioned earlier, I used to be a world-class shopper. But once I imposed the $100 ceiling on myself, I found that just "casually shopping" wasn't so much fun anymore. Items I had thought I "just had to have" no longer seemed so important once I got home and thought about them. Because I was buying less and less, shopping began to feel more and more like a waste of time. Before long I found myself going shopping less often. These days I only go shopping once or twice a year, and only with the specific purpose of getting something I need. I'm telling you, these exercises work!

The basic point of getting your spending under control is, of course, to allow you to save more. Ultimately, your goal should be to get your savings rate as high as 20 percent. For now, however, try to start saving at least 6 percent of your gross income and commit to raising that to 12 percent within 12 months.

The Magic of Compound Interest

You may wonder what good it will do to put aside less than an eighth of your income if your income isn't very big to begin with. But remember, even if you earn what seems to you like a modest salary, the amount of money that will pass through your hands during your life-time is truly phenomenal. For a quick reminder of just how phenome-nal, go back and review the chart on page 21 in Step One.

Pretty awesome, isn't it? And here's some more good news . . .

The sooner you start saving, the less you will need to put away!

Take a look at the following chart. It shows how quickly the magic of compound interest can help you accumulate a significant amount of assets. To me, "significant" means at least $1 million worth. Now, some skeptics may argue that $1 million doesn't go very far anymore, but regardless of how much it does or doesn't buy these days, wouldn't you rather have $1 million than not? In any case, given that the average mid-dle-age American has less then $10,000 saved, let's run with the idea that earning your "first" million is probably a worthy goal to shoot for.

What the chart illustrates is that simply by putting aside a couple of dollars a day and giving your money a chance to work for you, you can become a millionaire! While it is easy to think "a dollar here, a dollar there" is no big deal, it *is* a big deal. Depending on how quickly you decide to make your financial future a priority, it can be a *million-dollar deal!*

Stop reading for a second and think about the day you just had. What is your personal Latté Factor? What did you buy today that you could do without tomorrow and thus save a few dollars? Take a few moments right now and think of three things you could cut out of your daily spending tomorrow. What are they? How much money would you save a day? How much would it save you a month? While $100 a month in savings may not sound like a lot, look at the chart on page 99. Saving $100 a month can add up quickly to a lot of money.

Now, how do you make sure that this money you are now not going to spend on things you don't really need doesn't disappear down some other drain? It's simple, really. The trick to making sure your money goes where it's supposed to go—that is, that your spending matches up with your values—is to arrange things so you don't have any choice in the matter. There's no getting around it. We may like to think of ourselves as being self-disciplined and conscientious, and many of us actually are. But there is only one way to make sure you will consistently pay yourself first, and that is to put yourself on an automatic system. To put it another way . . .

Smart women pay themselves first . . . automatically!

What this means is that if you work for a company that offers some sort of contributory retirement program—such as a 401(k) plan—you should definitely sign up. (We'll discuss this in detail in Step Five.)

BUILDING A MILLION-DOLLAR NEST EGG

How to Accumulate $1,000,000

Regular Deposits Required to Accumulate $1,000,000 by Age 65 at Stated Rate of Return

$1,000,000
12% Annual Interest Rate

Starting Age	Daily Savings	Monthly Savings	Yearly Savings
20	$ 2.00	$ 61	$ 730
25	$ 3.57	$ 109	$ 1,304
30	$ 6.35	$ 193	$ 2,317
35	$ 11.35	$ 345	$ 4,144
36	$ 12.77	$ 388	$ 4,660
37	$ 14.37	$ 437	$ 5,244
38	$ 16.18	$ 492	$ 5,904
39	$ 18.22	$ 554	$ 6,652
40	$ 20.55	$ 625	$ 7,500
41	$ 23.19	$ 705	$ 8,463
42	$ 26.19	$ 797	$ 9,560
43	$ 29.62	$ 901	$ 10,811
44	$ 33.52	$ 1,020	$ 12,240
45	$ 38.02	$ 1,157	$ 13,879
46	$ 43.19	$ 1,314	$ 15,763
47	$ 49.14	$ 1,495	$ 17,937
48	$ 56.05	$ 1,705	$ 20,457
49	$ 64.08	$ 1,949	$ 23,390
50	$ 73.49	$ 2,235	$ 26,824
51	$ 84.58	$ 2,573	$ 30,971
52	$ 97.75	$ 2,973	$ 35,677
53	$ 113.53	$ 3,453	$ 41,437
54	$ 132.64	$ 4,035	$ 48,415
55	$ 156.12	$ 4,749	$ 56,984

The figures shown above represent the amount of money you would have to save (i.e. daily, monthly, yearly), at the stated interest rate, in order to accumulate $1,000,000 by the time you reach age 65. These figures DO NOT take into account any federal or state taxes that may be incurred. Monthly and yearly figures are rounded to the nearest dollar.

Source: "The Wise Investor: Ten Concepts You Need To Know to Achieve Financial Success" by Neil Elmouch (Dunhill & West Publishing)

Under most such plans, after you've signed up, you don't have to do a thing. Every pay period, your employer will take a portion of your gross pay (i.e., *before* taxes are withheld) and put it in a retirement account for you. No muss, no fuss, no chance to succumb to temptation.

If you don't have access to this sort of company-sponsored program, then you must set up the appropriate retirement account on your own. (Again, we'll provide details in Step Five.) You also must arrange your own automatic payroll-deduction system. You may be able to do this through your company payroll department. If not, you can do it on your own by telling your bank to transfer automatically a given amount from your checking account to your retirement account on the same day you deposit your paycheck.

The key is to make sure the transfer is done automatically. Otherwise, you probably won't do it consistently. Just as most people can't stick to budgets, most people who promise to "pay themselves first" don't . . . unless the money is taken out of their paycheck and put into a retirement account before they have a chance to do anything else with it. If you are married and your husband works, make sure he does this too!

It's Never Too Late

There's no question that the sooner you get started paying yourself first, the better off you will be. The following chart shows it plainly.

TO BUILD WEALTH . . . PAY YOURSELF FIRST AND DO IT MONTHLY

Your monthly investment	Your age	Total amount of monthly investments through age 65	At a 4% rate of return	At a 7% rate of return	At a 9% rate of return	At a 12% rate of return
$100	25	48,000	118,590	264,012	471,643	1,188,242
	30	42,000	91,678	181,156	296,385	649,527
	40	30,000	51,584	81,480	112,953	189,764
	50	18,000	24,691	31,881	38,124	50,458
$200	25	96,000	237,180	528,025	943,286	2,376,484
	30	84,000	183,355	362,312	592,770	1,299,054
	40	60,000	103,169	162,959	225,906	379,527
	50	36,000	49,382	63,762	76,249	100,915

Incredible, isn't it? But wait. If you study this chart closely, you might come to the conclusion that the key to success is to start young. What if you are older? What if you weren't fortunate enough to start saving when you were in your 20s or 30s? Don't worry. The miracle of compound interest does not depend on how old you are. The only thing that matters is how long your money has been invested and at what rate it is growing.

When students of mine who are in their 40s and 50s insist to me that it's too late for them to get started saving, I point out that simply by investing a mere $10 a day in a mutual fund that returns 15 percent a year (and plenty have exceeded this rate), over a period of 25 years they will accumulate well in excess of $1 million!

Remember—the combined power of the Latté Factor and the miracle of compound interest is truly amazing. The only thing that can short-circuit it is the all-too-human tendency to procrastinate. Too many people put off doing what they know they should, and as a result these two powerful tools never get the chance to work for them. Don't make this mistake.

Don't Label Yourself a Procrastinator

Even if everything I've just said makes sense to you intellectually, I know it is still very possible that you simply won't be able to pay yourself first. What many people say is "I know I should do this, but I'm just a procrastinator." Well, I have never met a real procrastinator. Whenever someone tells me she is a procrastinator, I respond by asking them, "Did you eat this week?" Of course, the person will always answer yes. The fact is, no one procrastinates *all* the time. What you may be is a selective procrastinator—which means that if something is important enough (like eating), you are perfectly capable of taking care of it right away.

So what makes us procrastinate about saving? Most of us do it for one reason: *fear of change.* Why do we fear change? Because we associate change with pain. Saving means reducing your spending. Reducing your spending means changing (however slightly) the way you live. And changing (however slightly) the way you live means . . . who knows what? *Probably something terrible!*

I often run into this when I address employee groups. Many people tell me they know my "idea" of contributing a portion of their gross pay to a retirement plan makes sense, but they just can't see how they could possibly get by if their take-home were suddenly reduced by 10 percent. I recall one incident in particular. I was at a Fortune 500 company, speaking at a sign-up seminar for the firm's retirement plan, when a gentleman named Dan stood up and challenged my assertion that it was possible "to give yourself a pay cut." "David," he said, very agitated, "I don't think you are in touch with reality. Many of us here today are in our mid-40s and 50s. We have expenses, like homes, car payments, and college costs. We are basically living from paycheck to paycheck, and when you are doing that, you can't take a 10 percent pay cut. It's simply not possible."

A murmur of agreement rippled across the room. Clearly many of Dan's coworkers shared his fears. Justified or not, those fears deserved to be addressed.

"What would you do," I asked Dan, "if your boss came into your office tomorrow and told you that because of a corporate restructuring, you had to choose between losing your job or taking a 10 percent pay cut?"

Dan looked startled, then stared at his feet and mumbled, "I'd take the 10-percent pay cut."

"And how would that affect you?" I continued. "Would it make you so depressed that you couldn't get out of bed in the morning?"

Dan looked at me a little strangely. "Of course not," he said. "I'd be bummed, but I'd still be able to get up in the morning."

"Good," I responded. "So we know that being forced to take a 10 percent pay cut wouldn't incapacitate you. Now, what about your house? Would you lose your home if you got a 10 percent pay cut?"

"No," Dan replied. "We'd figure out a way to cut back."

I told him that was good too. "Now we know that a pay cut will neither incapacitate you nor leave you homeless. What about your wife? Would she leave you if your pay got cut?"

"No, of course not," he answered.

"I didn't think so," I said. I went on to explain to Dan that the point of my questions wasn't to make fun of his concerns. What I was trying to do was show him and everyone else in the room that there are really two options in life: You can be either reactive or proactive to circumstances. And it's a lot more fun and a lot less painful to be proactive—to make decisions about your life before events take control of *you*.

It's Time to Give Yourself That Pay Cut!

If for any reason (a company restructuring, a war, a death, a divorce, whatever), you suddenly found yourself forced to take a pay cut, you'd manage to cope somehow, wouldn't you? So why wait for something to happen and then react to it? Why not take control over your own destiny and create your own future now?

Finally, remember that the key to the Latté Factor is recognizing that small things (like a $2 cup of coffee) can make a big difference. A dollar here, a dollar there, if invested regularly through an automatic pay-yourself-first system, can make you financially secure for life. And quite frankly, you deserve to be!

Congratulations, You've Completed Step Four

You've taken advantage of the Latté Factor to reduce your spending, you've made a commitment to pay yourself first, and you've arranged to put aside a portion of your gross income (ideally, 12 percent) automatically each month. You are now ready to move on to Step Five, in which we'll figure out exactly what to do with all this money you are now paying yourself.

PRACTICE GRANDMA'S THREE-BASKET APPROACH TO FINANCIAL SECURITY

As I mentioned in the introduction, it was my Grandma Bach who encouraged me to make my first investment—in three shares of McDonald's. I was seven at the time, and the idea of being a stockholder was so exciting to me that as soon as I managed to save up some more money, I bought another share. And then another. And another.

Finally my grandmother took me aside. "David," she said, "McDonald's is a fine company, but it's not the only one on the stock exchange."

"But I like McDonald's," I protested.

"I know," she replied, "but the sensible thing to do is to spread your money around. Haven't you ever heard the expression 'Don't put all your eggs in one basket'?"

I hadn't—not until then, at any rate. But once my grandmother explained it to me, it made complete sense, and to this day it remains one of the fundamental principles of my approach to financial planning.

Most people assume that financial planning is difficult, complicated, and exhausting. It's not. The fact is, if you do it correctly, actually it's pretty easy. One of the keys is to remember my grandmother's advice: Don't put all your eggs in one basket.

As it happens, there are *three* baskets into which you should put your eggs. I call them **the security basket, the retirement basket, and the dream basket.** The security basket protects you and your family against the unexpected (such as a medical emergency, the death of a loved one, or the loss of a job), the retirement basket safeguards your future, and the dream basket enables you to fulfill those deeply held desires that make life worthwhile. This three-basket approach may sound simple, but don't let that fool you. If you fill the baskets properly, you can create for yourself a financial life filled with abundance and, most important, security.

The "eggs" we're talking about are, of course, the extra dollars you learned to put aside in Step Four. You are going to use them to fill these three baskets—in some cases by investing the cash directly in money-market accounts or retirement plans, in other cases by buying things such as insurance policies.

We are going to discuss the security basket first—mainly because it involves a bunch of things that you need to take care of *immediately*. In practice, however, you will be filling up both your security basket and your retirement basket at the same time. Once you've taken care of your security and retirement baskets, you can start filling your dream basket.

We'll get to the details of exactly how retirement saving works in a little while. Right now, let's talk about security.

BASKET ONE: YOUR SECURITY BASKET

Your security basket is meant to protect you and your family in the event of some unexpected financial hardship, such as the loss of a job or some other major income source. It also can help you cope with life's little unplanned surprises, like the car breaking down, the refrigerator needing repair, or the dog eating your child's retainer, which just cost you $496! The security basket does this by providing you with a financial cushion—an air bag, if you will, that softens the blow in case of accident. Not only will having this sort of cushion contribute to your peace of mind, but when trouble strikes, it can (quite literally) buy you the time you will need to get back on your feet.

Seven Things to Do Right Away for Protection

In order to be properly protected, you must make sure that your security basket contains most—if not all—of the following seven elements.

> **SAFEGUARD NO. 1**
> YOU MUST HAVE AT LEAST 3 TO 24 MONTHS' WORTH OF
> LIVING EXPENSES SAVED IN CASE OF EMERGENCY.

The goal here is to put away "rainy-day money" to cover expenses in case you lose your income. Exactly how much money you need to put away depends on what you spend each month. (You can figure this out with the help of the Where Does Your Money *Really* Go? form in Appendix 1.) I generally recommend to my students and clients that they put away somewhere between 3 and 24 months' worth of expense money. By this measure, a Smart Woman whose basic spending runs about $2,000 a month should aim to have at least $6,000 in cash in her security basket.

That 3- to 24-month range covers a lot of ground. What's right for you depends in large part on your particular emotional makeup. Some of my clients simply do not feel safe if they have anything less than two years' worth of cash sitting in a money-market account. I happen to think that's a bit excessive, but if that's what it takes to make you feel comfortable, then by all means make it your goal.

In general, the size of your cushion should depend on how easy it would be to replace your current income. Say you currently earn $75,000 a year. If you suddenly lost your job, how long would it take for you to find a new one paying that much or more? If you are easily reemployable and are confident that you could land a new $75,000-a-year job relatively quickly, then you probably don't need to have much more than three months' worth of expenses in your security basket. If, on the other hand, you think it would take you six months to a year to find another job paying that much, then you should probably have a lot more money—at least six months to a year's worth of expenses—in your security basket.

DON'T LET THE BANKS RIP YOU OFF!

How much you save in your security basket is critical. But *where* you save it is equally important! As far as I'm concerned, there is only one sensible place to keep your security savings. They must be placed in a money-market account that pays a fair rate of return.

Many women today keep their rainy-day money in a bank savings account or in a low-earning checking account. In some cases, it's not earning any interest at all. Please, please don't make this mistake. The fact that banks can rip you off like this absolutely infuriates me. Quite frankly, I think Congress should make it illegal for financial institutions to pay you a less than competitive rate of return on your savings. But since it hasn't, you as a consumer need to protect yourself by shopping around for the best rate of return available in your area. I can't stress enough how important it is that you do this. Indeed, if the only action you take as a result of reading this book is moving your savings from a low-interest account to one that earns competitive money-market rates, that alone will earn you back what you paid for this book in just the first 30 days.

Most brokerage and mutual-fund firms today offer money-market checking accounts that are not only safe and pay competitive interest rates but also come with ATM cards and unlimited checking. As of this writing, these sorts of accounts are paying depositors around 5.5 percent a year. That's nearly four times the average bank checking-account rate of less than 1.0 percent!

If you have $10,000 sitting in a savings or checking account earning only 1.0 percent annually when it could be earning 5.5 percent, you are cheating yourself out of $450 a year in interest. The way I see it, that's a plane ticket to Hawaii or a fancy dream night out on the town or more money in your retirement account! In other words, that so-called free checking account at the bank really isn't. Quite the contrary, it's costing you a fortune.

FIVE-STAR TIP: *When in doubt about how much money to save in your security basket, always err on the high side. No one ever lost any sleep over having too much emergency cash. All the same, don't save more than two years' of expense money; that's overkill.*

SAFEGUARD NO. 2

YOU ABSOLUTELY, POSITIVELY, NO MATTER WHAT, MUST HAVE AN UP-TO-DATE WILL OR LIVING TRUST.

Two out of three Americans die intestate. That's legal jargon for dying without having written a will or set up a living trust that explains how your assets should be distributed after your death. Not taking steps to plan for what happens after you're gone is incredibly irresponsible. In effect, what you are saying to your loved ones is the following:

To those I love—

While I understand that I have the right to determine who will inherit my property when I die, I have decided to let the courts make that decision for me, even though that might mean that people I never knew or never liked could wind up as my heirs.

I also understand that there are perfectly legitimate ways of minimizing the estate taxes my loved ones will have to pay. However, because of the government's generosity to me throughout my lifetime, I have decided to let Uncle Sam take the biggest bite he can.

In addition, rather than deciding who should take care of my children, I've decided that I'd rather have my family fight about it and then let the courts just go ahead and appoint anyone they feel like.

Finally, I know that as a result of not leaving a will, a significant portion of my assets could be eaten up by lawyers' bills and that all the private details of my financial affairs will be made public.

Now, clearly, that's not what most people want to have happen when they die. Yet millions and millions of Americans have no will or living trust in place.

Please don't make this terrible mistake. Yes, making out a will or setting up a living trust can be difficult; it forces you to consider all sorts of contingencies you'd probably rather not think about. But remember—if you die without a will or living trust in place, it falls to the government to figure out what should be done with the fruits of your life's work. Do you really want the government to decide how your estate should be divided up? Even worse, by dying intestate, you make it possible for swindlers to lay claim to your estate, and you virtually guarantee that your entire private life will be made public.

The most common excuse for not having a will or living trust is laziness. Well, Smart Women aren't lazy! After you finish reading this chapter, call your family attorney and set up an appointment to draft a will or a living trust. Your lawyer can advise you on which would make the most sense for your situation. For what it's worth, I generally advise my clients in almost every case to go for the living trust.

WHAT IS A LIVING TRUST?

Before we go any further, I probably should explain a little about living trusts. A living trust is basically a legal document that does two things. First, it allows you to transfer the ownership of any of your assets (your house, your car, your investment accounts, whatever you like) to a trust while you are still alive. Second, it designates who should be given those assets after you die. By naming yourself the trustee of your trust, you can continue to control your assets—which means that as long as you live, the transfer of ownership will have no practical impact on your ability to enjoy and manage your property.

The main advantage a living trust has over a simple will is that if you create a living trust properly and fund it correctly, your assets won't have to go through probate—that is, the courts won't review your instructions regarding the distribution of your assets. This is very, very important. By avoiding probate, you can save thousands of dollars in attorney fees. In addition, you will be able to maintain your estate's privacy. (Once an estate goes through probate, all the details become a matter of public record.)

If your estate is likely to be worth more than $1 million—and, remember, even on a modest income, you can easily amass that much in an IRA or 401(k) plan—a good attorney may recommend setting up what is known as a bypass or A, B trust. By creating this type of trust, you can protect more of your assets from the dreaded drain of estate taxes, which can run as high as 55 percent. I have personally seen well-written trusts save families hundreds of thousands of dollars in estate taxes—in some cases, millions!

The cost of setting up a living trust typically ranges from $1,000 to $2,500, depending on the complexity of your estate. But setting it up isn't enough. The trick to making a living trust work for you is to fund it correctly. Many well-intentioned people set up a trust, but then they never get around to putting their house or their brokerage accounts in the trust. Say I set up the David Bach Family Trust. If I neglect to switch my brokerage account from my own name to the trust's name, that account will end up in probate when I die—all because I forgot to change the name on it. Changing the name on an account is called "replating." It's an easy process, and your financial advisor or attorney will be happy to help you with it.

WHAT TO DO IF YOU ALREADY HAVE A WILL OR LIVING TRUST

If you already have a will or a living trust, that's great. If it was written more than five years ago, however, don't assume it's still good. In all likelihood some things in your life have changed, and your will or trust probably needs updating. I have sat with clients reviewing wills that still talked about who would take care of the kids—even though the "kids" were now in their 50s. (People always laugh when I tell that story, but the situation is more common than you would believe.)

Once you've written or updated your will or living trust, make sure your loved ones know where you've stored it. And *don't* keep it in a safety deposit box. If your heirs don't have the keys to your box, they may need to obtain a court order to get it opened—and that could take weeks (sometimes even months). If you store important documents in a safe or strongbox in your home or office, make sure someone (like your attorney or your children) knows where it is and how to find the combination. You might think this is obvious, but even professionals sometimes forget. Not too long ago, my own father, who's been a financial advisor for over 30 years, casually happened to mention that he and my mother kept their wills and other important papers in a "hidden safe" in their house. It was the first I'd ever heard of it.

The point is, if you are hiding any valuables, make sure your heirs know where they're hidden. If you don't, they may well stay hidden after you pass away.

And don't be penny wise and pound foolish and try to draft a will or trust by yourself—not even with one of those "family lawyer" software programs that have become so popular. Why anyone would be willing to consign the value of their life's work to a $29 piece of software is beyond me. Just one mistake on a self-created will can make the entire document invalid—in which case your estate will end up in the courts, at a cost to your family of thousands of dollars and endless heartache. Spend the money (and time) to have your will drafted properly by a professional. As I mentioned, the bill may run from $1,000 to $2,500, but I promise you, it will be worth it.

> **FIVE-STAR TIP:** *If you have older parents and you don't know if they have a will or living trust in place, you really should have a talk with them about getting things organized. The conversation may be uncomfortable, but it will almost certainly spare you and your family much heartache later on.*

SAFEGUARD NO. 3
GET THE BEST HEALTH INSURANCE YOU CAN AFFORD.

This is nonnegotiable. Adequate health insurance coverage for yourself and your family is a basic necessity. The fact that millions of Americans are without health insurance is truly frightening. When it comes to your family's security, you don't ever want be in a position where you are "self-insuring" (meaning you're the one who pays the medical bills when you or a family member get sick or injured). Health care costs today are skyrocketing. Even a short hospital stay can cost thousands of dollars. And God forbid you need a major procedure, such as chemotherapy or a bone-marrow transplant. The bills for these can run to six figures. So no debating here. You must have health insurance. The only question in your mind should be how you get it and what your options are.

Most people fall into one of two categories. Either you or your spouse works for a company that provides you with some health care options, or you don't—meaning your company doesn't offer health insurance or you are self-employed. If you are one of the latter, you will need to search out a health care provider for yourself. This is not difficult to do. If individual coverage is too expensive, you may be able to get a group rate through a professional organization or association. You might even check with your church or synagogue.

In the end, however, everyone—even those whose companies do offer coverage—has to make some basic decisions on their own. For the sake of simplicity, I'm going to focus on the three major types of health insurance coverage that are available to most Americans. (If you work for a company, only the first two options may be available to you.)

OPTION 1: HMOs

Health maintenance organizations, or HMOs, are, in effect, large groups of health care providers who have joined together to provide comprehensive health care coverage for subscribers. HMOs are generally the oldest managed-care systems around, and while very large, they tend also to be the most restrictive.

When you sign up with an HMO, you are asked to select a primary-care physician from the organization's usually extensive roster of doctors. Once you have done so, you are free to see him or her as often as you need without it costing you anything beyond a small "copayment" charge (usually around $10). Generally, prescriptions are also covered at no additional cost, or with a small copayment.

The distinguishing feature of HMO coverage is that your ability to see doctors other than your primary-care physician is quite limited. For example, if you want your coverage to pay for the visit, you can't see a specialist without the approval of your primary-care physician. And even if he or she is willing to give you permission, as a rule your primary-care physician will refer you only to specialists who are affiliated with your particular HMO. The bottom line is that you are stuck with your HMO's doctors, even if the organization doesn't happen to have the particular specialist that you want or need to see.

In recent years, many HMOs have come under fire for allegedly making medical decisions on the basis of economic considerations rather than the client's best medical interest. Quite frankly, I think that's a persuasive argument against going the HMO route. My concern is that as an HMO subscriber, you can easily become just a number to them. These organizations are so huge that if you don't have a good relationship with your primary-care physician, you can get lost in the system and not get the medical attention you need or deserve.

I personally have dozens of clients who work for HMOs as doctors, nurses, and hospital technicians, and they tell me on a daily basis how difficult their jobs are becoming. As HMOs strive to improve profit margins, their medical personnel find themselves being forced to work longer hours for less pay, an unfortunate state of affairs that takes its toll on the quality of care. In the end, the person who loses out is you, the patient.

To be fair, many people absolutely love the HMO system. Certainly, there's no getting around the fact that HMOs are very affordable. They are by far the least expensive of the three main health care options— which is why so many employers promote them so enthusiastically. What's more, they are probably the easiest for consumers to use. They involve the least amount of paperwork, and you don't need to worry about complicated deductibles.

Still, if you are not truly struggling to make ends meet, I suggest you spend a little more money and take a look at the other health care options.

OPTION 2: PPOs

Preferred Provider Organizations, or PPOs, usually consist of a group of doctors, medical practices, and hospitals that have joined together to form a "group network." In some ways, a PPO is halfway between an HMO and a traditional fee-for-service plan (which we will talk about next). As with an HMO, you select a primary-care physician who refers you to doctors or medical practices within the group network. The major difference between a PPO and an HMO is that if you want to—and are willing to pay a little extra—you can see a doctor or use a facility outside the group. This flexibility gives you more choices. Personally, I like having choices.

The biggest problem with PPOs is the time and trouble it takes to get referred to a specialist. Depending on who your primary-care physician is, getting a referral may involve nothing more than a phone call—or you could be required to go in for an exam. Some PPOs will not cover you if you go to an outside doctor without first getting the referral approved by your primary-care physician. Still, while I don't love the PPO system, I do believe it is superior to the HMO alternative and definitely worth the additional cost.

As with so many other things I've talked about in this book, the key to making the PPO system work for you is to be proactive. You can't just let your medical care "happen" to you. Take what happened to me a few years ago. One day I noticed a spot on my leg. Worried that I might have skin cancer, I went to my primary-care physician to get a referral to a dermatologist. To my horror, he refused to give me one, insisting he could remove the spot himself.

"No way," I said. "You are not a skin specialist and I want a referral."

But the doctor was adamant. He would not give me a referral. Furious, I left his office and went straight to my word processor. Within two hours I had sent letters to every boss of his I could find in the managed-care facility. I also sent a copy to my lawyer. By the end of the day I had received by fax a written apology—and an appointment the next day with a dermatologist who normally had a waiting list of at least four weeks. Needless to say, I got myself a new primary-care physician.

The moral of this story is to remember that when it comes to your health, *you should be in charge*. Whether you're dealing with a PPO or an HMO, don't let them treat you like a number.

OPTION 3: FEE FOR SERVICE

Before there were HMOs and PPOs, most of us had what is known as fee-for-service health insurance. Some people call this traditional health insurance. Quite frankly, this type of health coverage was a lot simpler, and most people were much happier with it. Under fee for service, you can see just about any doctor or specialist you want (and go to just about any hospital as well). Typically, you pay the bills until you reach a certain preset level (the "deductible"), at which point your benefits kick in.

When I was self-employed, I chose this type of coverage. While it is more expensive than the others and requires the most paperwork, it also provides you with the most options. (In any case, you can reduce the cost by agreeing to a higher deductible.) The biggest advantage of fee for service is that you are totally in control over your medical decisions. You can decide which hospital you want to go to and which doctor or specialist you want to see.

The major downside of fee for service (besides the higher cost) is that your insurance carrier can force you to get a "second opinion" from a doctor of its choosing—and if you refuse, or if the company's doctor disagrees with yours, you can be denied coverage for a particular procedure. What's more, some fee-for-service plans require you to meet high deductibles before they will cover the cost of prescriptions.

WHICH PLAN SHOULD I CHOOSE?

In my view, if all three options are available to you and cost is not a problem, you should consider the fee-for-service plan. Fee for service offers subscribers the most flexibility and potentially the most control. If you must choose between an HMO and a PPO, as a general rule I would suggest that you go with a PPO. But it depends where you live. As I noted earlier, some people swear by their HMOs. Like everything else, not all medical groups are created equal. Ultimately, you need to research for yourself what sorts of health insurance are available to you and which you feel most comfortable with.

If you are self-employed or work for a company that doesn't offer health insurance, look into whether you belong to an organization that offers its members group coverage. If you don't, think about joining one. These days just about every organization imaginable seems able to offer members some sort of group coverage. If all else fails—or if for some reason you don't want a group policy—ask an insurance professional about obtaining independent coverage. The health care world is in the midst of a major transition, which makes things especially complicated. As a Smart Woman, you need to be very proactive in protecting your family, and that includes making sure you've got the best medical coverage you can afford.

FIVE-STAR TIP: *Don't wait until a problem arises to look into whether you have adequate health care coverage. Check it out now! If you currently have a health care policy, pull it out and read it. Look at the fine print. Is the plan portable (that is, do you lose your coverage if you leave your employer)? While many plans allow you to continue your coverage by paying for it on your own if you retire or otherwise leave your job, some don't—and getting a policy on your own can be prohibitively expensive. So review your situation today.*

SAFEGUARD NO. 4
IF YOU HAVE DEPENDENTS, YOU SHOULD HAVE LIFE INSURANCE.

If you have dependents—children or other relatives who depend on you financially—you must protect them by buying life insurance. Most people hate to talk about life insurance, but if someone is depending on you and your income, then you need to have some sort of protection plan in place in case something happens to you. And that's all life insurance is—a protection plan.

LIKE IT OR NOT, MEN DIE

One of the sadder aspects of my job as a financial advisor is how often I hear horror stories about women who thought their husbands had life-insurance coverage—only to find out after it was too late that they didn't. Remember, no one really knows when he or she is going to go. That's why you have to have insurance . . . to protect against the unexpected.

As I noted in Step One, men are the worst when it comes to dealing with this reality. So if you are married, put this book down right now and go find out if you and your husband have life insurance. Then find the insurance policy and read it. (By the way, when you pull out the policy, if the pages are yellowed and stick to the plastic folder they came in, chances are you have a really old policy that definitely needs to be reviewed.)

If you are a single mom raising kids on your own, it's even more essential that you have life insurance to protect your children's future. Indeed, as a single mother, getting adequate life insurance could be the most important thing you ever do for your children.

When you start reading your policy, the first two things you really want to know are who is covered and how much money will be paid out if the insured individual dies.

IF YOU ARE MARRIED WITH CHILDREN, DON'T INSURE JUST YOUR HUSBAND

Many family men naively assume that if their wife is a stay-at-home mom, she doesn't need to be covered. This is a huge mistake. After all, if you are a stay-at-home mom and something happens to you, who is going to take care of the kids? Your husband will have to hire a nanny or stay at home himself (and thus have to stop or cut back working). Either way that will require more money.

IF YOU ARE A SINGLE MOM, YOU'D BETTER OVERINSURE!

Life insurance is not the place to cut corners. Stop for a moment and think about it. If you were to pass away, who would take care of your kids? Would it be your parents? A relative such as a sister or brother? Or would your kids end up with your ex-husband? Whatever the case, you want them to be safe and secure, and this means, among other things, protecting them financially—that is, leaving them with enough money to live comfortably and ultimately with sufficient savings to pay for college.

So make sure you have enough life insurance not simply to provide for your children's needs over the next years if something were to happen to you but to cover their expenses straight through four years of college.

That's bound to be a lot of money, of course, but if you don't provide it, who will? Don't make the terrible mistake I personally have seen too many single moms make and assume that your parents will be able to handle the financial burden of taking care of your children. Over the last few years I have had to sit in too many meetings with clients who are now struggling because of the obligations they inherited when a grown child of theirs died, leaving them to take care of their orphaned grandchildren.

SO HOW MUCH IS ENOUGH?

In order to come up with a ballpark number, you should ask yourself the following questions.

1. Who will be hurt financially if I should die? In other words, who relies on my income? (By the way, if *you* could be hurt financially by a death in the family—your husband's, for example—then you definitely want to make sure you are protected yourself.)
2. What does it cost those who depend on me to live for a year? (This figure should include everything—mortgage, taxes, college costs, etc.)
3. Are there any major debts, such as a home or business loan, that would need to be paid immediately if I or my significant other were to pass away? (You'd be surprised how often smart people overlook these sorts of financial obligations. If you own a business, what costs would your family or children incur if you

died? Do you own a second home? If you do, make sure the mortgage payments are covered. What about funeral expenses, estate taxes, and probate costs? These can amount to tens of thousands of dollars.)

MOST PEOPLE ARE UNDERINSURED

As a starting point to determine the minimum amount of life insurance you need, take your gross annual income (that is, your total earnings before taxes) and multiply it by six. I say "minimum" because depending on the level of your debts and expenses, you might want a death benefit as high as 20 times your annual income.

Whether you insure yourself on the low or high end of that range depends on your situation. Some people like to have just enough insurance to cover their dependents' major expenses for a few years. Others want to make sure that if something happened to them, their family's independence would be assured indefinitely. As with the amount of your security savings, this is a decision you must make for yourself personally. I recommend that you cover your family's living expenses for at least ten years—more if your dependents happen to be very young.

NOT EVERYONE NEEDS LIFE INSURANCE

Life insurance is meant to protect dependents who can't otherwise take care of themselves and would be at risk if you weren't around. It's not meant to leave your significant other in the lap of luxury. Therefore, if you don't have kids (or some other relative who depends on you), there is no reason for you to make financial sacrifices to buy life insurance. I'd rather see you put the money away for retirement.

Indeed, if you are single and childless (and have no other dependents), then the only possible reason you should buy life insurance is because you want to leave an estate for a charity or you are using it as a retirement vehicle. As far as your security basket is concerned, the point of life insurance is to protect your dependents; if you don't have any, you don't need any.

SO WHAT KIND OF LIFE INSURANCE SHOULD I BUY?

If you are confused about life insurance, don't worry—you are not alone. Today there are more than 500 differently named types of policies. It's no wonder the public is confused. For the sake of your security basket, I am going to try to keep the insurance game simple.

First and foremost, there are really only two types of life insurance: term insurance and permanent insurance.

TERM INSURANCE

Term insurance is really very simple. You pay an insurance company a premium, and in return the insurance company promises to pay your beneficiary a death benefit if you die. Specifically, term insurance provides you with a set amount of protection for a set period of time.

The chief advantages of this type of insurance is that it is very cheap, and generally it is very easy to get. The disadvantage of term insurance is that it does not allow you to build any "cash value." What this means is that you never accumulate any equity in the policy no matter how long you pay premiums to the insurance company. All term insurance provides is a death benefit. You can literally pay premiums into a term policy for 30 years, but if you then decide you don't want it any more, you walk away with nothing.

Term insurance comes in two basic "flavors"—annual renewable term and level term.

Annual Renewable Term. With annual renewable term insurance, your death benefit remains the same while your premiums get larger each year. More than likely, this is the type of policy you have if you work for a company and signed up for life insurance through the benefits department. The biggest advantage of an annual renewable term policy is that it is really inexpensive when you are young. Indeed, it is by far the cheapest way to buy insurance when you are just starting out. The problem is that as you get older (and the likelihood of death increases), the premiums can become prohibitively expensive.

Level Term. Under a level term policy, both the death benefit and the premium remain the same for a period of time that you select when you first sign up. The period can range anywhere from 5 to 20 years. While this type of term insurance is initially more expensive than annual renewable term, it actually can turn out to be cheaper over the long run. If you choose this type of term insurance, I personally recommend you take it for a minimum of 15 to 20 years. If you are in your 30s or younger, a 20-year policy would at least protect your family in the years in which they are likely to have the greatest need for your income.

WHO SHOULD BUY TERM INSURANCE?

Unless you are looking for an investment vehicle, I would recommend that everyone with dependents to protect should buy term life insurance—ideally, a level term policy. Depending on your particular situation, you probably would do well to look into getting as long-term a policy as possible, at least 20 years. If better rates become available, you can always go shopping for a new policy. (If you do this, make sure you don't cancel your old policy before you've been approved for your new one.)

The great news about term insurance these days is that it has never been more affordable. In fact, if you have a life insurance policy that is more than five years old, you probably should get it updated. Typically, you should be able to buy a new policy that provides two to three times the death benefit for the same price you're paying now, or the same size death benefit at just half or a third of your current premium cost.

Why hasn't your insurance company told you about this? Come on. Do you really think your insurance company is going to phone you up and say "Hey, guess what? We've cut our prices 50 percent, and we'd like to send you some of your money back." Of course it won't—which is why you should be constantly reviewing your financial situation.

FIVE-STAR TIP: *As attractive as it may seem, don't get term life insurance through your employer unless the policy the company is offering is guaranteed renewable and portable. This means that if you leave your job, you can take the policy with you. If your policy isn't portable, you could find yourself without a job and without insurance—a bad combination.*

PERMANENT INSURANCE

Permanent insurance is known in the industry as "cash-value" insurance. Basically, it combines term insurance with a forced savings plan that can help you build a nice nest egg. The catch is that permanent insurance can cost up to eight times as much as term.

There are three main types of permanent insurance: whole life, universal life, and variable universal life.

Whole Life. With whole life insurance, the premiums remain level as you grow older (just as with level term), but a portion of what you pay in is funneled into a "basket" of tax-deferred savings, where it can accumulate and earn dividends. At first, the portion is quite small, but as time goes on, it increases. As your policy's cash value builds, you can borrow against it or cash out by canceling your coverage. The problem with whole life is that the dividends your savings earn are generally not that high; indeed, they may not even keep up with inflation. The returns on whole life insurance are comparable to what you'd get by keeping your money in a checking account, often running as low as 3 to 5 percent a year. As a result, it can take literally decades to build any substantial cash value in a whole life policy. In my opinion, this makes it a very poor vehicle for a retirement nest egg.

Universal Life. Universal life insurance is a lot like whole life, except that it is supposed to offer much better returns and it's a lot more flexible. Specifically, you can change the size of the death benefit—and thus the size of your premium payment—any time you want. This is a great feature if your income tends to go up and down; in years when you don't earn so much, you can reduce your premium by reducing the size of your death benefit.

The downside to universal life is that the projected rates of return that the insurance company quotes when it's trying to sell you on the policy are just that—projections. Nothing is guaranteed. Universal life works great when the insurance company invests well, but it can be a disaster when the company doesn't. Many people who bought whole life policies back when rates were in the high teens have been shocked in recent years by annual returns of just 6 percent—and they still have to make premium payments.

Variable Universal Life Insurance. If you are looking for life insurance that also can double as an excellent retirement vehicle, I'd recommend variable universal life insurance. With variable universal life you get a cash-value policy that allows you to control how the savings portion of your premium dollars is invested. A good variable life policy may offer over a dozen different high-quality mutual funds for you to select from. Your choices may include stock funds (both domestic and global), bond funds, money markets, and sometimes even fixed-rate securities. The advantages over a whole life or universal policy are plain. If you make good investment decisions, you can make significantly more money over the long term than you would with a whole life or a regular universal policy.

WHY HASN'T MY INSURANCE AGENT TOLD ME ABOUT VARIABLE LIFE?

If your insurance agent never told you about variable life insurance, chances are it's because he or she does not have the Series 6 or Series 7 license that allows him or her to sell a policy that involves stocks or other securities. This is not the sort of financial advisor or insurance agent a Smart Woman wants to have. In the twenty-first century, you want someone who can offer you every type of policy there is and is up-to-date on the newest policies available.

> **FIVE-STAR TIP:** *If you buy a variable policy, you must be prepared to accept a certain amount of risk and volatility. Because you are investing in securities that may go down as well as up, there is a chance you may lose a portion of your cash value and be forced to make additional premium payments. If you are extremely conservative and like "guarantees," don't consider a variable policy because you won't be happy with the volatility.*

If you do invest in a variable policy, don't make the mistake of investing too conservatively. You will just end up with a variable policy that looks and acts like a universal policy. I recently had a woman and her husband come into my office after both had purchased variable policies. The wife was invested in a money-market account, while the husband was in an S&P 500 index fund. In the roaring bull market of 1995 to 1997, the husband's policy generated a return of better than 72 percent, while the wife's earned just 11 percent! (In absolute terms, even though they each paid the same amount in premiums, the husband made $15,000 more than his wife in just three years.) When I asked the wife why she was invested in such a low-interest vehicle, she said, "Well, I told the insurance agent I didn't want too much risk, and that was what he suggested." Bad suggestion!

> **FIVE-STAR TIP:** *Permanent insurance only works if you are committed to it—and if you can afford to make premium payments over a long period of time. On average, it takes about 10 to 15 years for a permanent policy really to work as an investment vehicle. If you are not sure you can commit to fund a policy this long, don't buy one. Start with a level term policy instead. It will cost less and protect your family just as adequately. You always can get permanent insurance later.*

WHERE SHOULD I START?

Life insurance is so complicated that you probably should consult an insurance professional or financial advisor before making any final decisions. Still, it never hurts to do some research on your own. Here are some sources you can use.

Ameritas
(800) 552-3553
www.veritas.ameritas.com

Master Quote
(800) 337-5433
www.masterquote.com

Quote Smith
(800) 431-1147
www.quotesmith.com

USAA Insurance
(800) 531-8000

Wholesale Insurance Network
(800) 808-5810
www.feeforservice.com

SAFEGUARD NO. 5
YOU NEED TO PROTECT YOUR INCOME WITH DISABILITY
INSURANCE.

I used to think disability insurance was a waste of money. I was wrong. Although far more people have life insurance than have disability insurance, the chances of your becoming sick or hurt are much greater than the chances of your dying prematurely. Without disability insurance you are playing Russian roulette with your income.

Consider the following statistics. In one year . . .

- 1 out of every 106 people will die.
- 1 out of every 88 homes will catch fire.
- 1 out of every 70 cars will be involved in a serious accident.

But . . .

One out of every eight people will suffer a serious disability!

What this means to you and me is that the greatest threat to our ability to finish rich may be the risk we all face of serious injury or illness! And the younger you are, the greater your risk actually is. Indeed, it has been reported that between the ages of 35 and 65, the chances of suffering a disability serious enough to prevent you from working is 1 in 2. That's twice the chance of dying at that age.

Other than your health, your income is probably your most important asset. Lose it and you could be losing your primary means of financial security. That's why we all need disability insurance.

HOW MUCH DISABILITY INSURANCE DO I NEED?

Disability insurance is not designed to make you rich. Rather, it is a protection plan for your current earning power. Ideally, therefore, an adequate disability policy is one that would pay you the equivalent of your current take-home pay.

Most disability plans offer a benefit equal to about 60 percent of your gross (or before-tax) income. That may not sound like much, but if you've paid for the disability policy yourself, any income you receive from it will be tax-free, so 60 percent of the gross probably will be enough to maintain your standard of living. (After all, 60 percent of the gross is about what most of us actually take home after taxes.)

If your employer pays for your disability insurance, any benefits you receive from it will be taxed. This means that if the policy pays only 60 percent of your gross income, you're going to come up short. Indeed, once you've paid the taxes on your disability benefit, you're likely to find yourself with a only fraction of your normal take-home pay. To guard against this, you should consider purchasing what is known as a "gap policy" to make up the difference.

DON'T ASSUME YOU HAVE DISABILITY INSURANCE

Many people mistakenly assume they automatically get disability coverage from their employer. Don't assume anything. If you work for a company, first thing tomorrow check your benefits statement or phone your benefits department to find out whether you have disability insurance. If you don't, find out if you can get it through work and start the application process immediately. If you are a stay-at-home mom whose husband works, check to see if he is covered. If you are self-employed and don't currently have disability insurance, make getting it a top priority.

You should apply for disability insurance now while you are healthy. For some reason, people always seem to put this off, waiting until something is wrong with them before they start trying to get coverage. By then, of course, it is too late. And don't think you can fool the insurance company by fibbing on your policy application. Saying you're healthy when you know you're not, or that you don't smoke when in fact you do, is not only immoral, it's also pointless. Insurance companies will do just about anything they can to avoid having to pay out benefits—including hiring an investigator to thoroughly investigate your past medical history.

QUESTIONS TO ASK BEFORE YOU SIGN UP

1. **Is the disability plan portable and guaranteed renewable?**
   If you purchase your policy through your employer, you must make sure that you can take the policy with you if you leave the company. You also want a policy that is guaranteed renewable;

there is no bigger ripoff than an insurance company that makes you "qualify" each and every year. This is how a bad insurance company gets out of having to pay you when you file a claim!

2. **Under what circumstances will the policy pay off?** Specifically, you want to know whether the policy will cover you in the event you're no longer able to do the work you currently do, or whether it pays off only if you are rendered unable to do work of any kind. In the insurance industry, this is known as "owner occupation" and "any occupation" coverage. Make sure you buy an owner-occupation policy. Why? Well, take me, for example. I happen to make my living talking on the phone to clients. Now, if I lost my voice and couldn't talk, I would, for all intents and purposes, be out of a job. But unless I had owner-occupation coverage, the insurance company could say to me "So what if you can't talk on the phone? There are plenty of other jobs you could do—like digging ditches. So we are not going to pay you any disability benefits." With owner-occupation coverage, they can't do that to me. This sort of coverage is more expensive, but it is much, much safer.

3. **How long does it take for the coverage to kick in?** Most disability policies start paying benefits within three to six months after you've been declared disabled. The easiest way to reduce the cost of a disability policy is to lengthen that waiting period. The more cash you have in your security basket, the longer you can stretch it out.

4. **How long will the policy cover me?** Ideally, your disability policy should pay you benefits until you turn 65 at least.

5. **Is my coverage limited to physical disability, or are mental and emotional disorders also covered?** A major cause of disability these days is stress. Not all disability policies cover it, however. If you are in a high-stress occupation, make sure yours does.

FIVE-STAR TIP: *As with all good and important things, there is a catch to disability insurance. It is expensive (plans often cost between 1 to 3 percent of your annual income), which is why most people don't have it. In fact, less than 25 percent of Americans carry disability insurance. The reason it costs so much is that insurance companies know there is a good chance they will have to pay off on the policies they write. (This alone should convince you that you need disability insurance.) In any case, I recommend that you contact your company's benefits department first and see if you can get it through them. Group policies tend to be less expensive and easier to get. If your employer won't cover you—or if you are self-employed—check with the following companies that specialize in disability insurance.*

Once again, like life insurance, disability insurance is very complicated, and you may want to consider hiring a disability specialist to assist you.

Below I have listed a firm that specializes in disability insurance (Disability Insurance Services) and provides quotes for close to a dozen different disability companies. In addition, I have listed some companies that you can go to directly for a quote on a disability policy.

Disability Insurance Services
(800) 898-9641
(619) 284-8444

Provident Companies (Previously known as Paul Revere)
(800) 843-3426

Unum Life Insurance
www.unum.com
(800) 227-8138

USAA Insurance
(800) 531-8000

SAFEGUARD NO. 6
YOU NEED AN EFFECTIVE "ATTORNEY REPELLENT."

One of the more unfortunate realities of life in America today is that an attorney is born just about every six seconds. Okay, I'm exaggerating here a little, but chances are you personally know more people who have been sued than have died or become disabled.

To protect yourself against the tide of frivolous lawsuits currently washing over the land, you should consider buying lawsuit insurance, otherwise known as "umbrella" or liability insurance. The idea is that in the event someone sues you, the umbrella insurance will offer you and your assets additional protection beyond what your homeowners' insurance and car insurance normally provide. If you have more than $500,000 in assets, I would seriously consider purchasing a $1-million umbrella policy. Such policies are extremely inexpensive; often they cost less than $300 a year.

FIVE-STAR TIP: *The biggest reservation I have about recommending umbrella insurance is that the simple act of having it can motivate an attorney to sue you. For example, once it comes out that you are covered by $1-million umbrella policy, that guy you barely bumped into in the grocery-store parking lot may suddenly discover he has whiplash. Unfortunately, the only thing worse than this type of lawsuit is the one that's filed against you when you don't have an umbrella policy to protect you.*

SAFEGUARD NO. 7
IF YOU ARE 50 OR OLDER, IT'S TIME TO CONSIDER GETTING
LONG-TERM CARE COVERAGE.

As I often tell my female students, one of the great things about being a woman is that you probably are going to live a long time; the bad news is that you need to prepare differently for old age from how your mothers and grandmothers did.

Once upon a time, individual families provided their own support systems to take care of sick or aged parents. Today families often are spread out all over the country. As a result, there is no support system. With average life expectancies climbing, more and more elderly people are finding themselves in need of either home care or a long-term care facility. Indeed, studies indicate that no fewer than one out of every three Americans over the age of 65 eventually will need this sort of help. For women, the statistics are even more worrisome. According to the experts, there is a 50 percent chance that you will need to enter a nursing care facility some time after you turn 65.

The cost of such care today can be staggering—as much as $30,000 to $70,000 a year for residence in a long-term care facility. You may think that Medicare will cover your nursing care needs. Unfortunately, the reality is that in most cases it won't.

BUSTING THE MEDICARE MYTH

According to a poll taken by the American Association of Retired Persons, fully 79 percent of us assume that Medicare will pay for our basic nursing care needs when we get old. As I just noted, however, we are in for an unpleasant surprise. The fact is, of the billions of dollars in nursing home costs Americans incur every year, less than 10 percent are covered by Medicare.

The reason is simple. Most of the care that nursing homes provide to people with chronic, long-term illnesses or disabilities is *custodial,* and Medicare does not pay for custodial care. Rather, Medicare is meant to take care of what are known as acute-care needs. For Medicare to cover a nursing home stay, a person first must spend 3 full days in an acute-care hospital and require skilled care or rehabilitation therapy at least 5 days a week. And even then, Medicare will cover the person completely only for the first 20 days of your nursing home stay. (After that, it may pay a portion of care for the next 80 days, provided the person's health actually is improving as a result.)

And even if you turn out to be one of the lucky ones who meets the current qualification requirements, there's no guarantee that Medicare will still be around in 20 years. Many experts think that the government will not be able to continue the funding of Medicare in its current form for very much longer because there will be so many more elderly people who need it. (What about Medicaid? Well, Medicaid is welfare, and to qualify for it you must be legally categorized as "financially destitute." That's not how a Smart Women wants to end up.)

THE INS AND OUTS OF LTC COVERAGE

So to protect her future, a Smart Woman will want to buy herself some long-term care insurance. When you're looking for LTC coverage, the first thing you need to understand is what it will not do. Long-term care insurance will not pay for acute care that you get in a hospital (say, in the immediate aftermath of a heart attack or a broken hip). What LTC insurance will cover is the kind of care you get in a nursing home, a residential care facility, a convalescent facility, an extended facility, a community hospice or adult-care center, or in some cases in your own home.

There are basically four levels of assistance available: skilled care, intermediate care, custodial care, and home health care.

Skilled Care. This is the most comprehensive type of assistance. It is what you get when you need around-the-clock care provided by licensed professionals working under a doctor's supervision. While this type of care is often what we imagine when we think about what goes on in a nursing care facility, the fact is that only a small percentage of patients actually require such intensive attention.

Intermediate Care. People needing intermediate care also may require skilled medical staff; however, not on a daily basis. An example would be the services provided by a physical or speech therapist.

Custodial Care. Custodial assistance does not require skilled medical staff. Rather, it involves assisting patients with routine tasks such as eating, walking, bathing, and taking medication.

Home Health Care. Home health care assistance is becoming more and more common as patients choose to get their assistance in their own homes. This often includes assistance from a licensed nurse who makes regular visits to provide medical services that previously were available only in a facility.

TYPES OF COVERAGE

The type of LTC coverage you can buy varies from state to state. In California, where I live, insurance companies offer three different types of LTC policies: nursing facility only, home care only, or comprehensive long-term care.

All things being equal, when you check out what's available in your state, I recommend that you consider a comprehensive policy. The reason is that right now you are probably healthy and as a result can't really predict what type of coverage you will need in the future. A comprehensive policy typically will give you the most options. It will cost more, but should you eventually need the care. I'm confident it will more than justify the extra expense.

HOW MUCH DOES IT COST?

The cost of LTC coverage depends on a number of variables. They include the state you live in, your age, the level of care you want, the amount of coverage ($100 a day, $200 a day, and so on), the length of waiting time before your policy kicks in, your state of health and age, and how long you want your policy to last should you need to use it.

Not counting short stays of less than three months, statistics show that most people spend an average of about two to three years in a nursing care facility. Nonetheless, I recommend paying the extra 10 to 15 percent to get lifetime coverage. If the extra cost is too much for you, you can reduce the premium price by requesting a higher deductible on your policy. What this means is that your policy will take longer to go into effect. Most LTC policies start paying off within 30 to 60 days after you enter a nursing facility or put in a claim for home care. By stretching that out a bit, you can bring down your premium costs quite nicely.

Delaying the start of coverage may sound scary, but it's actually quite sensible, since you probably will be able to afford the first few months on your own. It's later on that you will need the most help. By taking a higher deductible and getting lifetime coverage you are covering the worst-case possibility, which is why you are buying this type of coverage in the first place. (By the way, the cost of this type of insurance can be tax deductible, so check with your accountant if you decide to purchase it.)

WHY I BELIEVE IN LTC COVERAGE

I went through the nursing care experience myself when my beloved Grandma Bach suddenly needed around-the-clock care. After years of walking five miles a day and going out dancing at night, my grandmother suddenly had a stroke at age 86. Within two weeks we were forced to move her into a nursing facility that could provide her with

24-hour care. Fortunately, we had the money (and so did she) to pay for the best nursing care available. Still, if where we sent my grandmother was "top of the line," I'd hate to see what "middle of the road" looks like.

Sadly, my grandmother passed away just a few weeks after she entered the nursing care facility. I personally believe she knew in her heart that she wasn't going get better and she didn't want to live in a nursing care facility.

The fact is, there are few decisions in life more brutal than having to decide whether the time has come to put a parent or some other loved one into a nursing facility. If and when that time comes, you won't want to have to worry about money. You will want to be able to afford the "top of the line"—and LTC coverage can make that possible. I should note that because my grandmother had built a nice nest egg, she didn't need to purchase LTC insurance. But unless you are similarly wealthy, I strongly suggest you look into purchasing LTC coverage for your parents—and for yourself if you happen to be over the age of 50. The younger you are, the easier it will be for you to get coverage, and age 50 is hardly too young to consider this type of coverage.

NO ONE NEEDS LTC COVERAGE MORE THAN WOMEN

As we've seen in other contexts, the fact that women live longer than men has both its upsides and its downsides. In this case, the downside is that it's much more likely that you will one day need a nursing care facility than the man in your life ever will. Realistically, if you are married and your husband gets sick, chances are that you will be the one who takes care of him. But who will take care of you after he passes away? The fact is, nearly three-quarters of all nursing care residents today are women. Indeed, I don't recall ever seeing a male patient at my grandmother's nursing care facility. I'm sure there were some, but they were definitely in the minority.

QUESTIONS TO ASK BEFORE YOU SIGN UP

1. **What exactly does the policy cover?** Remember, several difference types of coverage are available, and they vary from state to state. Make sure you know exactly what type of coverage you are being shown before you sign up.

2. **How much will the policy pay out in daily benefits? Will it be adjusted for inflation? At what point do my benefits kick in, and how long will they last?** Remember, I suggest that you keep your premiums down by requesting a higher deductible but that you also pay a little more in order to get yourself lifetime coverage.

3. **Does the policy contain a premium waiver, or will I still have to pay the premiums after I start receiving benefits?** You don't want to have to continue paying premiums while you are in a health care facility.

4. **Is there a grace period for late payments?** Make sure there is. You would hate to find yourself in a situation where you accidentally missed a payment and then discovered that you'd lost your coverage.

5. **Are there any diseases or injuries that are not covered?** The answer should be no. Don't ever buy a policy that excludes Alzheimer's or mental illness.

6. **How long has your insurance company been in the LTC business?** Long-term care insurance is still a relatively new product, and every year dozens of insurance companies enter and leave the business. The truth is that we haven't yet been able to gauge the financial impact of our rapidly aging population. If insurance companies find they can't make money on LTC coverage, they may well drop it. As a result, I feel strongly that you should *not* purchase an LTC policy from a company that has been in the LTC business for less than ten years.

You have now completed your security basket. In the process, you have done an amazing amount—far more than 95 percent of the population ever does—to protect both your future and that of your family.

BASKET TWO:
YOUR RETIREMENT BASKET

In Step Four we talked about the importance of paying yourself first—of putting aside a portion of your income (ideally, 12 percent of your income before taxes), and how you should have it transferred out of your paycheck automatically, before you even see it. Well, where this money actually goes is into your retirement basket.

Remember: Even though we discussed the security basket first, that doesn't mean you should put off funding your retirement basket until after you've funded your security basket. *You should be doing both at the same time!*

The point of paying yourself first is to put money away now so you can have a great retirement later. As you will see, accomplishing this is not only easy, it also can be a lot of fun. Why? Because nearly every dollar you put into this basket goes in tax-free! If that's not fun, I don't know what is. What's more, because your retirement money is not taxed as long as it stays in the basket, you are in essence getting "free money" from the government to invest. When was the last time that happened to you?

You may be wondering how this works. It's simple. When you put money into your retirement basket, you actually are putting it into what is known as a pretax retirement account.

What Exactly Is a Pretax Retirement Account?

A pretax retirement account is a retirement account into which you are allowed to deposit a portion of your earnings *before* the government takes its usual bite out of them. What's great about this is that normally that bite amounts to at least 34 cents out of every dollar you earn (roughly 28 cents for federal income tax, plus 7.65 cents for Social Security). If you live in a state that has its own income tax, the damage is even worse. For example, California imposes a 9 percent state income tax; as a result, my average client is lucky to keep barely 60 cents of every dollar she makes.

Funneling your hard-earned dollars into a pretax retirement account spares the money from this kind of shrinkage. When you put your earnings into a pretax retirement account, all 100 cents of each dollar goes to work for you, and as long as the money stays in the account, it can continue to work for you without any interference from the tax man.

The Wonderful World of Retirement Plans

There are basically two kinds of pretax retirement accounts: the kind your company provides for you (known as a employer-sponsored plan) and the kind you provide for yourself (known as an individual plan).

Over the next few pages, I'm going to describe how these work. Regardless of your status—that is, whether you are self-employed or on a company payroll—I suggest you read about both types of accounts. After all, self-employed people do wind up working for companies sometimes. And in this era of corporate restructuring, company people all too often suddenly can find themselves self-employed. What's more, even if you are lucky enough to have a secure job with a company that offers a good retirement plan, opening an individual retirement account of your own still might make sense for you. So please don't skip over a section just because you don't think it applies to your situation right now.

How Employer-Sponsored Retirement Plans Work

The most popular retirement program employers make available to workers these days is what is known as a 401(k) plan. Nonprofit organizations have 403(b) plans; some smaller companies may offer what is called a SIMPLE plan, a SEP-IRA, or a Defined Contribution plan (which used to be known as a Keogh plan).

Whichever type your employer offers, you should be able to join it at no cost. If you are not enrolled currently, go to your benefits or human resource department *first thing tomorrow morning,* ask if such a plan is available to employees, and if the answer is yes, say you want to sign up for it immediately.

If you've just started a new job, you may have to wait several months before you are eligible to join the retirement program. And even then, some plans allow new participants to enroll only at certain times of the year.

Whatever the case, once the "start" date has rolled around, the benefits person probably will give you what is called a sign-up package. Your job is to fill it out ASAP.

The most important piece of information you want to find out from your benefits person is the maximum amount of money is that you can put into the plan each year. Typically, the answer is 15 percent of your gross annual earnings, up to a maximum that changes each year. In 1998 the maximum allowable contribution for 401(k) and 403(b) plans was $10,000; for SIMPLE plans, it was $6,000. Usually the government raises this ceiling a bit each year, though not by much, and certainly not by enough. (Any congresspeople or senators listening out there?)

THE IMPORTANCE OF "MAXING OUT" YOUR RETIREMENT PLAN

Whatever your maximum allowable contribution happens to be, that's the amount you should be putting in. This is called "maxing out" your retirement plan, and it is by far the single most important thing you can do to create a secure financial future. There is nothing I know of that is better at transforming otherwise ordinary Americans into millionaires than the simple act of each month putting as much of their paycheck as they are allowed into a pretax retirement plan at work.

It's reported that less than half of Americans who are eligible for a retirement plan at work actually bother to sign up. And most of the people who do don't max out their contributions. Why? In a word, ignorance. I am convinced that if people knew what they were missing out on—how they were cheating themselves out of a secure and comfortable future—hardly anyone would fail to take full advantage of their retirement plans at work.

Here's a simple example that made a tremendous impact on me.

TWO WOMEN, SAME PLAN, BUT A $400,000 DIFFERENCE!

About three years ago, I held what is known in the investment industry as a IRA Rollover seminar for a local company. This is a seminar where you teach workers who are about to change employers or retire how to "roll over" the money they've saved in their company's 401(k) plan into an Individual Retirement Account.

After this particular class, two women came into my office. One was named Betty; the other, Lynn. Both had worked for the utility com-

pany for more than 35 years. Indeed, they were best friends who had
started work at this company the very same week.

I met with Lynn first, and after I reviewed her plan, I was able to tell
her that she was in great shape to retire. Her account balance totaled
more than $750,000—enough to produce plenty of income for her to
live comfortably for the rest of her life. Not surprisingly, Lynn left my
office with a big smile on her face.

Betty, by contrast, wore a worried expression when she came in.
"You know," she told me, "even though Lynn and I started at the same
time and have made close to the same amount of money, I'm not in
nearly as good as shape as she is financially."

"Oh, really," I said. "And why is that?"

Betty then took out her retirement plan and showed it to me. Her
balance was a little less then $300,000. Not bad, but not nearly as good
as her friend's $930,000. "David," she said with a sigh, "I can remember
it like it was yesterday. Sitting down at lunch 35 years ago, Lynn and I
discussed how much of our income we were going to put into the
plan. Lynn told me she was going to max hers out and put away the
full 15 percent. She figured it might hurt the first few months, but
after that she wouldn't really notice it. I said, 'Fifteen percent? No way!
That's just too much.' I figured I'd start with the minimum, which was
4 percent, and when I got a raise, I'd increase my contributions."

Betty shook her head ruefully. "You know what? So many raises
came and went, but I never got around to increasing the size of my
contribution. There always seem to be some new expense that came
first—a new car, a special vacation, college costs. Now Lynn gets to
retire and I have go find another job. I'll probably need to work for
another 15 years. Pretty stupid, huh?"

My heart went out to Betty. But there wasn't much I could do.
Don't make the same mistake she did. Maximize your retirement contribution now.

ARE YOU WHERE YOU SHOULD BE?

If you are currently enrolled in a retirement plan but don't know if
you are maxing out, you need to educate yourself immediately. Contact your employer's benefits person or meet with your accountant,
and with his or her help, figure out where you stand. If it turns out
that you're contributing anything less than the maximum, make it a
priority to get your contributions up to the ceiling as quickly as you

can. If you are not working but have a husband who is, make sure he's enrolled in his employer's retirement plan and that his contributions are maxing out.

FIVE-STAR TIP: *Government regulations concerning contribution ceilings are very complicated. For example, the maximum amount you are permitted to contribute to your retirement account is limited not only by the size of your own income but by how much money your fellow employees decide to put into their accounts. So don't assume you can figure out your maximum on your own. Ask the person in charge of your plan to calculate it for you.*

HOW DOES MY MONEY GET INTO THE PLAN?

Once you have completed your sign-up package and are enrolled in your firm's retirement program, your employer will begin taking your contribution out of your paycheck automatically. This automatic salary deduction has two tremendous advantages. First, because it is automatic, you don't have to worry about it (and run the risk of changing your mind). Second, the money you've decided to put aside goes directly into the plan, avoiding that 40 percent tax bite I mentioned earlier.

Oh, and don't worry: Your decision to contribute the maximum allowable amount is not chiseled in stone. If you find you need to reduce your contributions temporarily, at most companies you can do so on as little as 90 days' notice.

WHERE DOES MY RETIREMENT MONEY REALLY GO?

The application form you fill out to enroll in the plan asks you more than just how much you want to contribute. It also asks you where you want your money to be invested. Most plans today offer participants at least three choices: (1) your money can be invested in your company's own stock (assuming that you work for a company with publicly traded stock); (2) it can go into one or more mutual funds; or

(3) it can be put in some vehicle that offers a guaranteed fixed rate. It's up to you to decide what combination of the available options makes the most sense for you and how much of your contribution you want to put into each of them.

This decision is potentially one of the most important financial decisions you will ever make. Let me repeat that.

How you decide to invest the money in your retirement plan is one of the most important financial decisions you will ever make!

So take this decision seriously. Don't just turn to your neighbor at work and ask him or her, "What are you doing?" He or she may not have a clue.

Instead, study your options carefully and discuss them, both with your significant other (if you've got one) and with a knowledgeable financial advisor. At the end of this chapter, you will find a list of rules aimed at helping you make the smartest decision possible. Follow them, and I think you will be in great shape.

HOW DO I GET MY MONEY OUT OF THE PLAN?

As long as you remain employed by the company where you opened your 401(k) account, your funds typically stay in the company plan. You can take money out anytime you want, but if you're younger than $59^{1}/_{2}$, you will end up paying ordinary income tax on your withdrawal, plus a 10 percent penalty. (There are a few ways of avoiding this penalty; we'll cover them later in this chapter.) If you change jobs or leave the company for any other reason before you reach retirement age, you can "roll over" your 401(k) funds either to a new employer's 401(k) plan or to a new IRA of your own. If done properly, the IRS will not consider this transfer of funds a withdrawal, and you won't be subject to any taxes or penalties.

Once you've turned $59^{1}/_{2}$, you can start taking money out of your retirement plan. (You are not required to—not at least until you're $70^{1}/_{2}$ —but you can if you want.) Whatever money you withdraw from then on will be treated by the government as ordinary income, which means you will have to pay income taxes on it.

IF YOUR COMPANY DOESN'T HAVE A
RETIREMENT PLAN

In my view, companies that don't offer retirement plans are doing their employees a disservice. I happen to believe that employers have a moral obligation to provide programs that allow workers to secure their own financial futures by contributing to tax-advantaged savings and investment accounts.

Some employers—especially the owners of small businesses—complain that they simply can't afford to offer such programs. In recent years, however, the cost of setting up and administering retirement plans has dropped to the point where even small businesses should be able to manage it. Indeed, when you figure everything in, it's probably less expensive for an employer to set up a retirement plan than to replace a fed-up worker who has quit to join a competitor who cares about his or her people's futures!

As an employee, you should make sure your boss knows how unhappy you are about not having a retirement plan. You might add that if she expects you to make a long-term commitment to her company, she'd better do something about putting this sort of benefit in place.

That being said, it's still entirely possible to love your job even though your company does not now and never will provide you with a retirement plan. If that describes you, don't worry. You don't have to quit. But you do have to do something.

It's quite simple, really. If your employer won't provide a retirement plan for you, you must provide one for yourself. In other words . . .

You should open an Individual Retirement Account.

Opening an IRA is a relatively simple procedure. Indeed, as a result of recent changes in federal tax laws, it's easier than ever for individuals to put more money than ever before into tax-deferred retirement accounts.

Thanks to the massive Taxpayer Relief Act of 1997, there are now two types of IRAs, the traditional IRA and the new Roth IRA (named for its legislative sponsor, Senator William Roth of Delaware), into which you allowed to deposit a total of up to $2,000 a year. With a traditional account, your contributions may be tax deductible (depending on your income and whether you contributed to a 401[k] plan), and they get to grow free of all federal taxes until you take them out. With a Roth IRA, you pay income taxes on your money before you put it in, but that's it—if you follow the rules, you never pay a penny more in federal taxes on your nest egg, no matter how large it grows over the years (provided you don't touch the money until after you turn $59^{1}/_{2}$).

Let's go over the basics.

THE TRADITIONAL IRA

Originally created in 1974, the traditional Individual Retirement Account is meant primarily for people who work for companies that do not offer retirement plans. The rules governing this type of IRA are relatively straightforward.

1. **Who is eligible?** Anyone under the age of $70^{1}/_{2}$ who earns income from a job (as opposed to interest or investment income) or is married to someone who earns income from a job.

2. **What if my employer offers a retirement plan?** Even if you participate in a retirement plan at work, you still may be able to contribute to a traditional IRA, although how much of your contribution will be deductible depends on the size of your income. As with all tax issues, I strongly recommend you consult a tax advisor.

3. **How much can I put in?** You can invest up to $2,000 a year. Exactly how much depends on the size of your income. Under the new law, nonworking spouses also can contribute up to $2,000 a year as well (a significant increase over the old limit of $250). This means that a married couple can put away as much as $4,000 a year.

4. **What are the tax advantages?** Depending on how much you earn (or, if you are married, on your joint income), your IRA contributions may be fully tax deductible. As long as it stays in the account, your money can grow tax-deferred—meaning you do not have to pay any taxes on any interest earnings or capital gains.

5. **When can I take my money out?** Once you reach the age of $59^{1}/_{2}$ (or any time after that), you can withdraw any or all of your savings. The government will regard every withdrawal you make as ordinary income and will expect you to pay income taxes on it. (There is an exception to this rule: If you've funded

your IRA account with after-tax money—that is, you didn't take a tax deduction on the original deposit—then you'll be taxed only on the earnings and the growth your investment generated over the years, not on the investment itself.)

6. **Do I *have* to start taking money out of my IRA when I turn 59¹/₂?** No, but you can't leave it there forever. IRS regulations require you to start making what is called a mandatory minimum distribution from your IRA no later than six months after your seventieth birthday. To figure out exactly what your mandatory minimum amounts to, check with your accountant or call the IRS and ask for Publication 590, which explains how to calculate it. (By the way, if you have elderly parents, make sure they are aware of the minimum distribution requirement. Failing to take a minimum distribution can leave them liable to a penalty equal to 50 percent of the amount they should have taken out.)

7. **What if I need my money before I reach retirement age?** If you withdraw any or all of your IRA savings before the age of 59¹/₂, in additional to paying ordinary income tax on the money you have taken out, you may have to pay a 10 percent penalty on whatever interest or investment earnings your initial deposit generated over the years. This penalty does not apply if your withdrawal is used for one of three major "life events": to pay college bills for yourself, your children, or your grandchildren; to help finance a first-time home purchase (up to a maximum of $10,000); or to cover health insurance premiums, extraordinary medical expenses, or long-term disability costs.

There is another way to avoid the penalty—an obscure section of the tax code known as Internal Revenue Service Rule 72(t)(2)(A)(iv), generally referred to as "72T." According to this little-known regulation, you don't have to pay the early withdrawal penalty if you take your money in what the IRS defines as "substantially equal and periodic payments that are based on life-expectancy tables." This is an extremely complicated undertaking that you shouldn't attempt without professional guidance. Done correctly, however, it can be hugely valuable—especially if you are planning to retire in your early 50s. So if early retirement is a possibility for you, make a point of finding a financial specialist who knows the ins and outs of rule "72T." It could save you a bundle in tax penalties.

THE ROTH IRA

Not since IRAs were first introduced back in 1974 has any tax-deferred retirement account gotten as much attention as the new Roth accounts. The biggest difference between the Roth IRA and the traditional IRA is that with a Roth account, not only do your savings grow tax-deferred, but when you finally take them out, *you don't have to pay any taxes on them whatsoever!*

Sounds like a great deal, doesn't it? It is, but as always, there is a catch. In this case, it's that there's no tax deduction for the money you put into a Roth IRA. That deduction, of course, is what made traditional IRAs so popular in the first place. So it's a trade-off. Which is worth more to you: the money you'll save in taxes now by being able to deduct your IRA contributions this year, or the money you'll save later by not having to pay any taxes on your IRA withdrawals when you retire? The current rule of thumb on this is that if you are more than ten years away from retirement, you'll come out ahead with a Roth IRA.

COMPARING ROTH IRAs TO TRADITIONAL IRAs

	Non-Deductible IRA (balance after taxes)	Roth IRA (tax-free balance)
Annual Investment	$2,000.00	$2,000.00
Rate of Return	10%	10%
Tax Rate	28%	28%
10 Yrs	$30,844.88	$35,062.33
15 Yrs	$58,727.61	$69,899.46
20 Yrs	$101,923.60	$126,005.00
25 Yrs	$169,781.74	$216,363.53
30 Yrs	$277,358.53	$361,886.85
35 Yrs	$448,902.60	$596,253.61
40 Yrs	$723,466.61	$973,703.62

The first scenario shows the performance of a non-deductible IRA versus a Roth IRA over 10 to 40 years, assuming 28% tax rate, 10% return, $2,000 annual contribution, and $0 start balance.

Source: *Research* magazine, February 1998, page 48

Here is a rundown of the basic rules governing Roth IRAs.

1. **Who is eligible?** As with a traditional IRA, you must have earned income to be able to open a Roth IRA. The catch is that you can't have too much income. For singles, the ceiling is $110,000 a year; for married couples who file jointly, it's $160,000.

2. **How much can I put in?** Singles who earn less than $95,000 can contribute up to $2,000 a year; individuals who earn more than $95,000 and less than $110,000 may make a partial contribution. Married individuals whose joint annual income totals less than $150,000 can contribute up to $4,000 a year; the maximum contribution drops to zero as the couple's joint income approaches $160,000.

3. **What are the tax advantages?** While contributions to a Roth IRA are not tax-deductible, your money will grow tax-deferred—and provided it's been in the account for at least five years, you can take it out totally tax-free any time after you turn $59^{1}/_{2}$. This ability to take out money without paying any additional taxes is a tremendous advantage over a traditional IRA.

4. **When can I take my money out?** Once you reach the age of $59^{1}/_{2}$ (or anytime after that), you can withdraw any or all of your savings without penalty. Unlike a traditional IRA, however, you can leave your money in a Roth account as long as you like; you do not have to start making minimum withdrawals when you turn 70. This too is a significant advantage over a traditional IRA.

5. **What if I need my money before I turn $59^{1}/_{2}$?** The rules here are exactly the same as for traditional IRAs.

SO WHICH RETIREMENT PLAN IS BEST FOR ME?

Determining which plan makes the most sense for you depends on your income, your age, and your goals. That notwithstanding, company-sponsored plans are almost always the best way to go. If you want to put away more money for retirement, you always can supplement your company plan with an IRA. As to choosing between a traditional IRA and a Roth IRA, if you are more than ten years away from retirement, go with the Roth; the benefits of the tax-free distribution later probably will outweigh the benefits of the tax deduction now. Otherwise, a traditional IRA if it is deductible is probably preferable. In either case, if you are at all unsure of what's right for you, talk to your accountant or other professional financial advisor.

WHAT ABOUT CONVERTING MY OLD TRADITIONAL IRA TO A NEW ROTH IRA?

While Roth IRAs do offer some terrific advantages, especially for younger investors, that doesn't mean everyone under the age of 55 should convert all his or her old traditional IRAs to Roth accounts. I mention this because ever since Roth IRAs were first introduced many banks, brokers, and financial advisors have been enthusiastically urging their clients to do just that. I have two words of advice on this subject: Be careful. An IRA conversion is a very serious decision, and there isn't any one-size-fits-all answer. Often the only one who benefits from a Roth conversion is the financial planner who talks you into it—and as a result earns an extra commission.

Actually, that's not strictly true. Someone else also benefits: Uncle Sam, who gets to collect extra tax revenue from the poor suckers who make this ill-advised move.

The reason this move is ill advised is that in order to convert your old IRA, you in effect have to cash it out. While you won't be hit with any penalties, you will have to report as income all the money you have accumulated in the account, which means you will have to pay income taxes on your nest egg. Say you are in the 28 percent tax bracket and you convert an IRA with $50,000 in it. Some $14,000 of that will have to go to Uncle Sam. (Actually, your tax bill likely would be higher than that because having to report the $50,000 as income probably would push you into a higher tax bracket.) In any case, suddenly you'd lose well over a quarter of the money you have been working so hard to grow.

Now, some people will suggest that if you have "extra money" sitting around, you could use that to pay your tax bill. But seriously, who has "extra money"? In any case, if you use the tools this book provides, your money won't ever be "sitting around," it will be working hard for you. So be sure to get solid financial and tax advice before making any decisions about converting your old IRAs.

What If I Own My Own Business?

First, let me say congratulations! I say this because I admire entrepreneurs and because, as a business owner, you are eligible for the best retirement accounts around. Second, let me urge you to avoid a mistake that too many business owners make—deciding that setting up a retirement plan is too much of a bother.

Remember, you are in business to build a financially secure future for yourself and your family—and how can you do that unless you pay yourself first? As a business owner, the best way to pay yourself first is by setting up one of the three types of retirement plans meant for self-employed people:

- Simplified Employee Pension Plan (also known as a SEP-IRA)
- Defined Contribution Plan
- a Savings Incentive Match Plan for Employees (known as a SIMPLE IRA)

Establishing one of these may take a little effort on your part, but, hey, you're an entrepreneur—you should be used to going the extra mile. In any case, it's more than worth it. While the regulations regarding distributions and early withdrawals are pretty much the same as the ones that govern IRAs and 401(k) plans, the rules on contributions to retirement plans for business owners are much, much better, allowing you to put away up to $30,000 a year, tax-deferred—possibly even more. That's huge! We're talking big money here!

SIMPLIFIED EMPLOYEE PENSION PLANS (SEPs)

SEP-IRAs are very attractive to small business owners because they are easy to set up and require the least paperwork. If you run a small business, are a sole proprietor, participate in a small partnership, or are a Subchapter S corporation, this is probably the type of retirement account you'll want to set up. With a SEP-IRA, you can make a tax-deductible contribution up to 15 percent of your employees' annual compensation. (The annual percentage limit for self-employed individuals is 13.043 percent). In 1997 the maximum legal contribution was $24,000.

Certain obligations go along with establishing a SEP-IRA. If you have people working for you who are over 21 and have been on your payroll for at least three of the last five years, you also must include them in your SEP-IRA, contributing on their behalf the same percentage of their annual compensation that you do of your own. In other words, if you put in 13.04 percent of your compensation, you also must contribute an amount equal to 13.04 percent of theirs. (By the same token, if you decide not to put in any money for yourself one year, you don't have to put any money in for them.)

The one disadvantage of a SEP-IRA is that the contributions you make for your employees are immediately 100 percent vested (which means the money you put in for them is theirs to keep, even if they leave your employ the next day).

DEFINED CONTRIBUTION PLANS

If you run your own business and can afford to put away more than 15 percent of your income, a Defined Contribution plan may make the most sense for you. With certain Defined Contribution plans, you can make a fully tax-deductible contribution of as much as 25 percent of your income, up to a maximum of $30,000 a year!

Defined Contribution plans are especially good for business owners who earn significantly more than their employees. As a result of a feature called Social Security integration, highly compensated employees (which generally means the business owner—that is, you) are allowed to contribute a bigger percentage of their compensation than other workers. This means that you can put in, say, 25 percent of your compensation without having to make an equally large contribution on behalf of your employees.

There are three main types of Defined Contribution plans: Money-Purchase plans, Profit-Sharing plans, and Defined-Benefit plans.

MONEY-PURCHASE PLANS

With a money-purchase plan, you can put away as much as 25 percent of your annual income (20% of earned income for self-employed persons) to a maximum of $30,000 per participant a year. As with a SEP-IRA, you are required to make equal-percentage contributions for your employees, but you may create a vesting schedule for these contributions (meaning the employees must remain with your company for a set period of time before they can claim the money you have put into the plan on their behalf). The only downside to a money-purchase plan is that the size of your annual contribution is fixed; once you decide on a percentage of your income, you're stuck with it. If you want to change it later (say, because you had an especially good year and can afford to contribute more—or because times suddenly got tough, and you want to put aside less), you have to amend the plan document.

FIVE-STAR TIP: *If you change the size of your contribution, make sure you amend your plan document. Otherwise, the IRS could subject the plan (and you) to penalties.*

PROFIT-SHARING PLANS

These plans are wonderful retirement benefits that can be good for both owners and employees. As the name implies, a profit-sharing plan is meant to encourage business owners to share company profits with employees in a good year. Under this type of plan, you can contribute up to 15 percent of your income (to a maximum of $30,000). But unlike a money-purchase plan, which requires you to contribute the same percentage of your income every year, profit-sharing plans are flexible, allowing owners to change the size of their annual contribution—and even skip a year entirely—as conditions dictate.

Like all the Defined Contribution plans, profit-sharing plans also permit Social Security integration, meaning they can be structured so that the percentage you have to contribute for your employees might be less than you'd have to put in under a SEP-IRA. Another advantage to this type of a plan over a SEP-IRA is that it allows you to create a vesting schedule for your employee contributions.

DEFINED-BENEFITS PLANS

Business owners over the age of 50 who have no employees and enjoy a high level of dependable income should consider setting up one of these plans. The reason: Defined-benefits plans allow you to put away more money than any other plan around. If you can afford to contribute more than $30,000 a year and are confident that you can do this yearly until you reach $59^1/_2$, this plan is for you. This is not, however, a do-it-yourself kind of retirement plan. To set one up, you will need to hire a financial advisor who specializes in defined-benefits plans as well as a third-party administrator to write the plan document for you. You also will want to work closely with an accountant to make sure your plan conforms to all IRS guidelines and that you are filing the yearly reporting forms correctly. But don't let this extra work scare you. If your income is sufficiently high, in just ten years you could put enough into a defined-benefits plan to be able to retire!

THE SIMPLE IRA

The biggest disadvantage of Defined Contribution plans is that they don't allow your employees to put their own money into the plan. That's not a problem with the new SIMPLE IRA. Introduced in 1997, this plan is meant for small companies (those with less than 100 employees) looking for an easy and affordable retirement program—in other words, something simpler and cheaper than a 401(k) plan.

Under a SIMPLE IRA, you and your employees can each put as much as $6,000 a year into the plan. As with a SEP-IRA, the employer also must contribute to the plan on the employees' behalf, and these contributions vest immediately. Then again, they are relatively small—limited to between 1 and 3 percent of each employee's total compensation.

FIVE-STAR TIP: *Since SIMPLE IRAs are very new, the jury is still out on whether they are any easier or cheaper to set up and run than 401(k) plans. My guess is that they probably aren't. In most cases, these days setting up a small 401(k) plan has become so inexpensive that I can't fathom why any employer would prefer a SIMPLE IRA. For one thing, under a 401(k) plan, your employees can put away a lot more money (as much as $10,000 a year each)—and you are under no obligation to make any matching contributions, large or small. For another, 401(k) plans allow you to offer your workers a nice benefit in the form of matching contributions—and at the same time create a vesting schedule that will motivate them to stay with you.*

What Do I Do with My Contributions?

Okay, so you've decided what type of retirement account makes the most sense for you, and you've figured out how much you are going to contribute to it this year. Now comes the really big decision.

As I noted earlier, deciding where and how to invest your retirement money probably is the most important financial decision you ever will make.

Some of you may find that baffling. I can hear you asking "Haven't I just made that decision? I'm investing my money in a retirement account."

No, you are not. A retirement account—whether it's an IRA, a SEP-IRA, a Defined Contribution plan, a SIMPLE plan, a 403(b), or a 401(k)—is not an investment. It is, rather, just a holding tank for your retirement money.

People are often confused about this. They will tell you that they've gone to the bank and "bought an IRA." Sorry, but you can't "buy" an IRA. That's like saying you bought a checking account.

What you do with an IRA—and the same goes for employer-sponsored accounts like 401(k) plans—is this: You open it, and then you put money into it, and then you inform the bank (or brokerage or plan administrator) *how you want the funds invested*.

I once explained this to a class of mine, only to have a woman named Brenda stand up and tell me that I didn't know what I was talking about. "I've been buying IRAs at my bank for years," Brenda insisted.

When I asked her how she had invested her IRA funds, she shook her head angrily. "You're not listening to me, young man," she snapped. "I said I *bought* an IRA, I don't take risks with my money with foolish investments."

"Brenda," I said, "I'll bet you ten bucks that your IRA money is invested in a certificate of deposit that's paying you less than 5 percent a year."

"You're on," she replied.

As it turned out, I was wrong. When she brought her IRA statements to my office, I discovered that she was *not* invested in a CD. Rather, she was invested in nothing! It's true. When we called Brenda's bank to find out what exactly her IRA funds had been doing for the last ten years, the officer who answered the phone told us the money was sitting in a savings account.

"Great," I said. "And what rate of return is the savings account paying her?"

The bank officer stammered a bit. "Well," he said finally, "it's not actually paying her anything. It's just a place where we hold money until the client tells us how they want it invested."

Can you believe it? Brenda had her IRA money sitting in a holding account earning nothing for ten years! In other words, when you figure in inflation, her nest egg had shrunk, not grown.

If you think that's dumb, you are right. The only thing dumber is that there are literally thousands of Americans walking around right now thinking they "own" IRAs, when in fact they have no idea how their retirement money is invested or what it is earning. Equally bad is the fact that millions of Americans really don't know what their 401(k) money or 403(b) money is invested in.

Please, please don't be one of these people. Pull out all your IRA and/or company retirement-account statements right now and review them.

Make sure your retirement money is working as hard for you as you worked for it!

Don't let it sit in some miscellaneous bank account that pays you just 5 percent a year—or even worse, maybe nothing at all!

To help you make the most of your retirement money, here is a list of rules I've compiled over the years.

RULE NO. 1
WITH RETIREMENT FUNDS, ALWAYS INVEST FOR GROWTH!

This may strike you as painfully obvious, but it's so important that I think it's worth emphasizing. All too often, women come into my office and show me retirement accounts that are invested in certificates of deposit or other fixed-rate securities. Now, with their guaranteed returns, CDs are perfectly appropriate if your goal is what the professionals call "short-term capital preservation"—that is, you've got a bunch of money that you're going to need to use sometime soon, and you want to make sure nothing happens to it in the meantime.

Unless you are planning to retire in the next year or two, however, your goal with your retirement account is not short-term capital preservation. It's long-term growth. So don't make this mistake.

Review your retirement plan options carefully and make sure your choices include at least some growth-oriented investments.

If you are at all unsure about what the best available investment options may be for you, seek professional guidance. Speak with your company's benefits director or call your personal financial advisor and ask him or her to go over your retirement-plan options with you. At The Bach Group, we do this sort of thing for our clients all the time . . . at no cost. If your financial advisor isn't willing to review your 401(k) investment options, you probably should look for a new advisor.

WHY INVEST FOR GROWTH?

Many people make the crucial mistake of thinking that when it comes to their retirement money, the thing to do is play it safe. They couldn't be more wrong. Remember that inflation chart back on page 31? It showed that over the last two decades, the cost of living has been climbing steadily at an average of slightly more than 5 percent a year. Playing it safe will not allow you to beat that rate, and if your retirement account doesn't grow faster than inflation, you are not going to have very much to live on 20 or 30 or 40 years from now.

To secure your future, in other words, what you've got to do with your retirement money is go for growth. Yes, seeking growth requires you to invest in stocks, and they are generally more volatile and riskier over the short term than some other types of investments. But over the long term—and that's what we're concerned with here, the long term—they can be significantly more rewarding. Consider the following:

THE VALUE OF A HYPOTHETICAL
$100,000 INVESTMENT AFTER 25 YEARS

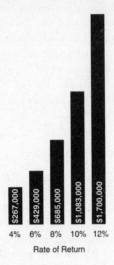

| 4% | 6% | 8% | 10% | 12% |

Rate of Return

AVERAGE ANNUAL TOTAL RETURNS: 1926–1996

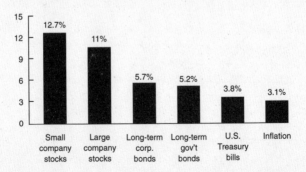

It's incredible, isn't it?

The obvious lesson here is that you should invest a significant portion of your retirement money in stocks or mutual funds that invest in stocks. How big a portion? Well, that really depends on your age, your personal goals, and your willingness to accept a certain amount of volatility.

ASSET ALLOCATION: CREATING THE PERFECT BALANCE

Figuring out the right mix of growth investments vs. fixed investments is what is known in the investment industry as determining your asset allocation. Asset allocation is a fancy way of saying "You need to put your eggs in different baskets." This may not sound like a big deal, but it is. In fact, it is a huge deal. *Studies indicate that more than 91 percent of all investment returns are attributable to proper asset allocation, as opposed to clever stock selection or good market timing.*

The first step in determining the asset allocation of your retirement plan is to decide how much of your money you want to put into growth vehicles (basically, stocks and stock-based mutual funds) and how much you want to put into safer but slower-growing fixed-income securities (basically, bonds or bond funds).

I use the following rule of thumb to help determine how much money a particular individual should invest in stocks vs. bonds:

Take your age and subtract it from 110. The number you get is the percentage of your assets that you should put in stocks or stock-based mutual funds. The rest of your assets should go into something less volatile, such as bonds or fixed-rate securities.

For example, let's say you are 40 years old. Following the rule, you subtract 40 from 110, which leaves you with 70. That means you should consider putting about 70 percent of your retirement fund into stock-related investments, with the remaining 30 percent going into bonds.

Obviously, the older you are, the smaller your stock investment will be. (According to the rule, a 50-year-old should have 60 percent of her assets in stocks, while a 30-year-old should have 80 percent.) This makes sense, since the closer you are to retirement age, the less risk you want to incur.

While this process may sound simplistic, it is widely used and based on a theory created by an acclaimed scholar named Dr. Harry

Markowitz, who was awarded a Nobel Prize in economics for his work on modern portfolio theory.

Once you have determined the ratio of stocks vs. bonds that is right for you, you will need to figure out more specifically what kinds of investments you should make in each category. This is something you should discuss in detail with a trusted and knowledgeable advisor. As a starting point, however, here are a few examples that you can use as a basic guideline to create your own plan.

CREATING YOUR MODEL PORTFOLIO THAT MATCHES YOUR GOALS AND VALUES

MOST CONSERVATIVE

CONSERVATIVE

Average annual return (1971-1997): 9.53%

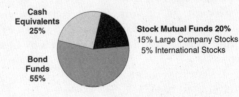

Cash Equivalents 25%

Bond Funds 55%

Stock Mutual Funds 20%
15% Large Company Stocks
5% International Stocks

MODERATELY CONSERVATIVE

Average annual return (1971-1997): 10.69%

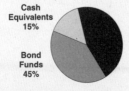

Cash Equivalents 15%

Bond Funds 45%

Stock Mutual Funds 40%
20% Large Company Stocks
10% Small Company Stocks
10% International Stocks

MODERATE

Average annual return (1971-1997): 11.55%

Cash Equivalents 10%

Bond Funds 30%

Stock Mutual Funds 60%
30% Large Company Stocks
15% Small Company Stocks
15% International Stocks

MODERATELY AGGRESSIVE

Average annual return (1971-1998): 12.17%

Cash Equivalents 5%

Bond Funds 15%

Stock Mutual Funds 80%
35% Large Company Stocks
20% Small Company Stocks
25% International Stocks

AGGRESSIVE

Average annual return (1971-1997): 12.61%

Cash Equivalents 5%

Bond Funds 0%

Stock Mutual Funds 95%
40% Large Company Stocks
25% Small Company Stocks
30% International Stocks

AGGRESSIVE

WHAT ABOUT INVESTING IN MY COMPANY'S STOCK?

If you are enrolled in a 401(k) plan, your employer may allow you to invest all or part of your retirement funds in your company's own stock. (Generally speaking, this will be an option only if you work for a company whose stock is publicly traded.) Before you do so, however, do some research. As with any potential stock purchase, first you must determine if the company is well run and what its long-term prospects are.

Finding out the answers to these questions shouldn't be too difficult. First, contact your company's investor relations department. Publicly traded companies almost always employ people whose job it is to answer investors' questions. Ask to be sent an investor's kit, along with an annual report and the company's most recent 10-K, which is a company's filing given to the SEC annually.

Now, you may be thinking, "An investor kit? A 10-K? I wasn't a business major. What good is this stuff going to do me?"

Well, first of all, it will make you a much more knowledgeable employee. Most likely, the investor relations kit will include press clippings about your company along with research reports from brokerage firms that follow your company's stock. The press clippings may tell you a lot about your company that you never knew, while the research reports can give you a good idea of what Wall Street experts think of it. (These reports are written by professional securities analysts whose job is to follow specific companies and make predictions about their future performance.) If, for some reason, your investor kit doesn't contain any research reports, ask the investor relations department for a list of brokerage firms that "cover" your company's stock. Then call these firms and ask for a copy of their most recent report on your company. They should be happy to mail it to you at no cost.

Basically, what you want to find out from a research report is whether the analyst thinks the stock is a "good buy," and if so, why. The 10-K, which is a detailed financial report that the Securities and Exchange Commission requires every publicly traded company to file each year, will provide you with an enormous number of facts and figures about your company's operating results, current problems, and future prospects.

But you should do more than just read reports. Look around at work. Are key employees buying the company's stock? Is your boss? Ask him or her. At good companies, the answer is usually a resounding yes. Finally, ask yourself how the company feels to you on a "gut" level.

Is morale good? Are its customers happy? Does management seem to have a coherent strategy for the future?

If you discover that your company is not particularly well run and that no one is buying its stock because it's losing money, then changing your 401(k) investment strategy may turn out to be the least of your worries. Indeed, you might want to reconsider why you're working there. Maybe you should get your résumé together and find yourself a new job before some sort of corporate restructuring is announced and you find yourself laid off.

FIVE-STAR TIP: *Regardless of how confident you are of your company's long-term prospects, my personal feeling is that you should never put more than 50 percent of your retirement funds into its stock. After all, even great companies occasionally stumble. A 50 percent investment in your company stock is more than enough; it will allow you to participate in your company's growth while still leaving you protected if something were to go seriously wrong.*

RULE NO. 2
TAKE ADVANTAGE OF THE FREE MONEY YOUR EMPLOYER MAY GIVE YOU!

In many cases, employers will supplement your retirement plan contributions with contributions of their own. These "matching" contributions, as they are called, usually start at 20 percent of what you've put in and sometimes go as high as 100 percent! For example, say you work for a company that matches 50 percent of your contributions. If you earn $50,000 a year and you max out your retirement contributions, you should be putting away at least $5,000 a year for your retirement. But on top of that there's your employer's 50 percent matching contribution, which will add $2,500 to your retirement fund. So in just one year you'll have put away $7,500, and that doesn't include any investment growth your fund may have enjoyed over the year.

What's particularly great about this is that you now have $7,500 socked away that didn't actually cost you $7,500. It didn't even cost you the $5,000 you contributed to your retirement plan. Why not? Because if you hadn't put this $5,000 into your pretax retirement account, you would have had to hand over about $1,500 of it to the government in the form of income taxes. What that means is that this $7,500 investment really costs you only $3,500! That adds up to a 100 percent return on your investment in the first year alone—and once again, that's without counting any investment growth. Say you enjoyed a 15 percent return for the year (not unrealistic given the stock market's performance over the last few years). Fifteen percent of $7,500 is $1,125, which brings your balance to $8,625. So from a measly $3,500 investment, you are up more than $5,000! And that's in just one year. See how this can get to be fun?

FIVE-STAR TIP: *Don't make the huge mistake of contributing only the percentage of your paycheck that your company will match. A lot of people think they are being smart when they do this. They are not. The reason to max out your retirement contributions is to build a secure financial future and avoid taxes! Whether your company matches is irrelevant. If your employer does happen to add some money to your contribution, that's icing on the cake. You still need to bake that cake, which means maxing out your contributions!*

RULE NO. 3
DON'T BORROW FROM YOUR RETIREMENT PLAN.

Many retirement plans allow you to borrow money from your account—that is, take money out without having to pay taxes or penalties—as long as you eventually return it with interest. This may sound like a good deal, but in reality it can be a terrible trap. In short, don't do it. The money you are putting away for retirement is just that—money for your retirement.

People who borrow money from their plans to make down payments on homes, cover college costs, or—worst of all—pay off credit-card debt are only asking for trouble. Why? Because at some point they are going to have to pay the money back, and when that time comes, they may find they can't afford to. And then they are really in trouble.

I once had a client named Sally who quit her job shortly after filing sexual harassment charges against her boss. The moment she left the company, she received a letter demanding that she remove all her retirement savings from the company's 401(k) plan. (Because she was no longer an employee, the company had the right to do this.) What it meant was that she had to either transfer the money to a personal IRA account or withdraw it in cash (which would mean paying taxes on it and incurring the 10 percent federal penalty).

Normally, this wouldn't have presented a problem, but Sally was in a bind. A year earlier she had borrowed $15,000 from her 401(k) in order to settle some credit-card debt, and she wasn't yet in a position to pay the loan back. Unfortunately, as I explained to her, if she couldn't repay it before she left the 401(k) plan, the IRS would consider the loan a premature IRA distribution subject to taxes and penalties.

In desperation, Sally tried to borrow money from a bank, but it said no. She turned to her parents. They too were unable to help her. In the end, Sally had to pay income tax on the $15,000 she had borrowed, plus a 10 percent penalty. The total bill came to over $7,000. Lacking the cash, Sally ended up having to negotiate with the IRS, which eventually agreed to let her pay off her liability in installments. All of this was the result of borrowing money from a 401(k).

The point is, none of us knows what the future holds. Ideally, your 401(k) plan should be the last place you turn to for money. If you can, leave your retirement money alone until you are ready to retire.

RULE NO. 4
CONSOLIDATE YOUR ACCOUNTS.

Many people remember Grandma's advice about not putting all your eggs in one basket, but they often misunderstand it. Not putting your eggs in one basket means diversifying your risk—putting your money into different kinds of assets, such as different types of stocks, bonds, mutual funds, and other investment vehicles. It doesn't mean opening an IRA at a different bank or brokerage firm each year.

Every day I meet people who have four, five, or six—sometimes more than a dozen—different retirement accounts. The record in my office currently is held by a client named Ben. Ben always had been what we call a CD shopper. Every year he would literally spend days going from bank to bank to find the best rate on certificates of deposit for his new IRA. The trouble was, he was so focused on "buying" his next IRA that he never thought about the pitiful rates his old IRAs were earning. (Those "terrific" rates he got lasted only for a year; when his "premium" CDs matured, the bank would roll them over into new certificates that didn't pay nearly as much.) When I met with Ben he had over $160,000 in CDs in 18 different banks—earning an average of less than 5 percent a year! I showed him how much better off he would be consolidating all his CDs into one IRA account and then managing his money for a combination of growth and income.

The fact is, there is simply no way you can do a good job managing your retirement accounts if they are spread all over the place. If that's what you've done, consider consolidating them into one IRA custodial account. Not only can you completely diversify your investments within a single IRA, but you'll also find it much easier to keep track of everything.

RULE NO. 5
BE CAREFUL WHOM YOU LIST AS THE BENEFICIARY OF YOUR RETIREMENT ACCOUNT.

I find it terrifying how many well-intentioned people decide to create a living trust to protect their estates—and then either misunderstand their attorney's advice or are given bad advice.

Many lawyers instruct clients who've just established a living trust to make sure to put all their assets in it. As a result, people go out and reregister the beneficiary of the retirement accounts in their trust's name. Big mistake. Never, ever, ever put your IRA in the name of a trust or make your beneficiary of the IRA a trust. When you do this, your spouse loses the ability to do what's called a spousal IRA rollover. A spousal IRA rollover allows a widow to take over her late husband's IRA and put it in her name, without having to pay any taxes on it until she actually starts taking the money out (presumably when she reaches retirement age). If the husband has transferred ownership of his IRA to a trust, the wife can't take it over in the event of his death; instead, the account goes to the trust and the proceeds become taxable. (If you are single, putting your IRA in the name of a trust similarly could limit the ability of your children or your siblings to enjoy the tax-deferred benefits of your retirement savings.)

For much the same reason, you shouldn't make a trust the beneficiary of any of your IRAs or 401(k) plans. Doing so can lead to catastrophe. Take the case of Diana, a recent widow who came up to me in a panic after I made this point to a class of mine. Diana had just lost her husband to cancer. In an effort to get their financial house in order before he died, she and her husband had consulted a discount brokerage firm, which referred them to a local attorney who created a living trust for them. The attorney, she told me, had recommended that her husband make the trust the beneficiary of his 401(k) plan.

When I heard that I just about went white. Swallowing hard, I asked her how much money was in the plan.

She said her husband had accumulated close to half a million dollars.

"Well," I said, "then you have a potential $250,000 problem."

That, I explained, was how much money she was likely to lose to estate and income taxes immediately as a result of the attorney's bad advice. But that wasn't all the lawyer's mistake would cost her. Diana was only 38, meaning she had nearly 20 years to go before she reached retirement age. If you figured in how much less she probably would earn over the next two decades because she would no longer be able to defer taxes on the rest of her husband's 401(k) money, you'd come up with a total loss closer to $500,000. A very costly mistake.

Diana looked at me desperately and asked if there was anything she could do. I called her attorney and discovered that he had created more than 100 trusts that year—and given the same bad advice each time. He didn't even understand what he was doing wrong until I explained it to him!

Fortunately for Diana, there was a solution to her problem. We got her late husband's trust to decline his 401(k) money, as a result of which Diana was able to do a spousal IRA rollover the way it should be done.

The moral of the story is twofold: Be careful where you go for legal advice, and be careful whom you make the beneficiary of your retirement account. If you leave your retirement account to a trust, the proceeds will be taxable. What you and your husband should do is leave your accounts to each other first and then to your children. As a spouse, whoever lives the longest will be able to do a spousal IRA rollover and then the children can, when they inherit the IRA elect how they want to take the money out.

As long as we're on the subject of beneficiaries, if your husband has been married before, you might want to make sure his ex still isn't listed as the beneficiary on any of his retirement accounts. I've seen this happen more than a half dozen times in the last five years—and not just on retirement accounts, but on insurance policies too!

In addition, you also should make sure you have a "contingent beneficiary" listed on your retirement account—that is, a second choice in case your primary beneficiary dies before (or at the same time) you do. For example, let's say you are married with children, and you and your husband are killed together in a car accident. If you had listed your kids as contingent beneficiaries on your IRA, they would automatically get control over your retirement money. (They could then either leave the money in the account for five years or arrange a yearly minimum distribution based on their life expectancy; in either case, the tax benefits of the IRA would be preserved.) If, on the other hand, you hadn't listed a contingent beneficiary, the courts might be forced to have your accounts distributed, which would mean subjecting them to tax.

RULE NO. 6

ALWAYS TAKE YOUR RETIREMENT MONEY WITH YOU.

When you leave a company where you've been contributing to a 401(k) plan, don't leave your retirement money behind. Rather, immediately inform the benefits department that you want to do an *IRA rollover*. What this means is that your former employer will transfer your retirement funds either to a new custodial IRA that you have set up for yourself at some bank or brokerage firm or to the 401(k) plan at your new employer (assuming there is one and that it accepts money from other plans).

Leaving funds in a old 401(k) plan can be disastrous. In the event of your death, your beneficiary would have to go back to a company where you may not have worked in years in order to get your money. This process can take months—in many cases as long as a year—and it's possible that the money could be subject to taxes before your beneficiary could collect it. By contrast, if you've moved your money to an IRA, all your beneficiary has to do is take your death certificate to the brokerage firm or bank, and the IRA will be rolled over to his or her account—tax-free—usually within three days!

Another reason not to leave your money in a former employer's plan is that companies are constantly changing their 401(k) providers. If your old company changes plans, your money will have to be transferred to the new plan—and if for some reason the company is unable to find you (say, because you moved), you won't be able to tell it how you want your funds invested in the new plan. Lacking instructions, the company could wind up parking your money in a low-interest money-market fund, which could potentially cost you tens of thousands of dollars in lost earnings. Don't lose control of your money. Do an IRA rollover and take it with you when you go!

RULE NO. 7
DON'T SHORTCHANGE YOURSELF.

Whatever else you do in your financial life, please take retirement planning seriously. I know I sound like I'm preaching here, but as I said before, there is really nothing you can do that will have more impact on your future financial security than maximizing your contributions to a retirement account and then making sure that money works really hard for you.

The fact is, if you are not currently maxing out your retirement contributions—whether to a company-sponsored 401(k) or 403(b) plan, to your own IRA, or to a retirement account for self-employed people—you are living beyond your means. This is not meant to be harsh; it is meant to be a wake-up call. Contributing to a retirement plan is not a luxury; it is a necessity! Please give yourself the opportunity to retire as early as you would like, with enough money to have all the fun you deserve.

BASKET THREE:
YOUR DREAM BASKET

Pretend for a moment you had a magic lamp with a genie inside. As we all know, genies are obliged to grant their masters (or mistresses) three wishes. So what would yours be? If you could have—or be—anything you wanted, what would you wish for?

That may seem like a childish question, but it's not. What it's really asking is something quite important—namely, what dreams of yours currently are going unfulfilled? Do you long to see the world? Quit your job? Start your own business? Devote yourself to some charitable organization?

It is one of the sadder facts of life that most people stop dreaming as they get older. The number-one reason, I'm sorry to say, is money. For the most part, it takes money to make our dreams come true, and most of us simply don't have enough. Lacking the necessary resources, we find ourselves frustrated; eventually, we stop bothering to dream at all.

That's the bad news. The good news is, it doesn't have to be that way. You *can* make your dreams come true . . . and you won't need a magic lamp—or its modern-day equivalent, a winning lottery ticket—to do it. Nor will you be restricted to just three wishes.

To make your dreams a reality, you have to do only two things: identify what your dreams are and create a plan to finance them. That may sound pretty obvious, but you know what? Most people never do it.

Smart Women, however, aren't like most people. So let's get started . . .

Recapture Your Wide-Eyed Optimism

You know why so many people play the state lottery? It's because for the price of just $1, they get the opportunity to dream. Unfortunately, that's generally all a person gets. The reality is that you have a better chance of being hit by lightning than actually winning a lottery.

Even though most of us know that, we play anyway. That's how powerful our need to dream is. Dreams energize us. They add passion to our lives. It's hard to be depressed when you are excited about your future, and that's what dreams do: They make us believe that tomorrow is going to be better than today.

Think back for a moment and recall, if you can, what it was like when you were a kid. Can you remember a time in your life when you believed you could be anything and have anything you wanted? Do you remember what it felt like not to have to worry about bills and work and family responsibilities? Try to imagine that for a moment. Pretend you are a little girl who feels she can have or be anything she wants. What would it be? Who would you become?

Try to pursue these questions more deeply than you did in Step Three, when you were coming up with goals for yourself. We are not talking here about earning 10 percent more income or losing ten pounds. We are talking about *dreams*. Do you want to climb the pyramids of Egypt? Study painting in Paris? Open a shelter for battered women?

Remember, you are trying to be young and imaginative like you were when you were a kid, not stressed-out and conventional like you are now. (Just kidding!) Seriously, though, what do you want to see happen in your life? What's missing? Where do you want to go? Perhaps your dream is to own your own home. Or to take off from work for a whole month and not call the office once! Maybe you would like to write a book.

Whatever your dreams happen to be, I want you to write them down. On the following Dream Sheet, list your five top dreams. If you don't have the time to do this right now, then set up a time later to meet with yourself and create your dream list. That's right—make an appointment with yourself to reserve somewhere between 30 and 60 minutes in which you will write down the dreams that excite you. And don't make excuses. Your dreams are worth half an hour of your time.

DREAMS
Designing and Implementing the Fun Factor!

THERE ARE TWO PARTS TO THIS EXERCISE:

- Ten blanks for writing down your most important dreams
- A form in which you specify your five most important dreams over your lifetime

STEPS:

- On this page, below, fill in the ten blanks with as many dreams as possible that you want to accomplish during your lifetime.
- On the next page specify:
  1. Five Most Important Dreams
  2. Make Specific, Measurable, and Provable
     (i.e.: How much will it cost?)
  3. Immediate Action in the Next 48 Hours
  4. Who Will You Share Your Dreams With
  5. What Values Does It Help You Accomplish
  6. What Challenges Will You Face
  7. Strategies to Overcome Anticipated Challenges

1.   6.
2.   7.
3.   8.
4.   9.
5.   10.

TOP 5 DREAMS	MAKE SPECIFIC, MEASURABLE, AND PROVABLE	IMMEDIATE ACTION IN THE NEXT 48 HOURS	WHO WILL YOU SHARE YOUR DREAMS WITH	WHAT VALUES DOES IT HELP YOU ACCOMPLISH	WHAT CHALLENGES WILL YOU FACE	STRATEGIES TO OVERCOME ANTICIPATED CHALLENGES
1						
2						
3						
4						
5						

Making Your Dreams a Real Part of Your Life

Once you have written down your top five dreams, the next step is to spend a little time thinking about what it would take to make them a reality. How much money will be required? How long will it take you to save that much?

The more defined your dreams are, the easier it will be to estimate what it will cost to realize them. You definitely should spend a little time on this, for as I explained back in Step Three, the key to getting what you want in life is to be specific about it. Once you have a good idea of what it will take, you can determine how much you need to put away each month. By putting money away each month, you will feel your dream come closer to reality, and as it does, you will find yourself getting more and more excited about your future.

WHAT IF I DON'T HAVE ANY SPECIFIC DREAMS RIGHT NOW?

I usually suggest to my clients that they should fund a dream basket whether they are able to come up with a list of dreams or not. After all, just because you don't have a specific dream right now doesn't mean you never will. And wouldn't it be nice to have some money already put aside when something comes along (as it inevitably will) that falls into a "dream" category?

Sometimes dreams are not what we expect. I once suggested to a young woman named Lisa that she start funding a dream basket even though she didn't have any specific dream in mind. Six months later Lisa's dog Brandi got really sick. Without an operation that cost $1,500, Brandi would die. Lisa immediately turned to her dream basket for the money, and today Brandi is wagging her tail and doing whatever else happy dogs do. As Lisa explained to me later, "I had no idea what my dream was at the time I started putting money aside, but when Brandi got sick, I knew that my dream was to help her live. If I hadn't funded my dream basket, I would have lost Brandi. My dream basket kept her alive!"

How to Fund Your Dream Basket

Your dream basket is the place where you put aside the money you will need to make your dreams (other than security or retirement) come true. You should fund it the same way you fund your retirement basket—that is, with a fixed percentage of your income that you automatically contribute every month. As I said earlier, making the process automatic is the best way I know to ensure that you actually stick to your savings plan. Set up a systematic investment plan, in which a set amount of money either is deducted directly from your paycheck or is transferred from your checking account the day after you are paid.

The size of your regular contribution should be determined by the likely cost of your dreams. As a rule of thumb, it probably should be at least 5 percent of your after-tax income (which is to say, a lot less than the 12 percent of pretax income that you should be putting into your retirement basket). While 5 percent of your after-tax income isn't a huge amount, it is certainly big enough to create a very powerful long-term savings vehicle. Needless to say, if your dreams happen to be of the particularly expensive variety, you will want to put away a larger percentage of your income. The key here is to realize that it's up to you; the more money you put away, the faster your dreams will become a reality.

The form in which you keep this money will depend on how long you expect it will be before you're ready to make your dream a reality. Some dreams require just a year or two of planning and saving; others may take half a lifetime. Over the next few pages, I will discuss a variety of different investment vehicles and explain which are right for what time frame.

In order to keep things simple (and there's certainly no point in making them more complicated than they need to be), you should think of your dreams in terms of how long it will likely take you to realize them. Specifically, you should categorize them as being either short-term, mid-term, or long-term dreams. Short-term dreams are those that can be accomplished within a year or two. (An example might be getting yourself in a position to be able to take a luxury vacation.) Mid-term dreams take a bit longer to fulfill—say, between two and five years. (A typical mid-term dream might be having the funds to put a down payment on a house). Long-term dreams require even more time than that. Some (such as being able to quit your job so you can move to Tahiti and live on the beach) may take decades.

Obviously, you don't fund a short-term dream with a long-term investment strategy. Here are my recommendations for the best ways to construct your dream basket.

FOR SHORT-TERM DREAMS
(LESS THAN TWO YEARS)

If you're saving to finance a short-term dream, you need to keep your funds as safe and liquid as possible. As far as I'm concerned, that means investing in cash or cash equivalents. In this case I consider three kinds of cash investments to be appropriate: money-market accounts, certificates of deposit, and government Treasury bills.

Money-Market Accounts. A money-market account is a mutual fund that invests in short-term securities (typically, U.S. Government Treasury bills). Most major brokerage firms, banks, and credit unions offer them—often with such perks as unlimited check-writing privileges and a debit card that you can use to get cash from an ATM machine. Generally opening money-market accounts require a minimum investment of $500, and as of this writing interest rates of around 5.5 percent a year are not uncommon. (Then again, some money-market accounts pay only 1 percent and don't come with any perks. So be sure to shop around.) While money-market accounts usually are not federally insured, they are nonetheless among the safest investments around.

Certificates of Deposit. CDs are bank-issued securities that promise to pay you a given rate of return over a given period on a deposit that can range from $500 to $100,000. CD maturities can be as short as one month or as long as ten years; as of this writing, rates for one-year CDs are running at about 5 percent. Unlike money-market accounts, CDs are federally insured up to $100,000. That's their big advantage. Their disadvantage is that if you need to get your cash out before your CD matures, you may have to pay a penalty that can run as much as half the interest your were supposed to earn. (Money markets, by contrast, are always immediately liquid, without any penalty.) For this reason, if you can find a money-market account offering a better return than a one-year CD, you shouldn't even consider buying a CD.

> **FIVE-STAR TIP:** *CDs can be purchased through brokerage firms as well as from banks. The advantage to buying through a brokerage firm is that a brokered bank CD is liquid—which is to say, it can be sold prematurely without incurring any penalty fees. You will have to pay a small commission, but that won't run you anywhere near the outrageous interest-rate penalty that the bank will charge you!*

Treasury Bills. Issued by the federal government, Treasury bills (T-bills) are fixed-income securities that can be purchased either directly from the Treasury Department or through a bank or brokerage firm. They are issued in increments of $10,000 and mature in a year or less. The main difference between a Treasury bill and a CD is that technically T-bills do not pay interest. Rather, they are issued at a discount and then can be redeemed at full price (known as par value) when they mature. For example, if the one-year T-bill rate happens to be 5 percent, you would pay $9,500 for a certificate that a year later you could redeem for $10,000.

There are a number of reasons why people like Treasury bills. For one thing, they are backed by "the full faith and credit of the United States Government," which makes them just about the safest investment you can buy. For another, T-bill earnings are exempt from state taxes. Finally, if you buy them through a broker, T-bills generally can be sold on a moment's notice simply by making a phone call, and you usually can collect your money within three days. (As with brokered bank CDs, there is no penalty for selling a T-bill this way before it matures, though you will have to pay a small commission.)

> **FIVE-STAR TIP:** *As a result of modern telecommunications, it's now easier than ever to buy T-bills, notes, and bonds directly from the government. To find out about the Federal Reserve Board's Treasury Direct program, you can telephone them toll-free at (800) 943-6864 or visit their Web site at www.publicdebt.treas.gov.*

FOR MID-TERM DREAMS (TWO TO FIVE YEARS)

Given the slightly longer time frame, liquidity should be less of an issue for mid-term dreams than for short-term ones. The same goes for safety. You've got a little more time to play with, so you can afford to take a bit more risk—which means you can expect a bit more reward. Not that you should take any big chances, mind you; the idea, after all, is to protect your money, not gamble with it.

With that in mind, I generally recommend mid-term dream money be invested in bonds. Although bonds are slightly less liquid and slightly more risky than cash equivalents, they are still relatively safe, and they pay better interest.

Essentially, a bond is an IOU; when you buy one, you literally are lending money to the issuer (usually a company or a government agency). The bond specifies when you will be paid back (the maturity date) and how much interest you will be paid in the interim (usually in two installments a year).

Bonds typically are issued in increments of $1,000, $5,000, or $10,000. Maturities can be as quick as 1 year and as long as 30 years. The shorter the period, the less risk for the bond buyer—and the lower the interest rate.

You can invest in literally hundreds of different kinds of bonds, from super-safe government savings bonds to high-yield "junk." For our purposes, I suggest you restrict your choices to one of the following three categories.

Treasury Notes. Issued by the United States Government, Treasury notes are issued in increments of $1,000, $5,000, $10,000, $50,000, $100,000, and $1 million and come with maturities ranging from two to ten years. As with T-bills, the interest you earn on these securities is exempt from state taxes. As of this writing, Treasury notes are paying between 5 and 5.75 percent a year, depending on the maturity. You can buy Treasury notes directly from the government or through a broker. While buying direct will save you the price of the broker's commission, it also will make it more difficult for you to liquidate your investment before it matures. For this reason, I suggest you buy Treasury notes through a broker; the increased liquidity more than justifies the slight extra cost.

Corporate Bonds. While a Treasury note is backed by the wealth and majesty of the U.S. government, a corporate bond is only as solid as the particular company that issued it. That's not to say there aren't some very safe corporate bonds. There are. But there are also some very risky ones. Before you buy any bond, you need to check out the grade it has received from one of the major rating firms, such as Standard & Poor's or Moody's (see the chart below). At The Bach Group, we almost never buy for our clients corporate bonds that are less than A-rated. Of course, the higher the rating, the lower the interest rate. (To sell their bonds, healthier companies don't need to offer as much interest as riskier companies do.) But that's okay. The extra interest you can earn from a lower-rated bond is generally not worth the extra risk. As of this writing, rates range from 5 to 10 percent, depending on the company's creditworthiness and the bond's maturity.

KNOWING THE RATING BEFORE YOU BUY IT!

Two recognized agencies that assign credit ratings to corporate issues are *Moody's* and *Standard & Poor's*. Their *investment grade* rating levels, which reflect the credit quality of an issue, appear below.

RATING/QUALITY	MOODY'S	S&P
Highest grade— smallest degree of investment risk.	Aaa	AAA
High grade— slightly more risk than highest grade.	Aa1 Aa2 Aa3	AA+ AA AA–
Upper medium grade— interest and principal regarded as safe, but not risk-free.	A1 A2 A3	A+ A A–
Medium grade— adequate security, but susceptible to changing economic conditions.	Baa1 Baa2 Baa3	BBB+ BBB BBB–

Municipal Bonds. Generally issued by local governments, municipal bonds (munis) offer the hard-to-beat advantage of being double tax-free. That is, the interest you earn from them is exempt from both state and federal taxes. As a result, they make great sense for investors in high tax brackets. (Tax-free municipals pay lower interest rates than taxable bonds, so unless you're in a high tax bracket—and thus can enjoy major tax savings—they may not be such a good deal for you. Before you invest in one of these bonds, have an accountant or a financial advisor review your tax situation to determine whether you will come out ahead with a tax-free rate.) Although municipalities rarely default on their bonds, I nonetheless recommend that you stick to AAA-rated munis. These pay lower interest, but they are insured against default, which means you will never lose any sleep over them.

INTEREST RATES MAKE BOND PRICES FLUCTUATE

Most investment-grade bonds are fairly liquid, meaning you don't necessarily have to wait until they mature to get your money back. While you probably won't be able to get the company that issued your bond to pay you back early, you always can sell the bond to another investor. There is, of course, no guarantee that it will fetch the same price you originally paid for it. Bond prices at any given time depend on the general level of interest rates. If rates have risen since your bond was first issued, you'll probably have to sell at a bit of a discount. On the other hand, if rates have fallen, your bond will likely fetch a bit of a premium.

$10,000 BOND PAYING 8%
(30-YEAR MATURITY)

IF INTEREST RATES STAY EVEN

$10,000
Price
(PAR)

8%
Rate

FACE
VALUE
$10,000

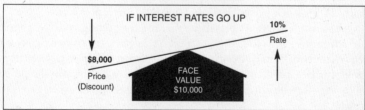

IF INTEREST RATES GO UP

10%
Rate

$8,000
Price
(Discount)

FACE
VALUE
$10,000

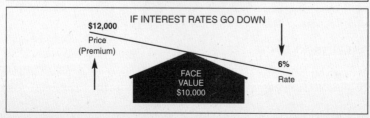

IF INTEREST RATES GO DOWN

$12,000
Price
(Premium)

6%
Rate

FACE
VALUE
$10,000

Of course, none of this matters if you hold your bond until it matures. Assuming that the company that issued the bond is still solvent, you will be repaid in full regardless of where interest rates are or what the market is doing.

THE SIMPLEST WAY TO INVEST IN BONDS

One of simplest ways for a nonexpert to invest in bonds is through a bond fund. The advantages of this approach are numerous. Not only are bond-fund portfolios managed by full-time professionals, they are also diversified, with a typical fund owning literally hundreds of different bonds. What's more, while you generally can't buy an individual bond for less than a $1,000, you can buy into a bond fund with an initial investment of as little as $500. And unlike individual bonds, which usually pay interest only twice a year, you can arrange to get a payout from a bond fund every month if you like. As a result, I typically recommend bond funds to people with less than $50,000 to invest in bonds.

FOR LONG-TERM DREAMS
(THREE TO TEN YEARS)

Nothing has created more millionaires in this country than the stock market. While no investment is a sure thing, over the long haul stocks are hard to beat. As I noted earlier, since the late 1920s, stocks have generated an average annual return of close to 11 percent. Since the early 1980s, stock prices have risen nearly 15 percent a year.

It's statistics like these that make the case for putting your long-term dream money into the stock market. Yes, stocks are riskier than cash equivalents or bonds, but if you can wait out the inevitable market downturns—and if you're saving for a long-term dream, you should be able to—for the long-run stocks are the best investment game in town.

WHAT IS A STOCK?

When you buy a stock, you are purchasing a piece of a publicly traded company. (How big a piece depends on how many shares you buy.)

There are two ways to make money from stock ownership. The most obvious way is to buy a stock at a relatively low price and then have it appreciate in value. In addition, some companies pay dividends on their stock, in effect distributing part of their profits to their shareholders.

There are basically three ways to invest in stocks. You can purchase individual stocks directly, you can invest through a mutual fund, or if you've got at least $100,000 to invest, you can use a managed-money portfolio. For greater simplicity for you, the investor, I am going to focus the dream basket investments on mutual funds.

10,000 MUTUAL FUNDS AND COUNTING . . .

To say that we have seen an explosion in mutual fund investment over the past decade is to understate the situation wildly. In the last ten years, the mutual-fund industry has seen its assets base grow from less than $150 billion to more than $2 trillion.

I often joke in my classes that a new mutual fund is born just about every seven hours. Actually, that's not so far from the truth. Currently more than 10,000 mutual funds are available to American investors. Although these funds were created originally as part of an effort to simplify the investment process, their enormous proliferation has left most of us more confused than ever. Over the next few pages, I'll try to clear up some of the confusion.

WHY BUY A MUTUAL FUND?

The reason you want to consider investing in a mutual fund is that as an investor, your goal is going to be to put away money each month regardless of what the outside world is doing. Remember the pay-yourself-first concept we discussed in Step Four? Now I want to suggest that you also should fund your dream basket automatically. Whether you make $3,000 or $30,000 a month, my goal for you is to put money away automatically each month that represents a specific percentage of your income. You can do this very easily with what is known as a systematic investment plan, an automated process by which your checking account is debited (typically once a month) to fund an investment (typically a mutual fund).

Now, whatever the dollar amount that you select to invest monthly turns out to be, it needs to go into an investment. Let's say that after taking the seven-day financial challenge of tracking your money (you are doing this, right?), you find $200 that you can save each month. If you automatically put this money into your dream basket and your dream is five years out, then you want the money to be invested for growth. If it goes into a mutual fund that invests in stocks, your money will be put to work for you immediately and a professional money manager will be spending his or her full time investing your $200 in a pool of money to make it grow. This mutual-fund manager has at his or her disposal the best research and support that money can buy and access to information that you and I do not have unless we want to spend hundreds of hours a month becoming investment savvy. Now, how realistic is it that you are going to start focusing even ten hours a month on the stock market looking for investments? Pretty unlikely, right? But even if you did want to do this and you felt you could pick stocks yourself, are you going to want to do it each and every month? Even if you have $3,000 a month to invest—do you want to invest it in just one stock each month, and then have to worry if you picked the right stock? Chances are you'll want to do other things with your life. That's why mutual-fund investing has become so popular in the last ten years.

Entire books have been devoted to the question of how to pick a mutual fund, so I am not going to pretend that I can tell you all you need to know about mutual fund investing in just a few pages. The truth is that you probably should consider hiring a financial professional to assist you in the critical process of selecting and building a mutual-fund portfolio. In the meantime, however, I can suggest a few basic steps you can take.

I happen to be a believer in building from the ground up. When it comes to mutual funds, that means you should stock your portfolio with five different types of mutual funds. Listed in order in which you should buy first, from the most conservative to the most aggressive, they are: a growth and income fund, a growth fund, a value fund, an aggressive growth fund, and a global fund.

Growth and Income Funds. The first type of fund in which you should invest is what is known as a growth and income fund. This type of fund typically invests in "blue-chip" stocks—those issued by the nation's top corporations, including household names such as AT&T, Exxon, Ford, General Electric, and Procter & Gamble. These top-tier companies produce annual revenues that are generally well in excess of

$1 billion and are referred to as large-capitalization (or "large cap") companies.

Growth Funds. A growth fund invests in companies that typically do not pay dividends because they prefer to reinvest their profits in their own continuing development and expansion. The best of these growth-oriented companies—outfits like Home Depot, Microsoft, Dell Computers, McDonald's, and Intel—usually enjoy a steady (sometimes spectacular) increase in the market price of their stocks. Growth funds are slightly riskier than growth and income funds, but over the long term they generally outperform them.

Value Funds. Typically, a value fund will focus on buying both large and mid-capitalization companies whose stock is undervalued or down in price. Often a fund manager of a value fund will focus on purchasing stocks that have a low price-to-earnings ratio and pay dividends. I myself love to invest in these types of funds. If you pick the right type of value fund, you usually can get great returns with low risk. That's music to my ears!

Aggressive Growth Funds. An aggressive growth fund will invest in companies that typically have annual revenues ranging from a $100 million to $1 billion. While that may sound like a lot, in the investment world these types of companies are still babies waiting to grow up. Their potential for huge growth is great but so is the potential for problems. Ultimately an aggressive growth fund is just that—aggressive! Investors are hoping to get big returns but are taking potentially significantly more risk here than with the other three types of funds. I suggest that you invest no more than 20 percent of your dream basket in this type of a fund.

Global Fund. The United States is not the only country with a stock market. Indeed, fully 60 percent of all the world's stock-market activity takes place abroad. Global funds reflect this financial fact of life, investing in both foreign and U.S. stock markets. In this increasingly interconnected world of ours, you need to have some global exposure in your portfolio. I generally recommend to clients that they invest about 15 percent of their dream-basket money in global funds. That gives you good exposure to the global markets but not too much risk.

AVERAGE FUND PERFORMANCE
For the Period:
12/31/84–3/31/98

Portfolio Investments	Period's Average Annual Return
Dow Jones 30 Industrial Average w/ divs.	19.86%
S & P 500 Composite Index w/ divs.	18.75%
Mid Cap Funds Average	17.42%
Small Company Growth Funds Average	16.72%
Growth Mutual Fund Index	16.70%
Growth & Inc. Fund Index	16.57%
International Mutual Fund Index	15.86%
Global Fund Average	15.67%
Balanced Mutual Fund Index	14.20%
High Yield Bond Fund Index	11.27%
General Municipal Fund Index	9.21%
General U.S. Gov't Fund Index	8.24%
Money Market Fund Average	4.63%

* Source: 1998 Lipper Analytical Services, Inc.

THE CONTROVERSY OVER LOAD OR NO LOAD

Some financial magazines (mainly those whose advertisers are primarily "no-load" mutual fund companies) will tell you that the only way to invest in mutual funds is through what are called no-load mutual funds.

It's not my goal here to take a swipe at any particular financial magazine. I simply want to point out that many of our information sources are not objective. In fact, some of them are flat-out biased. No-load mutual funds (those that, in effect, do not charge a front-end or back-end sales charge) are not free!

Charles Schwab, whom I both admire and respect, built the no-load concept of mutual fund investing almost singlehanded by persuading the public that it could invest successfully without professional help.

Well, Charles Schwab is a marketing genius, but he didn't become a billionaire by giving out mutual funds for free. No-load mutual funds *do* cost money. On average, when you invest in a no-load fund, you incur about 1.5 percent in annual fees. This money is deducted from the fund's performance (which is why you never see the charge). That's what it costs to have your money supposedly managed for "free."

The fact is, the industry that Charles Schwab created with no-load mutual funds is undergoing massive change. Over the last five years, people have realized that they do need help managing their investments. As a result, the no-load firms like Charles Schwab, Vanguard, and Fidelity are all rushing out to provide advice to their clients. They are doing this not because it's cost effective (in fact, it's expensive for them to hire advisors or share fees with the advisors they recommend), but they have to. Studies have shown that people are more confused than ever about investing, and many who have invested on their own are not doing well.

Now, if you hire a financial professional to help you build a custom-tailored mutual-fund portfolio that takes into account your goals and objectives—a professional who will help you manage your money for the rest of your life—the annual cost to you should be about 1.5 to 2.50 percent of the total value of your assets (this includes mutual fund fees). So how much more expensive is it to get professional help on the most important aspect of your life other than your health? About 0.5 to 1 percent of your assets. Not only should a good financial advisor be able to make up that cost by giving you smart advice, but you will be able to sleep better at night because you will have a professional "sounding board" to help you make smart decisions about your money.

FOR REALLY LONG-TERM DREAMS
(TEN YEARS OR MORE)

There are long-term dreams and then there are *really* long-term dreams. Say your dream is to have a second home in Hawaii, but you know it won't be possible until your kids are out of college, which is at least ten years away. Where should you put your dream-basket money in the meantime?

Consider the variable annuity. It's one of my favorite investment vehicles for money you won't need for a decade or more. (Note: This is *not* a substitute for a retirement plan. You should make sure your retirement basket is fully funded before you start putting money into a variable annuity.)

Basically, variable annuities are mutual funds with an insurance policy wrapped around them. The insurance wrapper, as it's called, allows the money in the fund to grow tax-deferred. In this, variable annuities are like nondeductible IRAs—with two big advantages: There are no income limitations on who can buy them, and you can put in as much money as you want.

You fund a variable annuity by contributing after-tax dollars, which are allowed to grow without Uncle Sam taking his annual bite. When you reach the age of $59^1/2$, you can elect to start taking money out. As with regular IRAs, you have to pay income taxes on your distributions, but only on the portion attributable to growth of principal and interest earnings.

Sounds like a good deal, doesn't it? Well, it is. Indeed, the closest thing to a catch here is the fact that you have to pay for the insurance wrapper. As a rule, the insurance fee runs about 0.5 to 1 percent of the annuity's asset value. (In other words, if you've invested $100,000, the insurance will cost you between $500 and $1,000 a year.) Some people regard this as a terrible disadvantage. I disagree. In most cases, the money you save by having your funds grow tax-deferred more than offsets the extra cost.

Think about this for a second. Say you had $100,000 in a regular, taxable mutual fund. Most likely, an account of that size would generate about $7,500 in capital gains and distributions each year. If you're in the 30 percent tax bracket, that would mean you'd have to pay the government $2,250 in taxes. On the other hand, if you had the same amount of money in a variable annuity, you would have to pay about $500 to $1,000 a year in insurance fees, but you wouldn't have to pay the $2,250 tax bill.

To my way of thinking, that's a no-brainer.

THERE'S MORE TO VARIABLE ANNUITIES THAN TAX AVOIDANCE

The insurance wrapper does more than defer taxes on the money you invest in a variable annuity. It also guarantees the principal for your beneficiaries.

Let's say you've put $100,000 worth into a variable annuity and invested it in stock-based mutual funds. Suddenly the market completely falls apart, dropping 30 percent. As a result, your investment is now worth only $70,000. What do you think your beneficiaries would get if you picked this particular moment to die?

If you said a $70,000 variable annuity, you'd be wrong. What actually would happen is that the insurance company would pay your beneficiaries the full $100,000 that you originally invested. This feature is known as a guaranteed death benefit. Some insurance companies offer features that increase this guaranteed death benefit each year to keep up with the growth in the value of your annuity.

Another advantage to keeping your money in a variable annuity is that should you die, in most cases the annuity proceeds will pass directly to your beneficiaries and avoid probate.

THE DOWNSIDE OF VARIABLE ANNUITIES

Many annuities impose what is known as a seven-year deferred sales charge. What that means is that if you sell your annuity or take any distributions from it within seven years of the purchase date, you will have to pay a penalty fee. The fee usually starts at 7 percent of the amount withdrawn and drops by 1 percent a year until seven years have gone by. At that point, you can take your money out without incurring a sales fee.

Because of this, when purchasing an annuity, you should make sure to ask your financial advisor to explain in detail if there are any "back-end" sales charges. These days a good annuity shouldn't impose a premature sales charge of more than 7 percent, and the deferred sales charge should be totally gone after seven years.

The point here is that taking your money out of a variable annuity in one of the early years can be prohibitively expensive. But remember—I'm suggesting that you don't even consider buying a variable annuity unless you are confident that you won't need to get your hands on the money for at least ten years. In most cases, by then this issue of the sales cost will be entirely moot.

And finally, the money you put into a variable annuity needs to stay there until you reach $59\frac{1}{2}$ (just like a retirement account). If you take it out early, you will have to pay a tax penalty of 10 percent on the profits. So ideally, look to put money into a variable annuity when you know you won't need it for at least ten years and ideally until after the age of $59\frac{1}{2}$.

There's Nothing Wrong with Asking for Help

We've covered an awful lot of ground in this chapter. Between all the recommendations I've made about how to fill your three baskets, I'm sure your head must be spinning. But remember—financial planning really isn't that complicated. For the most part, smart investing (which is the only kind of investing Smart Women do) is simply a matter of knowing what steps to take and in what order.

The fact is, becoming financially secure and being able to fund your dreams is a lot like opening a safe. Unless you know what numbers to turn to and how, you'll never get inside. With the right combination, however, the world's strongest safe can be opened with very little effort. You now know the combination to your financial safe. Use the tools I have given you, in the right order, and your financial dreams will become a reality.

While I believe that every Smart Woman is capable of managing her finances on her own, if that is her goal, I still strongly suggest that before you start making investments, you consider getting some professional guidance. Now, hiring a professional to help you does not mean you are weak or lazy or lacking in confidence. It's like hiring a coach—and there's nothing wrong with hiring a coach. The most accomplished people in the world hire and work with coaches on a daily basis. Take Barbra Streisand. She is one of the greatest singers in the world, yet she still has a voice coach. Same with Tiger Woods. Perhaps the greatest golfer on the planet, he's got a golf coach. Michael Jordan works with basketball coaches as a matter of routine. Meryl Streep, the brilliant Oscar-winning actress, uses drama and dialect coaches.

Why do these people, all of whom are at the top of their respective games, still rely on coaches? Because they want to keep improving—and because a coach can give you something that is very difficult (if not impossible) to give yourself: accurate and objective feedback on how you're doing.

So consider hiring a financial coach. Not only will he or she make the job of managing your finances much easier, but if you hire a good one (which is the only kind you should consider), you probably will end up achieving better results than if you tried to do it on your own.

How do you find a good financial advisor? The interesting thing is that, while this may be one of the most important people you ever hire to help you in your lifetime, most investment books don't discuss how you should specifically go about hiring a real financial pro. Having grown up in the financial world my entire life, there are a couple of things I know for a fact. One, if I did not stay in the investment business, I would not continue to manage my own money. I'd hire someone to help me because within a few years of leaving the business, the laws and financial arena would change, and if I was not managing money full time, I'd lose my edge and ability to really manage my money well. So I would be forced to go out and do what you may need to do right now, which is to start interviewing a financial advisor. Knowing what I know now, having managed money for years, here are the rules I would use if I was going to go out and interview someone to help me manage my money. While these rules may seem basic and even obvious, most people don't use them. If you use these rules and really apply them, I am confident that you will be able to find a financial professional who can help you and your family (if you have one) make smart decisions with your money. Most important, you'll be able to hire the best advisor possible and get the best attention possible.

The 14 Golden Rules to Hiring a Financial Pro

> **RULE NO. 1**
> GO WHERE THE MONEY IS.

Rich people do not manage their own money. As a rule, they work with top-notch financial professionals. So why reinvent the wheel? Go to someone you know who is wealthy and ask her who she works with. She doesn't have to be a close friend. Maybe it's the owner of the company you work for. Maybe it's someone you have read about in the local paper. Ask her if she is happy with the financial guidance she receives and why. Ask her how she pays for this financial guidance and if she would refer you to her advisor. Then call the financial professional and ask if you can set up a meeting to discuss the possibility of hiring him or her to help you make smart decisions with your money.

You might think, "Well, a top-notch financial advisor won't work with me. I don't have millions of dollars." You might be wrong. Here's how the real world works. Let's say I have a client named Margaret with a $5-million portfolio. Let's also say that Margaret happens to be the president of the company you work for and that you've asked her to recommend a financial advisor. So Margaret calls me up and asks if I would be willing to meet with an employee of hers (namely, you) who wants some advice. Well, what type of service do you think you're going to get? Million-dollar service, that's what! Why? Because regardless of how much or how little money you have, I'm going to want to keep the million-dollar client who referred you happy.

So go out and find someone who is wealthy and ask if he or she would be willing to refer you to a financial advisor. I guarantee you will start out an "A" client, even if you don't have a lot of money to invest.

RULE NO. 2
GO TO YOUR FIRST MEETING PREPARED.

A real professional will insist that you come to your first meeting prepared. That means he or she will ask you to bring copies of your investment statements, net worth, current expense breakdowns, and your most recent tax returns—in short, the kind of information called for in the worksheets in Appendices 1 and 2. There are 500,000 people in this country who call themselves financial advisors. They are not all equally excellent. A professional who doesn't ask you to bring this sort of information is not the kind of professional you want to hire.

If you are not willing to take the time to get organized prior to your first meeting with a financial advisor, or if you are reluctant to show your personal financial documents to a professional, then you probably are not ready to work with one. That's not intended to be harsh; it's intended to be realistic. Some people are very uncomfortable showing their financial documents to anyone and have a deep-rooted problem with trust. A person like this will not be happy hiring a financial professional regardless of how good the advisor may be.

RULE NO. 3
DURING YOUR FIRST MEETING, YOU SHOULD DO MOST
OF THE TALKING.

Your first meeting with a financial advisor is like a financial checkup. The goal is for the advisor to determine your financial health and to discover (or help you discover) what your financial goals and values are. A good financial professional will conduct the meeting in such a way that you end up doing most of the talking. If the advisor spends a lot of time telling you how great he is, how much money he makes for his clients, and how powerful his firm is, thank him politely for his time and continue with your search. This is not the type of financial advisor you want.

RULE NO. 4
A GOOD FINANCIAL ADVISOR SHOULD BE ABLE TO EXPLAIN HIS OR HER INVESTMENT PHILOSOPHY.

Ask the financial advisor about his or her investment philosophy. He or she should be able to explain it quickly and in simple terms. A real professional should have this part of the process down to a science and be able to explain it both easily and comfortably.

What you don't want is someone who says "Oh, you like stocks—I specialize in stocks! Oh, you like mutual funds—I'm a mutual-fund specialist! Oh, you like gold—I think gold sounds great!" What you are getting with this kind of financial advisor is a salesperson, not a financial pro. A financial pro has a set philosophy, a long-term plan or strategy, that shapes all his or her dealings. What you should look for is someone whose philosophy coincides with yours, not someone who is willing to do whatever you want.

RULE NO. 5
FIND OUT WHAT THE FINANCIAL ADVISOR CHARGES.

Some financial advisors are paid by commission (that is, they take a small percentage of every transaction they make on your behalf). Some are paid a flat annual fee on assets managed. Some are paid on an hourly basis. Some are paid a combination of commissions and fees. Don't be reluctant to ask the advisors you are considering to explain how they are compensated and what their services will cost you. Get them to list and explain all the associated fees they charge, including hidden costs such as internal mutual-fund fees. (I call these "hidden" because many financial advisors—and even some no-load mutual-fund companies—often don't explain them in detail. A good advisor will.)

RULE NO. 6

DECIDE HOW YOU WANT TO PAY YOUR ADVISOR.

The financial services industry is in the midst of dramatic change. For decades, financial advisors worked on commission. But those days are ending. As a result of technological change and increased competition, commissions on stock and bond trades are getting smaller and smaller, and more and more advisors are moving toward fee-based compensation. Under a fee-based arrangement, you generally pay a financial advisor an annual fee of 1 to 2.5 percent of the value of the assets he or she is managing for you. In other words, to manage a $100,000 portfolio, a fee-based advisor will charge you somewhere between $1,000 and $2,500 a year.

For that annual fee, you should receive a comprehensive financial plan that includes an investment policy statement (this is a written agreement of understanding that explains how your money will be invested and highlights your goals and objectives). In addition, you should receive full-time professional money management, the ability to speak with your advisor and meet regularly (at least twice a year and more if needed), and quarterly performance reports that show you a detailed breakdown of how your invested money is doing. Lastly, all transaction costs (meaning the costs to buy or sell) should be included in this annual fee.

Overall, I believe that the fee-based system makes more sense than paying your advisor a commission per transaction. That's because with a fee-based relationship, there is no conflict of interest. The advisor is not paid to move your money around, as he or she is under a commission system. Rather, the advisor makes more money only if he or she grows your portfolio effectively. If the advisor does not do a good job managing and servicing your account, you'll take your business elsewhere and the fees stop. This puts you totally in the driver seat, which is where you should be.

Five years ago, the average fee to have your money managed professionally was about 3 percent a year. Now, as a result of competition, fees are averaging only about 2 percent. My personal prediction is that within three to five years, almost all financial advisors and stockbrokers will be fee-based, and the going rate will be down to 1 percent annually. This will be great for the consumer and good for the financial advisor who has built a sound business by serving his or her clients well. Many financial advisors, myself included, are in the process of changing over from charging commissions to being fee-based. Those who are doing it now are on the cutting edge. It is only a matter of time before the rest will be forced to follow suit or become like the dinosaurs, extinct.

RULE NO. 7
MAKE YOURSELF AN IMPORTANT CLIENT . . . BY SAYING "THANK YOU."

It is not enough simply to hire a good financial advisor. You want whoever you hire to pay attention to you—ideally, to consider you one of his or her most important clients. Most people think that in order to be important to a financial advisor, you need to have lots of money. Nothing could be further from the truth. I have clients with assets that range from $25,000 to $100 million, and I can assure you that some of the smaller ones are just as important to me as the biggest ones.

The fact is, it's not just money that determines how much your financial advisor cares about you. It's how you treat your financial advisor that matters. As an example, I have a client, Francine, who opened an account with me with just $1,000. I put Francine's money into a stock that tripled in value, so all of a sudden she had $3,000. I also bought this stock for more than a half-dozen other clients. Most of them made significantly more money than Francine, because they had more invested. Unlike any of them, however, after the stock took off, Francine showed up at my office one day with four bottles of wine as a gift for me and each of my assistants. Now, I don't know what the wine cost Francine. I don't even remember whether it was red or white. What I do remember is that this small gesture of hers was talked about in our office for weeks. We couldn't believe how special it was. I'm still talking (and now writing) about it three years later.

So when your financial advisor makes you some money, take a moment to say "thank you." Sure, it's his or her job to make you money. But that's no reason not to show your appreciation. No matter how small your portfolio, a small gesture like a simple thank-you note or a bottle of wine can transform you to an "A" client.

Another great way to say "thank you" to your advisor—and become as a result an "A" client—is to refer the advisor some new business (that is, to recommend that a friend hire your advisor). Not only will this show your advisor how much you appreciate what he or she has done for you, it may turn out to be just what your friend needs to get her financial life together.

And it's not just financial advisors who should get this sort of consideration. When Francine gave me that little gift, it made me realize that I had never once expressed my appreciation to any of the professionals on whom I depend: my attorney, my CPA, my doctor, my haircutter, the mechanic who looked after my car—the list goes on and on. So three years ago I started sending them all thank-you notes and in some cases a gift basket at Christmas. The first time I did this, my doctor called me personally to say "thank you." Guess what? Even though my doctor is routinely booked up three months in advance, I never have to wait for an appointment anymore. I just seem to get right in. My car mechanic framed my thank-you letter and posted it on the wall of his waiting room. My CPA seemed to find more deductions the next year.

I'm not kidding. Because of my small gifts and notes, my relationship with all these professionals is now different. They remember me because I made a small gesture to say "thank you." Try it. Our parents were right: Saying "thank you" goes a long way.

RULE NO. 8
HIRE A FINANCIAL ADVISOR WITH A STRONG SUPPORT TEAM.

Many financial planners run a one-person shop. They answer their own phone, get your coffee, validate your parking, prospect for new business, service clients, and then—if there's any time left—manage your money.

The fact is, the support staff of a good financial advisor is often as important to you as the advisor him- or herself. In my office, all I do is meet with clients and manage money. Everything else—service, correspondence, statement requests, dividend checks, newsletters, seminars—is handled by my support team. There are nine people on my team, four brokers and five assistants. This depth of trained support staff ensures that our clients receive the attention and service they deserve. So when you hire someone to manage your money, make sure he or she has a good team. Ultimately a good support staff will mean better service for you and, ideally, better investment returns long-term.

RULE NO. 9

CHECK OUT A PROSPECTIVE ADVISOR'S BACKGROUND.

As I said earlier, there are more than half a million people in this country who call themselves financial advisors. How can you tell if the one you are talking to is someone you can trust? The newspapers always seemed to be filled with stories about dishonest financial managers who swindle their clients out of their life savings. Recently in the Bay Area there was a case of a man who called himself a financial planner and allegedly fled the country with over $10 million of his clients' money. He was even said to have conned his own employees. The worst thing about this tale is that it was totally avoidable. This man had a record of negligent financial behavior, as a result of which he had been fired by a major brokerage firm. This fact was documented on what is known as his U4—a record that the National Association of Securities Dealers (NASD) keeps on every licensed financial professional in the country. Most reputable firms will not hire a financial advisor who has any sort of black mark on his or her U4.

Therefore, what you want to do before you hire a financial advisor is check out his or her U4. To do this, telephone the NASD at (800) 289-9999, or visit their Web site at www.nasdr.com, and ask them if the advisor is clean or not. Also take a look at the firm where the advisor works. If you hire someone from a large firm, you are buying built-in safety. Large firms have what are known as compliance departments, which see to it that all employees of the firm observe the highest ethical and legal standards when it comes to investing and money management. At the investment firm where I work, every single piece of mail that comes in or goes out is photocopied and reviewed. Every single transaction we make is monitored. If an advisor seems to be trading a client's account too actively, the firm checks with the client to confirm that he or she is aware of what's going on.

Of course, hiring a financial advisor who works for a large firm does not guarantee performance results. But it does provide you with one very important protection against the damage an unethical advisor can do—namely, deep pockets. If a broker somehow slips under the compliance department's radar and you get burned by unethical or illegal investment practices that should have been caught, there's a much better chance that firm will compensate you for the damage done. The same cannot always be said of a small independent financial planner.

FIVE-STAR TIP: *If you use the Internet to do this search, when you get to the advisor's page that shows his or her information, there will be a section that reads* **disclosure events**. *If this term is highlighted it may mean your advisor has had past legal problems. You will be able to request additional information on this, and the NASD will mail it to you within ten days. This is extremely important. One advisor I know of who was hired by a major investment firm had a police record for assault and battery on his mother. He is not required to advise prospective clients of this, but it is listed on his U4 and available to those who do their homework.*

RULE NO. 10
NEVER, EVER HIRE AN INVESTMENT ADVISOR WHO BRAGS ABOUT PERFORMANCE.

In recent years, with the stock market's unprecedented run-up, many investment portfolios and mutual funds have had little trouble producing double-digit returns. As a result, currently it is quite easy for a financial advisor or mutual-fund company to come up with a recommended portfolio that's generated earnings of better than 20 percent a year over the last 5 years.

Looking back at the last 5 years means very little going forward. I call it "rearview mirror" investing, and it does not make for good solid financial forecasts. A good financial advisor will talk to you about historical returns going back not 5 years but at least 20 to 30 years. That's important, for by looking at the returns generated by different investments and asset classes since the 1960s and 1970s, you will see that over the long term, investing in the stock market is more likely to produce annual returns of about 11 percent, not 20 percent.

The key to creating an intelligent financial plan is to use realistic projections—which is to say ones that are based on more than just the last 5 to 10 years. Often a prospective client will ask me why some other advisor is promising her returns of, say, 18 percent a year, while I'm willing to project only 8 to 12 percent over the next 5 years. My answer is that I am being honest and the other guy is not; he's basing his projections on the last 5 years, while I base mine on the last 50. No one knows what the future holds. All we know is what history has

ASSET ALLOCATION - RISK & REWARD
One-Year Returns
January 1950 - March 1998

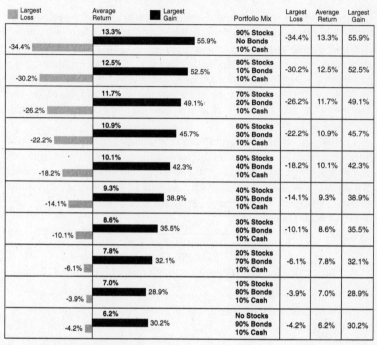

Largest Loss	Average Return	Largest Gain	Portfolio Mix	Largest Loss	Average Return	Largest Gain
-34.4%	13.3%	55.9%	90% Stocks / No Bonds / 10% Cash	-34.4%	13.3%	55.9%
-30.2%	12.5%	52.5%	80% Stocks / 10% Bonds / 10% Cash	-30.2%	12.5%	52.5%
-26.2%	11.7%	49.1%	70% Stocks / 20% Bonds / 10% Cash	-26.2%	11.7%	49.1%
-22.2%	10.9%	45.7%	60% Stocks / 30% Bonds / 10% Cash	-22.2%	10.9%	45.7%
-18.2%	10.1%	42.3%	50% Stocks / 40% Bonds / 10% Cash	-18.2%	10.1%	42.3%
-14.1%	9.3%	38.9%	40% Stocks / 50% Bonds / 10% Cash	-14.1%	9.3%	38.9%
-10.1%	8.6%	35.5%	30% Stocks / 60% Bonds / 10% Cash	-10.1%	8.6%	35.5%
-6.1%	7.8%	32.1%	20% Stocks / 70% Bonds / 10% Cash	-6.1%	7.8%	32.1%
-3.9%	7.0%	28.9%	10% Stocks / 80% Bonds / 10% Cash	-3.9%	7.0%	28.9%
-4.2%	6.2%	30.2%	No Stocks / 90% Bonds / 10% Cash	-4.2%	6.2%	30.2%

shown us. The more history we use—that is, the farther back we go—the safer our projections are bound to be.

Once your potential advisor gives you a proposal on how to invest your money, ask the advisor what the breakdown in his proposal is between stocks, bonds, and cash. Then compare what you're told to the chart above. If you are meeting with someone who tells you he can earn you 18 percent a year when the chart shows that, historically, the asset breakdown he is suggesting has achieved just 10 percent, you know you are dealing with a less than ethical person. Find someone else.

RULE NO. 11
A GOOD FINANCIAL ADVISOR EXPLAINS THE RISKS
ASSOCIATED WITH INVESTING.

It's easy to forget about risk when the stock market is running the way it has been lately, but that doesn't mean you should. A good advisor will spend time explaining and educating you about the risks associated with investing. At The Bach Group, before we implement an investment plan, we show our clients exactly how often in the past the market has dropped, how long it has stayed down, and, based on the history of the last 45 years, what we believe the risks associated with our proposal to be.

This is incredibly important because many people today do not fully understand—nor are they being prepared for—the risks inherent in any stock-market investment. If you meet with an advisor who does not discuss the notion of risk with you and ask you specific questions to get a feeling for your comfort level, thank her for her time and continue on with your search.

RULE NO. 12
LOOK FOR AN ADVISOR WHO HAS MANY SATISFIED CLIENTS.

A first-rate financial advisor is like a good doctor or a great restaurant—hard to get in to. The fact is, a good advisor is bound to be busy—so busy, in fact, that he or she may not be able to see you for at least a few weeks.

So don't be put off by a tight schedule. And don't be impressed by someone who is overly accommodating. A financial advisor who is available to come to your home on a moment's notice is not a professional. (When was the last time a doctor came to your house?) You should expect to have to take time out of your workday and go meet with a financial advisor at his or her office. Someone who will meet with you either at night or on a weekend either does not have enough clients or has no personal life. Both are bad signs.

RULE NO. 13
GO WITH YOUR GUT INSTINCT.

When you interview a financial advisor, ask yourself if you feel comfortable with this person. Is this the kind of person you want to open up to and work with for years to come? Do you feel deep down inside that this is someone you can trust? The answer should be a "gut level" yes. If it is not, continue your search. You have not yet found your trusted advisor.

RULE NO. 14
KEEP IN REGULAR CONTACT WITH YOUR FINANCIAL ADVISOR.

If you haven't heard from your financial advisor by phone or by letter in the last 12 months (statements don't count), then you may have fallen into what we call the client abyss. Get out quick. Either go in immediately and reacquaint yourself with the professional with whom you are working, or start interviewing for a new advisor. As a rule, your advisor should contact you at least twice a year, and you should sit down together to review your financial situation at least once every 12 months.

In Conclusion

These 14 rules are meant to make your search for a lifelong financial guide easier. Don't let anything I have said scare you off from searching for one. There are many, many good and ethical professionals out there who can help you with your financial decisions.

Remember, it's now time for you to move on your decision. If you have decided that you do want professional help, make hiring an advisor a priority. Your ultimate goal should be to hire an individual or a team that you could see yourself working with for a long time—perhaps even the rest of your life. Therefore, the hiring process is something you should take very seriously. Ask around your community, talk to friends and wealthy people you know and respect, and ask who they are working with. Spend time, interview more than one professional, ask for references, and then follow up and call those references.

I promise you—it will be worth the effort.

LEARN THE NINE BIGGEST MISTAKES INVESTORS MAKE AND HOW TO AVOID THEM

When I was five, my friend Marvin and I thought it would be fun to see what was behind those electric sockets our mothers were always warning us not to touch. I think I was the one who found the screwdriver, but it was definitely Marvin who stuck it in the socket.

Wham!

Before either of us had a chance to react, Marvin went flying backward across the room and all the power in the house went out. "Wow," I said, gaping at my friend, who was now lying in a heap against the opposite wall. "Was that fun?"

Poor little Marvin looked at me with a dazed expression, then burst into tears.

I can't remember what lame story we eventually concocted to cover up what we'd done, but I do recall clearly that the experience taught me two important things. The first was never to stick a screwdriver in a light socket. The second was that while it's important to learn from your own mistakes, it's probably a better idea (and certainly a much safer one) to learn from other people's.

I bring this up because both these lessons are important to remember when you're trying to decide how to invest all that money you should now be putting in your three baskets. The fact is, when it comes to investing, many of us act like five-year-olds sticking screw-drivers into electric sockets. That is, we experiment ignorantly—and invariably wind up making some horrendous mistake that sends us reeling across the room in financial shock.

Over the course of this chapter, we're going to focus on what I consider to be the nine most "shocking" mistakes that investors generally make. My hope is that as a result of studying other people's mistakes, you'll be able to avoid the painful and expensive experience of having to learn from your own.

MISTAKE NO. 1

BECOMING AN INVESTOR BEFORE YOU ARE ORGANIZED AND HAVE SPECIFIC GOALS IN MIND.

Back in Step Three, we talked about the importance of knowing exactly where you are today financially and what eventual destination you've got in mind before you go charging down the road to riches. Well, I hope you don't mind if I repeat myself a bit here. The fact is, going off half cocked—that is, without having a clear idea of how you stand and where you want to go—may well be the most common (and most avoidable) mistake investors make.

There's no getting around it. Before you invest any of your money, you must invest some of your *time*. The rule is simple: *In order to become a successful investor, you first have to get your values and goals written down on paper and your finances organized.* You absolutely *must* do a family financial inventory and balance sheet and determine precisely your current net worth. You also must get a good handle on what you earn and what you spend. This is not a guessing game or a time for estimates. Remember, until you know where you stand financially, you should not invest in *anything*. As I noted earlier, use the worksheet in the Appendix 2 to get a solid grip on where you stand today financially.

I can already hear you protesting: "Worksheets? Financial inventories? This stuff takes time. What if I miss out on a great investment opportunity while I'm busy getting my finances organized?"

Believe me, I know that doing the foundation work is not nearly as exciting as investing in a hot stock. No one goes to a cocktail party and brags about the fact that she spent the weekend cleaning her financial house. Rather, people like to talk about the hot new investment they just bought—and now with all those personal-finance magazines, television shows, investor newsletters, and Internet chat rooms, it's very easy to be tempted into investing without first getting your money in order and your investment goals down on paper.

Resist the temptation. You can't invest successfully without knowing where you are starting from and what your investment goals are. Only after you have figured out these things will you be able to evaluate intelligently the opportunities around you and figure out whether (and how) they might make sense for you.

MISTAKE NO. 2
BUYING AN INVESTMENT YOU DON'T UNDERSTAND.

You'd be surprised how many otherwise smart people make this mistake. Take Marilyn. When I first met her, I was impressed with her sophistication and the fact that she had a degree from one of the nation's top business schools. By the time I finished looking at her portfolio, however, I was a lot less impressed. Nearly every single stock she owned had dropped significantly in price since she had bought it—an amazingly bad record, given the stock market's incredible performance over the last few years.

As I studied Marilyn's portfolio, I realized that the loser companies in which she had invested had one thing in common. I had never heard of any of them. Thirteen stocks, 13 companies—and not one single name was familiar. When I asked Marilyn where she had come up with these companies, she said her broker had picked them.

"Do you know what any of them do?" I asked her.

No, she said, but that didn't matter because her broker had assured her that they all had great "upside potential."

"Marilyn," I said, "why would you invest your money in a company you have never heard of when there are so many great companies that you have not only heard of but whose business you understand?"

"Well, isn't that what sophisticated investors do?" she asked me.

The answer, of course, is no. What smart, sophisticated investors do is buy what they understand.

Peter Lynch, the legendary money manager who helped create the Fidelity Investments empire, was once quoted as saying "I don't buy investments that I can't explain using a crayon and one piece of paper." Lynch's point was that if he can't easily explain an investment, then he doesn't understand it—and if he doesn't understand it, he doesn't want to own it.

About three years ago I ran into Lynch at a seminar. Not being one to pass up an opportunity to get advice from the best, I asked him if he believed his "crayon" philosophy still made sense in today's technology-driven economy.

Lynch laughed. "No," he told me, "I've changed it. Now I only buy stocks that a *seven-year-old* can explain to me with a crayon!"

He meant that literally. For the last few years, Lynch has been teaching third-graders in his hometown how to buy stocks. And his approach has clearly worked. In each of the last three years, the kids in his classes have outperformed the market!

Were Lynch's seven-year-olds investing in biotech companies, index fund derivatives, the latest initial public offerings? Quite the contrary. They've been buying stock in companies that make or do things that make sense to them—companies like McDonald's, Coca-Cola, Pepsico, Colgate-Palmolive, Apple Computers, Toys 'R' Us, and America Online.

Kids are smart. They are suspicious of things they don't understand. Grown-ups, on the other hand, tend to be impressed. Certainly, that seems to be true when it comes to investments. Most of us will spend more time researching a purchase of a new stereo or refrigerator or planning a vacation than researching an investment or designing a retirement plan.

This is why so many investors fail so miserably. They literally don't know what they are doing. *Never, ever buy an investment you don't understand.* Remember my little friend Marvin: Investing in something you don't understand is like sticking a screwdriver in a light socket. Chances are you're going to get shocked. If the person pushing the idea (whether it's your broker, your financial planner, or your best friend) can't explain the investment to you clearly—showing you why you should buy it, how you can benefit from it, and, most important, how much risk is associated with it—then *don't buy it*.

MISTAKE NO. 3
TRYING TO TIME THE MARKET.

What's the secret to making money in the stock market? If you're like most people, you'd probably answer "Buy low, sell high."

You'd also be wrong.

There is a widespread notion that the way to do well as an investor is to buy when the market is low and sell when it is high—what's known as timing the market. This notion probably was created by some marketing company to promote its market-timing newsletter. The fact is, trying to improve your performance by trying to anticipate market swings is a recipe for ulcer-producing anxiety, if not outright disaster.

Just ask Jim.

When Jim came to my office to discuss his personal financial situation, I was immediately curious. A 49-year-old architect, he had more than $500,000 (his entire retirement savings) sitting in a money-market account. By now you know that retirement money does not belong in a money-market account. But Jim apparently didn't. "So what's the deal?" I asked him. "What's your retirement money doing in a cash account earning just 4 percent a year?"

Jim's story was heartbreaking, but it wasn't uncommon. Back in 1994, when the Dow Jones Industrials hit 4000, he became convinced that stock prices were due for a fall. The smart thing to do, he thought, would be to pull his money out of stocks and park it in a safe money-market account until the market correction had run its course.

Unfortunately, the correction never came. For the next four years, Jim's money sat on the sidelines as the Dow climbed past 9000. "I'm literally sick over what a mistake I made," Jim told me. "If I had just left my money where it was, my retirement account would now be worth about $1.2 million! I could be retired by now!"

Jim's mistake was that he didn't know his history. Consider the following.

Over the 50 years from 1946 to 1996, the stocks that comprise the Standard & Poor 500 have grown in value at an average annual rate of 12 percent. To put it another way, if you invested $100 in the S&P 500 back in 1946 and let your money ride, reinvesting all the dividends, by 1996 your portfolio would have been worth some $31,000!

That sounds pretty good, doesn't it? But suppose instead of leaving your investment alone, let's say you actually believed those people who claim they can foresee the future of the market and make their money selling market-timing newsletters. So in 1946 you set out to grow your nest egg by trying to time the market—that is, buying only when you felt the market had bottomed out and selling only when you thought it had reached a top.

Now, even if you were a really good guesser, you have to admit there's no way you could guess right all the time. Over the course of

50 years, there were bound to be some occasions when you guessed wrong—times when you sold because you thought the market was about to go down and instead it went up (or when you bought because you thought it was about to go up and instead it went down). Suppose you were wrong just 5 percent of the time. Actually, that's a pretty amazing track record. Think about it—we're assuming you guessed right 19 out of every 20 times you tried; stock market experts tell us we're doing a great job if we're right just 60 percent of the time, or on 12 out of every 20 guesses.

So how would you have done? Well, according to the records, if you missed only 5 percent of the market's best growth months over the last 50 years, your average annual return over that period would have been just 6.5 percent. What that means is that instead of growing to $31,000 by 1996, your initial investment of $100 would have grown to only $2,000. In other words, your decision to time the market would have cut your ultimate return not merely in half but by more than 93 percent!

And that's if you guessed *right* 95 percent of the time. What if you were right only 90 percent of the time? In that case, your $100 investment would have produced a measly 2.7 percent annual return, growing to only $325 by 1996. Your nest egg would be worth just 1 percent of the value it would have had if you'd simply left it alone all those years.

Whether you're a beginning investor or a seasoned professional, the statistics speak for themselves. The chart on page 200 illustrates exactly what I mean.

As you can see, it's literally impossible to do well timing the market. Most investors who try it not only drive themselves crazy with worry, they often lose significant amounts of money.

To make matters worse, many would-be timers seem to fall prey to what I call investor's dyslexia—instead of buying low and selling high, they end up buying high and selling low. There's an old saying that two things drive the stock market: greed and fear. Greed causes people to go stampeding after overpriced "hot" stocks, while fear causes them to panic and dump their investments at the first sign of trouble. Obviously, this is a recipe for failure.

So what's the real key to long-term investment success? It's quite simple, really: *Buy quality . . . and hold on to it!*

If there is a secret to long-term success with stocks, it's not timing the market but time *in* the market. When I first started writing this book in January 1996, the Dow Jones Industrial Average was below

MARKET TIMING
VS.
BEING CONTINUALLY INVESTED

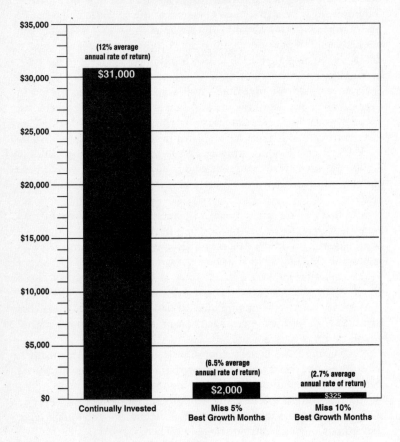

Time period 1946-1996
$100 original investment

5000. Twenty-six months later it was over 8600. How long will it keep rising? I don't know. No one knows—and you personally should not care. Yes, the best time to get in the market was 30 years ago, but if you missed that chance, then *the best time to get in the market is now.*

The catch, of course, is that if you do get in, you have to invest for the long term. Let the stockmarket have its ups and downs, but don't you go and panic along with it. As long as you invest in quality companies that consistently produce a profit, you can hold on to your stocks for years and watch your fortune keep growing and growing and growing . . .

MISTAKE NO. 4
PUTTING OFF SAVING FOR RETIREMENT.

At the beginning of this book, I noted that 95 percent of Americans age 65 or older have an income of less than $25,000 a year. As I pointed out, that means that fewer than 5 percent of us are in any position to lead a life of comfort when we reach our so-called golden years. In fact, the government tells us that only 2 percent of retirement-age Americans are truly wealthy, which is defined as being in a financial position to do more or less what you want when you want.

This failure rate is not only totally unacceptable, it's also totally unnecessary. The difference between a comfortable future and destitution is literally a matter of no more than a few dollars a month. The problem is, by failing to plan, most of us in effect plan to fail.

The problem is not complicated. The longer you wait to get started, the more you need to save. The following chart illustrates this quite dramatically. It shows the savings records of two women, Susan and Kim. Susan began saving for retirement at age 19. For eight years she put $2,000 a year into an investment account; then, at age 26, she stopped, never putting in another dime. Kim, on the other hand, waited until she turned 27 to begin putting money away for retirement. Starting then, and continuing right up through the age of 65, Kim put $2,000 into an investment account every year. Who came out ahead? The following chart shows the answer, and I'll bet you'll find it surprising.

THE TIME VALUE OF MONEY
Invest Now Rather Than Later

SUSAN Investing at age 19 (10% Annual Return)			S	KIM Investing at age 27 (10% Annual Return)		
AGE	INVESTMENT	TOTAL VALUE	E	AGE	INVESTMENT	TOTAL VALUE
19	$2,000	2,200	E	19	0	0
20	2,000	4,620		20	0	0
21	2,000	7,282		21	0	0
22	2,000	10,210		22	0	0
23	2,000	13,431	T	23	0	0
24	2,000	16,974	H	24	0	0
25	2,000	20,871	E	25	0	0
26	2,000	25,158		26	0	0
27	0	27,674		27	$2,000	2,200
28	0	30,442	D	28	2,000	4,620
29	0	33,486	I	29	2,000	7,282
30	0	36,834	F	30	2,000	10,210
31	0	40,518	F	31	2,000	13,431
32	0	44,570	E	32	2,000	16,974
33	0	48,027	R	33	2,000	20,871
34	0	53,929	E	34	2,000	25,158
35	0	59,322	N	35	2,000	29,874
36	0	65,256	C	36	2,000	35,072
37	0	71,780	E	37	2,000	40,768
38	0	78,958		38	2,000	47,045
39	0	86,854		39	2,000	53,949
40	0	95,540		40	2,000	61,544
41	0	105,094		41	2,000	69,899
42	0	115,603		42	2,000	79,089
43	0	127,163		43	2,000	89,198
44	0	130,880		44	2,000	100,318
45	0	153,868		45	2,000	112,550
46	0	169,255		46	2,000	126,005
47	0	188,180		47	2,000	140,805
48	0	204,798		48	2,000	157,086
49	0	226,278		49	2,000	174,094
50	0	247,806		50	2,000	194,694
51	0	272,586		51	2,000	216,363
52	0	299,845		52	2,000	240,199
53	0	329,830		53	2,000	266,419
54	0	362,813		54	2,000	295,261
55	0	399,094		55	2,000	326,988
56	0	439,003		56	2,000	361,886
57	0	482,904		57	2,000	400,275
58	0	531,194		58	2,000	442,503
59	0	584,314		59	2,000	488,953
60	0	642,745		60	2,000	540,048
61	0	707,020		61	2,000	596,253
62	0	777,722		62	2,000	658,078
63	0	855,494		63	2,000	726,086
64	0	941,043		64	2,000	800,895
65	0	1,035,148		65	2,000	883,185

EARNINGS BEYOND INVESTMENT $1,019,148

EARNINGS BEYOND INVESTMENT $805,185

SUSAN EARNS	$1,019,148
KIM EARNS	$805,185
SUSAN EARNS MORE	$213,963

Susan invested one-fifth the dollars but has 25% more to show

START INVESTING EARLY!

As we discussed in Step Five, the best way to get started saving for retirement is to arrange to have it done without your having to think about it—that is, to have your monthly contribution either deducted directly from your paycheck or automatically transferred from your checking account each month. The benefits of this approach are enormous. First (and most important), you can't spend what you don't see in your checking account. Second, it spares you having to debate with yourself whether you *really* need to make a contribution this month. Third, contributing once or twice a month is a lot easier than writing a big check at the end of the year. The fact is, most people who wait until the end of the year to fund their retirement plans end up either not doing it or putting too little away.

Remember, the sooner you start saving for retirement, the sooner you will be able to finish rich and go play!

MISTAKE NO. 5
SPECULATING WITH YOUR INVESTMENT MONEY.

Show me a gambler and I will show you a future loser. The reason Las Vegas is America's fastest-growing city, with new casinos being built there every month, is that the odds favor the house. People who gamble eventually lose.

The same holds true when it comes to investing. In the investment world, of course, we don't call it gambling. We use the word "speculation," but it really means the same thing. A speculator, like a gambler, is someone who is looking for a quick hit, a fast buck, a big payoff. And just like at a casino, every once in a while someone does get lucky. But over the long haul, nothing will more effectively prevent you from ever becoming financially secure than speculating with your investment money. This should be obvious, but it's not; otherwise, millions of Americans wouldn't be speculating in the market every day.

Here are four of the most common ways to speculate—all of which you should avoid.

Investing in Options. One of the easiest ways to speculate in the stock market—and in the process probably lose everything you've invested—is to buy what are called *options*. Options allow you to speculate on the future price of a given stock. Essentially, you're placing a bet that the price of a certain stock will reach a certain point by a certain date. The problem is, if you bet wrong and the stock doesn't reach that price by that particular date, your option could expire worthless—and the money you paid for it is down the drain. (An amazing thing about options is that they are one of the only investments where you are actually told in advance what day your investment could be worthless. It's called option expiration day.)

There's a lot more to options than this, of course. However, unless you are willing to put in the considerable time required to master the complexities—or if you happen to work with a professional who has a *proven* track record in option trading—I recommend you avoid them altogether.

Investing in Companies That Don't Make a Profit. It may sound obvious, but the second easy way to lose money in the stock market is to invest in companies that don't make a profit. When you buy a stock, you are making an investment in a business. Some businesses are well run and make money year after year; some are poorly run (or just new) and lose money. Now, all things being equal, doesn't it make more sense to invest in a company that consistently makes money rather than one that doesn't? Of course it does. Nonetheless, thousands of people buy stock every day in companies that have never shown a profit—or even produced a proven product. Most recently, we've seen this phenomenon in Internet-related stocks. Lately, it seems all you need to do is put the words "Internet" or "cyber-something" in your prospectus, and the investing public will go bananas. As a result, some companies that have been in business for only a year or two are worth billions of dollars on paper—even though they consistently lose money. Eventually, of course, most of these "hot stocks" will cool off, and the investors who were sucked in by all the excitement may well end up losing their shirts.

Some people argue that investing only in proven companies with solid earnings records is a great way to miss the next Microsoft. That's ridiculous. You don't have to get in on the absolute ground floor of a promising new company in order to do well with it. You can easily wait to buy into it until after it has compiled four or five years of steady profits. Take Microsoft itself. Let's say you decided to be really cautious and wait for it to report profits for ten years in a row before you were willing to invest. Could you have made any money on the stock? Absolutely. Between 1995 (ten full years after the company reported its first profits) and 1998, the price of Microsoft stock more than quadrupled.

So why take chances? Leave the high-tech start-ups and other risky businesses to the venture capitalists. As long as you are investing to secure your future, you should stick to solid companies with proven track records.

Actively Trading Your Account. One thing that makes women potentially better investors than men is that women generally are better at committing to the long term. When men buy stocks, they tend to get fidgety; they are constantly looking around, wondering if some better investment isn't waiting for them just around the corner. And while actively buying and selling investments may sound like a great way to stay on top of market developments, the fact is that there are only two winners when you trade frequently: the firm that executes your trades (because it earns a commission on every one of your transactions) and the IRS (because it gets to collect a piece of your profits every time you sell an investment for more than you bought it). There's no getting around it; under current tax laws, you simply cannot win over the long term by actively buying and selling stock in the short term.

Let's say you buy a stock at $10 a share and less than a year later you sell it at $12. You might think you made a 20 percent return, but you really didn't. First off, it probably cost you 25 cents a share to buy the stock and 25 cents a share to sell it. Right there, your $2 profit is cut to $1.50. Second, if you sell a stock at a profit within 12 months of when you bought it, you could end up paying as much as 40 percent of your earnings in short-term capital gains taxes. So there goes another 40 cents. Suddenly your 20 percent return has been reduced to around 7 percent. And that's assuming you actually did everything right and bought a stock that went up and then sold it at a profit.

The point is this: When it comes to investing in stocks, the key word is *investing*. You don't invest in a business by making a speculative stock purchase in the hope of a favorable short-term movement. You invest for the long term, with the goal of owning a particular company's stock for years. Trust me—this philosophy will make you significantly more money. At the very least, you'll end up paying far less in commissions and taxes.

Throwing Good Money After Bad. I can't tell you how often I've seen people persuaded to put more money into an investment that has just suffered a significant drop in price—the so-called logic being that having fallen in price, the investment must now be a bargain. This is known in the investment world as buying on dips. Often financial advisors will suggest that if you liked a stock at $20 a share, it must be an even better buy at $10. But just because the price of a stock has dropped, that doesn't mean it's now "on sale." That's true only if the company is well run and its stock happens to be down simply because of some short-term market gyration, rather than business problems that could prevent it from making money in the future.

I learned this the hard way. I once owned a stock that hit $65 a share and then started falling like a rock. When it reached $3, I said the stupidest thing I've ever said to myself: "Gosh, $3 sure seems cheap. If management can turn things around, it will be back to $10 in no time." With that in mind, I bought a thousand more shares—and watched the price go straight down the tubes to zero. And this was a company with a board of directors whose membership read like a "Who's Who" of American business.

The point of this expensive lesson was clear: When a stock price falls through the floor, and the company doesn't have a convincing explanation for the collapse (or a specific plan in place to correct the problem), don't add to your financial misery by doubling down. As investment guru Warren Buffett once put it: "The most important thing to do when you find yourself in a hole is to stop digging."

MISTAKE NO. 6
PAYING TOO MUCH IN TAXES.

The biggest enemy of your financial future is taxes. Yet when I review the financial situation of new clients, you'd be amazed how often it turns out that their previous advisors never did any tax planning for them. To my way of thinking, that's financial malpractice. If you currently work with a financial advisor who has not reviewed your tax situation with you, fire that advisor and find one who will.

When you are building an investment portfolio, it is absolutely imperative that you take into consideration your potential tax liability. The reason I spent so much time in Step Four and Step Five talking about retirement accounts is that the money in them grows tax-deferred, which helps you to grow your nest egg much faster. The difference in not paying taxes on your investments over a 10- to 30-year period can be huge! It can mean the difference between financial pain or financial pleasure. The following chart shows how much faster your money will grow if it is invested in tax-deferred vehicles. Over a typical 30-year period, you could literally be talking about millions of additional dollars in your pocket!

NOTICE THE DIFFERENCE
TAX-DEFERRED INVESTING CAN MAKE

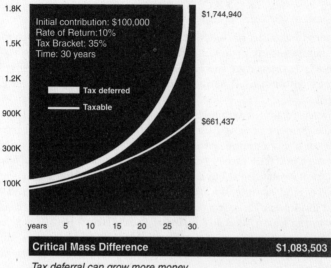

Initial contribution: $100,000
Rate of Return:10%
Tax Bracket: 35%
Time: 30 years

Tax deferred
Taxable

$1,744,940

$661,437

| Critical Mass Difference | $1,083,503 |

Tax deferral can grow more money.

Turning Growth into Income

From	Taxable	Tax Deferred
Accumulation	$661,437	1,744,940
Rate of Return	at 10%	at 10%
Annual Earnings	$66,143	$174,494
Tax Bracket	at 35%	at 35%
Annual Income	**$42,993**	**$113,422**

Tax-deferred growth can lead to more income.

As you can see, your money grows significantly faster when the profits are not drained away by taxes. Always seek to minimize your taxes when investing; ideally you should seek investments that grow tax deferred.

MISTAKE NO. 7
BUYING AN INVESTMENT THAT IS ILLIQUID.

An illiquid investment is one that you cannot sell immediately. To me, immediately means in less than five business days. If I can't sell it within five business days, I won't buy it. Why? Show me an investment you can't sell for a fixed period of time and I'll show you a potential problem.

Now, don't get me wrong. I'm not arguing against buying a home, or an investment such as a government bond that takes ten years to mature, or a mutual fund with an annual sales fee. All of these things may have a perfectly proper place in your investment portfolio. What I'm warning you against buying is something that is not salable for a specific period of time, no matter what. An example of the kind of illiquid investment I hate is a *limited partnership*—the two most dreaded words in the Smart Woman's financial vocabulary. When I bring up limited partnerships in my classes, I often hear moans and groans from a few of the older students. That tells me they have some experience with the subject.

Limited partnerships generally are set up to pool investors' money in order to purchase certain types of investments, typically real estate. The problem is that most limited partnerships are not salable—that is, not liquid—usually for as long as 10 to 15 years. "Don't worry about it," the salesman typically tells a potential investor. "The money you're investing is for retirement and you won't need it for 20 years anyway." Sure, but what happens if an emergency arises and you've got to get your hands on your money early?

Now, I know some people will dispute me on this and insist that limited partnerships can make sense. Well, I'm sorry; I have seen too many account statements and heard too many firsthand stories from people who were burned by this kind of investment. As far as I'm concerned, limited partnerships are a bad idea for ordinary investors. They are not liquid, so don't buy them. Period. (If for some reason you come across a limited partnership that you feel you just have to be a part of, then my rule of thumb is don't put more than 10 percent of your investable assets into it. This way if you lose your whole investment, your financial world won't be completely devastated.)

Limited partnerships are hardly the only illiquid investment out there, so don't let down your guard. For example, there are investment companies (offering everything from collectable coins to second mortgages) that claim to make a "secondary market" in the investment they are selling. That's all well and good, but in many cases they slip into the fine print a disclaimer saying they are not obligated to buy out your investment if you want to sell. If that's the case, then what you're buying is not really a liquid investment.

One of the worst cases I know of in this regard concerns a former client of mine named Barbara. Back in 1991, a devastating fire wiped out over 2,800 homes in the hills above Berkeley, California. Barbara's home was one of them. Fortunately, she had adequate fire insurance. Her insurance company settled her claim for more than $500,000 and Barbara went about planning to rebuild her home.

Since construction wouldn't be ready to start for six months, Barbara put the money in a bank CD (a great place, you will remember from our discussion of the dream basket, for short-term funds). A few weeks later a neighbor who was in a similar situation asked her what she'd done with her insurance money. When Barbara told him it was sitting in a CD earning 5 percent, the neighbor rolled his eyes. His insurance money, he claimed, was earning 15 percent.

That got Barbara's attention. The neighbor explained that a friend of his who invested in secondary mortgages had let him in on a deal. Barbara was impressed, and to make a long story short, she wound up giving her neighbor's friend half her insurance money—$250,000 in all—to invest in secondary mortgages. The friend's pitch was simple. The money would be safe because it would be backed by real estate. In any case, Barbara didn't need to worry because short-term investments in secondary mortgages were very easy to buy and sell. She would be paid 180 days' worth of interest up front and then get her principal back at the end of the 180 days. It sounded too good to be true.

It was. Barbara got her interest payment up front, but when the 180 days were up, she found herself waiting in vain for her $250,000 principal to be returned. When she went to ask her neighbor's friend what was going on, she discovered he was nowhere to be found. In a panic, Barbara ran to local courthouse to check the records on the property she supposedly had a second mortgage on. The property was in foreclosure—as a result of which, Barbara's investment was unsellable.

Had Barbara used the rule of not investing in illiquid investments, she never would have had this problem. The fact is, secondary mortgages are almost never easily liquid because they are backed by real estate that would have to be sold for you to get your money back.

Liquid means that the public (that is, anyone you choose to sell to) can buy you out easily and quickly—ideally, in less than five business days. Examples of liquid investments include stocks, bonds, mutual funds, money markets, certificates of deposit, Treasury bills, and annuities. In fact, most investments are liquid. Just remember to ask the question: "If I absolutely had to, could I sell this and get my money within five business days?" If the answer is no, think hard before you put any money into the investment.

MISTAKE NO. 8

HAVING A 30-YEAR MORTGAGE.

In my opinion, without question the biggest single scam perpetuated on the American buying public today is the 30-year mortgage. A typical 30-year mortgage at 8 percent inflates the real cost of a $250,000 home to more than $660,000. That's more than two and a half times the actual price of the house!

What's the alternative? Well, if you paid off your mortgage in 15 years, the total cost of your house would come to just under $493,000. That's still a lot, but it is nearly $168,000 less than it would have been with a 30-year mortgage. Is it really difficult to pay off a home in 15 years instead of 30 years? I honestly don't think so.

To begin with, you don't have to run out and get a new mortgage. All you need to do is the following.

First, call your mortgage holder and ask him to tell you how much you would need to add to your principal payment each month in order to pay off your mortgage in 15, 18, or 20 years. Ask also how much you would save in reduced interest costs. Once you see the savings in black and white, you will be motivated to start making extra principal payments. Trust me on this. This one phone call could end up saving you literally hundreds of thousands of dollars. So make the call.

Once you have decided how much more quickly you would like to pay off your mortgage, you need to decide whether you want to reach your goal by making a small extra payment each month or by forking over a larger lump sum at the end of the year. I recommend you do it monthly; the smaller bites make it more likely you will stick to your plan. If you can manage it, consider making an extra 10 percent payment each month and then adding an extra month's payment at the end of the year. This would almost guarantee that your 30-year mortgage will be paid off in close to 18 years (maybe even less, depending on whether your loan is fixed or adjustable). Just think, that's 12 years' worth of mortgage payments that you would now be able devote to something else—such as your retirement fund, or maybe even a vacation home.

"But wait," I can hear you say, "what about the great tax write-off I get?" Well, what about it? More than likely, you bought your home because you needed a place to live, not because you needed a great tax write-off. The tax benefits of home ownership are nice, but they don't outweigh the amount you can save by paying off your mortgage early.

If you need another reason to consider speeding up your mortgage payments, think about this: The faster you pay off your home, the sooner you can retire.

Now, there are some experts who disagree with this philosophy. Indeed, one school of thought suggests that rather than trying to pay off a 30-year mortgage more quickly, you should take a 40-year mortgage and strive to never pay it off. Well, that sure sounds like a lot of fun. What woman wouldn't look forward to making mortgage payments for the rest of her life just so she can have a tax write-off?

Even crazier, some financial planners say you should cash out whatever equity you happen to have in your home and invest the proceeds in the stock market or in an insurance policy. In my opinion, this advice is totally out of touch with reality. The reality is that you need a place to live in which you can feel safe and happy. You can't live in a mutual fund or in an insurance policy. I don't care how great the return is, you can't park your car in it. And despite what these experts would have you believe, there are going to be years when the stock market goes down and that "perfect" mutual fund actually appreciates less than your home.

Let's get back to basics. Most people dream of owning their own home. Most people also dream about being able to retire early so they can enjoy their lives and spend time with their loved ones. If you buy a home and pay it off early, you can accomplish both of these dreams. So pay off your mortgage sooner rather than later, and don't ever let some slick salesman tell you that having money in your home is like having cash "in them thar" walls or under your mattress. Cash in a home is your ultimate equity and your ultimate security. In my opinion, the sooner you own your home free and clear, the better.

MISTAKE NO. 9
GIVING UP.

I once asked my grandmother if she had ever made any major mistakes investing. She told me that the first stock she ever bought went straight down and she lost everything she had invested. As she explained it, she had gotten a "tip" and just jumped in. She actually invested only a couple of hundred dollars, but at the time that represented a full year's worth of savings. She told me she felt sick and embarrassed, and was afraid to tell my grandfather.

"Well, what did you do?" I asked her.

"What could I do?" she replied with a smile. "The money was gone." Still, she realized one important thing: The problem was not the stock market, the problem was her inexperience with investing. "So I set out to become smart about investing and do it right the next time," she told me.

And that's just what she did. She read books (like the one you're reading now) as well as financial magazines and newsletters, she took classes, and in general she made an effort to get smart about investing. Did she invest perfectly from then on? Of course not. She made plenty of mistakes at first, but she learned from them, and over the years she built a million-dollar portfolio.

People often make a financial mistake, get bad advice, and then give up on their dream of financial security. *Don't let this happen to you.* You now know more than most people about how to avoid the most common mistakes that can be made with your investment dollars. Are there more pitfalls out there? Absolutely. Might you stumble into one of them? Possibly. But don't let that keep you from getting where you want to go. As you continue on your journey and acquire more knowledge of and control over your finances, you will start to be able to spot bad money decisions a mile away. It will be as if they have a huge sign on them reading "Kiss your money good-bye!"

Yes, you should be careful, but don't become overcautious. By learning to avoid the common pitfalls investors make, you can minimize your risk and put yourself on the road to financial security. But remember—*the biggest mistake you can make is* not *to become an investor.*

FOLLOW THE 12 COMMANDMENTS OF ATTRACTING GREATER WEALTH

So far on our journey to financial independence, we've concentrated mainly on how to make the most out of the financial resources you have—the best way, in other words, to slice up your financial pie. Now let's talk about how to bake a bigger pie.

The thing to keep in mind in this regard is that it's a mistake to separate your "money life" from your personal or professional life. It's not that your life should revolve around money. It's that your personal financial situation is inextricably linked to everything else that's important to you: your goals, your dreams, your health, your security, your freedom.

The fact is, the tools I hope you have acquired in the course of reading this book apply to much more than just money management. The good habits you should be developing as part of your journey to financial independence—things like focus and discipline and values-based behavior—can reinforce success in every aspect of your life. Indeed, as you change your financial behavior to match your values, you'll probably start noticing positive things happening in other areas of your life as well: your health, relationships, career, hobbies. At the very least, you're bound to become a lot more aware of the extent to which the choices you're making in your work life and personal life reflect (or *don't* reflect) your values. And that, in turn, will enable you to make more intelligent decisions about which professional and personal options make the most sense for you.

Remember, though, that it's not enough simply to understand intellectually the concepts we have discussed in this book. It's not enough simply to believe that by following the steps I've laid out, you can take control of your financial destiny. You have to apply what you've learned here. You have to go out and actually do it.

Now, that doesn't mean you have to climb Mount Everest. One of the most common misconceptions people have is the belief that in order to make massive changes in their lives, they have to do incredibly difficult and special things that require enormous effort and complicated skills. As a result of this misconception, most people get defeated—*they defeat themselves*—before they even get started. Don't let that happen to you! The point of this book is that you can make dramatic changes in your life—and ultimately help and support the people around you—just by using the simple tools I've provided.

But you have to *use* them.

The last tool I'm going to give you may be the most powerful one of all. That's because it possesses the ability to make it much easier for you to accomplish everything we've set out to do in the first six steps of our journey. The tool I'm going to give you now will enable you to earn more money quickly.

Now, I know what you're thinking. Didn't I say that income didn't matter?

That's true; I did, and I still believe it. But as I said, the whole point of this book is that financial success is based on the cultivation of good habits—that to be financially secure and able to achieve your dreams, you need to have the right habits, tools, and beliefs. Now that you have them all, I want to make the process of getting where you want to go that much easier.

GETTING PAID WHAT YOU'RE WORTH

One of the defining characteristics of a Smart Woman is that she is paid what she is worth. But getting paid what you are worth doesn't just happen to you; you have to act to ensure that you get what should be yours.

I am convinced that most people earn 10 to 30 percent less than they could be earning if they just took control over their careers. Think about this for a second. What if you could easily increase your paycheck by 10 to 30 percent over the next few months? Before you read this book, you might have thought about rewarding yourself with a fancy vacation or some new clothes or maybe even a new car. But now, with your new insights, think about what amazing things you could do with your extra income: go back to school, travel the world, have enough to retire on by the time you're 55. Rather than making one-time purchases that satisfy instant cravings, you will be making an investment in yourself that's permanent. It is these lasting contributions to your life that reflect a real, substantive change in *you*.

Now, how do you increase your wealth so that you can make these critical investments?

You don't have to get this extra money just through a paycheck, of course. Whether you are a career woman in a corporation, are self-employed, own your own business, or are managing an inheritance or alimony payments, there are certain behaviors and habits that will allow you to attract the wealth you deserve—as long as you decide to take control. These "rules"—which I call the 12 Commandments of Attracting Greater Wealth—aren't all about earning, however. One is even about giving it away! But, as you'll see, they are all about taking an active role in your life and making intelligent decisions rather than allowing fate to control you.

The 12 Commandments of Attracting Greater Wealth

Back in the introduction, I told you a story about a woman named Lauren whom I had coached on both her personal finances and her career. As a result of my coaching, Lauren was able to double her income in less than six months. Today she earns a six-figure salary and is significantly happier than she used to be. What I taught her can be boiled down to the following.

> **COMMANDMENT 1**
> WHATEVER YOU EARN RIGHT NOW IS EXACTLY WHAT YOU
> ACCEPTED.

People constantly complain about how much money they make—or, rather, how much they *don't* make. I call them the gripers. They say things like "My boss doesn't appreciate me," or "I haven't gotten a raise in over a year," or "All my hard work and effort goes unnoticed," or "If only I worked for XYZ Company, I'd make twice what I'm a making now," or—and this is the classic line—"I'm in a dead-end career going nowhere."

I'm sure you know someone who's said something like that. As a friend, you probably nodded in sympathy and empathized about his or her situation. This sharing process is what I call group griping, and it is a national phenomenon that seems to take place at lunch, by the water cooler, or (God forbid) during a cigarette break. I'm sorry, folks, but I've got no sympathy for gripers. And I don't think you should either. Indeed, for the next 30 days I want you to say to yourself whenever you hear one of these people going on about how lousy his or her situation is: "If their work is so unappreciated, they should get off their collective butts and change their destiny."

That's basically what I told Lauren after listening to her complain for the thousandth time about how she was working 70-hour weeks and not being paid what she was worth. I politely but firmly pointed out that I had been hearing her tell me the same story for more than two years. "You should either stop griping," I said, "or go out and get a job that pays you what you think you're entitled to."

Lauren was earning $55,000 a year, and she insisted she knew people in jobs similar to hers whose salaries topped $80,000. The problem, she said, was that even if she could prove she was underpaid, her bosses were too cheap to give her the raise she deserved.

"In that case," I said, "you're working at the wrong company. You should find yourself a new employer."

"But how?" Lauren wailed.

I asked her to name one company that was paying the people who did what she did $80,000 a year.

She did.

"Well," I said, "that's where you should be working." I suggested she call this company, explain that she worked for the competition but was exploring other opportunities, and ask if they thought it might make sense for her to come in and talk to them.

Lauren did just that. Within five weeks, she had a job offer not for $80,000 but for $115,000 plus a signing bonus! The moral of this story is simple. You get paid what you are willing to accept. If you think you are worth more than you are being paid, then go out and discover if you are right. If you are, you will find someone willing to pay you significantly more than you're currently earning. If it turns out you are wrong, then at least you'll have a good reason to stop your griping and start focusing on ways to add more value.

> ### COMMANDMENT 2
> SOCIETY REWARDS PEOPLE WHO ADD VALUE.

The single greatest way to increase your income is to add value. This is one of the most important lessons I ever learned. I learned it from motivational speaker Zig Zigler. Zig says that in order for you to get out of life what you want, you have to help other people get out of life what they want.

It doesn't get any more simple than that. If you run a business, you need to determine what it is that your customers want and then you need to give it to them. In other words, you must add value to their lives. Businesses that are failing generally have one problem in common: They are not adding enough value to their customers' lives.

This concept applies every bit as much to employees as to entrepreneurs. If you work for a boss, you need to ask him or her what specifically you can do to "add more value" to the company. (The same holds true if you are a professional with clients.) Don't ask if you are doing a good job. That means nothing. Sit down with your boss or client and say, "I'm making it a goal to improve who I am and I need your help. I want to become even better at what I do. In other words, I want to add more value to our relationship. What can I do specifically to accomplish that?"

Trust me on this. Even if you never did anything else of note, this one action would boost your standing with your boss or client. (By the way, this works with significant others and children too. Just thought I'd mention that.)

> ### COMMANDMENT 3
> DISCOVER WHAT MAKES YOU UNIQUELY VALUABLE.

We are all blessed with special talents that make us unique. Some people discover their talent at a young age and from then on focus their lives on honing it until they are rewarded by society. We call the most successful of these people stars.

I'm not just talking about sports or movie stars. Stars exist in every realm. There are star salespeople, and star mothers, and star accountants, and so on. The question you need to ask yourself (or ask others who know you) is what makes you uniquely valuable. What is it that you have to offer?

Chances are there is something that you love doing. Most likely it's something you're good at. (Most of us tend to like doing stuff we do well.) The point is, if you focus on this thing you love doing, you can become uniquely valuable enough at it that you can be paid significantly to do it. There's a book called *Do What You Love and the Money Will Follow* written by Marsha Sinetar. It's an excellent book I recommend, and I also think that it is a fair statement.

> ### COMMANDMENT 4
> DON'T WASTE YOUR TIME ON THINGS OTHER PEOPLE
> SHOULD BE DOING FOR YOU.

Time is our most precious asset. Yet most people waste it doing stuff that someone else can do. Figure out what you make an hour and then never do something that you can pay someone else less to do.

When I say figure out what you make an hour, I mean figure out how much of your time you actually spend doing the thing that you get paid to do—the thing that makes you uniquely valuable. Let's say you earn $3,000 a month as a salesperson. The fact is, you're not spending every minute of the 200 or so hours you work each month meeting with prospects. Most likely you spend only a fraction of your time doing that—say, just 5 hours a week, or 20 hours a month. But that's what you're being paid for. So what you really make is $150 an hour (when you're selling).

People in business often confuse the hours they spend at work with the hours they actually work. They are not the same thing. Work is the thing you do that gets you a result. If you are in sales, only a small portion of what you do actually produces a result. Everything else is process. You are not paid for process. You are not paid to type letters, seal envelopes, photocopy documents, make phone calls, and so on. You are paid to get results.

Most people major in what I call minor stuff; in other words, they fritter away their time on trivialities. A Smart Woman focuses on what she does that makes her uniquely valuable. Everything else, she delegates.

If you happen to have a job that involves the process of typing letters, photocopying documents, answering the telephone, and so on, then you need to focus on what it is you do that adds the most value. Once you've figure that out, see if you can get your boss to let you delegate some of your nonessential tasks. The best way to persuade your boss is to get him or her to explain how you might add more value to the company. Then you can make a case for how delegating nonessential tasks could help you accomplish this.

COMMANDMENT 5
CLEAN UP THE MESSES IN YOUR LIFE.

Most people are drowning in paper at their office. Open the average workers' file cabinets and you'll find them crammed with papers that have not been read in years. The result is more than just a mess. According to time-management expert Jeffrey Mayer, author of *Time Management for Dummies,* most people spend about an hour a day looking for papers that are lost on the top of their desks—60 percent of which aren't needed anyway!

Now, think about this for a second. If the average person is really spending an hour a day looking for stuff, that's about 22 hours a month, or 264 hours a year, down the drain. That's a whole month of working time. For some people (maybe even you) it could be worse.

So throw yourself a life preserver. First thing this weekend, go to your office and start cleaning it out.

Here's a series of hints on how to get the job done quickly and easily.

1. Start with the drawers. Open every file and ask yourself three questions: Have I looked at this in the last 12 months? Do I

need to hold on to it for legal reasons? Is this file or paper of critical value? If the answer is no, throw it out.

2. Do the same thing with all the newspapers and magazines in your office. If you have been saving anything to read for more than 30 days, throw it away. Period. Just get rid of it. Obviously it's not as important as you thought it was; if it were, you'd have gotten to it by now

3. Commit to the following creed: "I will not keep anything on my desk for more than one week. At the end of the week, I'll either take it home to read or I will throw it away."

4. Make keeping your office clean a priority. A clean office shows whomever you work for—your boss or your clients—that you are organized and on top of things. Don't kid yourself into believing that it's okay to be messy. The excuse "But I've always been a slob" simply does not fly in the working world. A clean office not only makes an immediate impression, it also makes you feel better about yourself and allows you to be more productive.

The messes in your life don't stop at the office. You should clean up your home as well. To make the process of getting your home cleaned fast, let me make a simple suggestion that I learned from my personal coach, Dan Sullivan, at his program Strategic Coach. Go through your home (closets, drawers, etc.) and garage and ask yourself three simple things: Have I used this item in the last six months, do I love it, is it irreplaceable? If the answer to any of these questions is no, seriously consider throwing it out. Trust me on this—giving both your office and your home a good solid top-to-bottom cleaning (meaning a massive throwing-away of nonessential items) is one of the most instantly motivating and empowering things you can do to take immediate control over your life.

COMMANDMENT 6
POST YOUR GOALS IN YOUR OFFICE FOR EVERYONE TO SEE.

Remember those goals you worked out in Step Three? Well, in addition to putting them on the bathroom mirror at home and in your Day-Timer, put them up in your office. That's mainly for your benefit, but chances are your bosses, coworkers, or employees will see them as well. Don't be embarrassed to have your goals in view. Be proud. At the very least, if your coworkers or employees know your goals, you may feel more motivated to stick to them. At the most, your coworkers or boss may offer to help you make your goal attainable.

COMMANDMENT 7
INVEST IN YOURSELF.

For some reason, once most people leave school (and it does not matter whether we're talking about high school, college, or graduate school), they stop valuing the process of learning. This is a big mistake. The fact is, you should seriously consider putting aside some money each year to improve what you do and who you are. The common denominator among really successful people is that they consistently seek new skills and better tools. The self-help movement is not a fad. Successful people know that the power of one idea can change your life forever. But less than 5 percent of Americans read books like this one. That's because they have stopped investing in themselves and their ability to grow. Make a commitment to take classes, read new books, and listen to motivational tapes. They can propel you to a higher quality of life and happiness.

COMMANDMENT 8
LEARN TO BE A "GO-GIVER."

John Templeton, the billionaire investor and renowned philanthropist, once said that the key to life is not to be a go-getter but a "go-giver." This one statement changed my life. It is so easy to get caught up in whatever it is we are trying to accomplish, which often leads us to believe that we should be a go-getter. But a go-getter focuses on getting. A go-giver focuses on giving.

Ultimately, it gets back to the concept of adding value. What the truly successful person does is to add value and give back. I'm not just talking about giving financially to charity but also about giving time to the people who need it. This can even start at home with your children or at the office with a new employee. Seek to be the person who is there with a helping hand. People remember this, and ultimately what you give (both good and bad) does come back—in spades.

COMMANDMENT 9
MAKE A DECISION.

Your financial future can be shaped the moment you make a financial decision.

Remember the basic philosophy on which this book is built: When it comes to your future, you can be either proactive or reactive. Most people never make up their minds about the things that are important to them. They let their life happen to them rather then making it happen.

Right now, I'll bet, there are decisions involving your career or your personal life that you have been putting off. Well, get off the fence and make a decision. The only way you go forward is to decide to. So ask yourself: What one big decision have I been avoiding? I suggest that you stop avoiding it and act.

COMMANDMENT 10
FOCUS ON BEING A "GO-TO GAL."

In sports, certain athletes are known as "go-to guys." These are the players who can be counted on to deliver in a pinch. The idea is that when the game is on the line, others give the ball to the guy who can make the play—the go-to guy.

These days more and more women are making names for themselves in both sports and business. That's what a Smart Woman wants to do. She wants to become known as the type of woman who rises above the competition, who can make it happen. She wants to be a "go-to gal."

Whether you own your own business or work for someone else, you want to be someone other people can count on. What does it take to accomplish this? Fortunately, not a whole lot.

One of the amazing things about the business world today is that it is filled with people who are satisfied with being mediocre. As depressing as that may sound, it's also great news for Smart Women, because it means you don't have to do all that much to stand out. In fact, here's all it takes to make more money, earn the respect of your colleagues, and become known as a **"go-to gal."**

1. Show up early.
2. Have a plan and implement it.
3. Always do what you say you will do.
4. Take total responsibility.
5. Be polite.
6. Smile.

These six things may not seem like much, but the fact is, most people don't bother to do them, either personally or professionally. So give it a try. How could it hurt to be a woman who shows up early with a plan, always follows through on what she promises, takes responsibility, acts politely, and does it all with a smile? You may be stunned to discover how lavishly the world rewards such simple good manners and behavior. Remember—simple is good, simple works!

COMMANDMENT 11
TO MAKE MORE MONEY, YOU HAVE TO ASK FOR MORE MONEY.

In sales, they say the key to success is learning that you have to ask for the order. But salespeople aren't the only ones who need to learn that lesson. Everything in life that's important requires you to "ask for the order." From getting promoted to getting your children to pick up their clothes, you're not going to get what you really want if you don't ask for it. Yes, if you do all the other commandments I've listed, you're bound to be rewarded in some way or another—but if you are going to be able to charge your customer more or get that raise you want and deserve, ultimately you're going to have to ask for it.

But here's what not to do. Don't go and tell your customer or boss, "I want more money." What you must do is remember Commandment 2, which says that you should add more value. Once you are adding more value, you will be entitled to ask for more pay. If, like my client Lauren, you believe you already are adding significant value, then go make your case. Show how you add value and what you believe that value is worth in the marketplace today. Cost is an issue only when value is lacking. Employers and customers will gladly pay top dollar for top services that produce top results. The key is that you must add that top value, top service, and top results—and then ask for the money you have earned the right to receive.

COMMANDMENT 12
LIVE BY THE PHILOSOPHY OF MIHN!

MIHN stands for Make It Happen Now! In life I believe there are really four types of people. Those who watch things happen, those who wonder what happened, those who complain about what happened, and those who *MAKE THINGS HAPPEN NOW!* As you go about your life, ask yourself regularly which person are you being. Life is not a dress rehearsal. You get in life exactly what you go for. I say the heck with being a spectator and jump in.

TAKE THE TIME TO SMELL THE ROSES

We have now reached the end of our journey together—though your individual journey to financial security and independence is just beginning. I want to close this book with a reminder of something that I myself often neglect. In our efforts to build a secure future and protect our financial destiny, we should never forget that the greatest asset we have is life. Unfortunately, life is of limited duration and is not guaranteed. There is no insurance we can buy that will give us back our life or make it possible for us to bring back those we love.

My point is that you shouldn't get so consumed with your financial journey that you don't spend enough time sharing moments with the people you love. As you take control over your finances and your career, please remember to let those you really care about know how much they mean to you. The words "I love you" are three of the most powerful and underutilized words in the English language. If you love someone, let that person know. Not only will it make you feel better, but you will add more value to them spiritually than you will ever know.

Now that you've learned what it takes to become financially secure and reach your dreams, my final wish for you is that you enjoy the journey. The *Smart Women Finish Rich* process is not about pain or sacrifice. You don't have to give up the fun part of life to become a women in total control of her financial future. You can become financially secure, reach your dreams, and still be a woman who has time to smell the roses.

Live Your Life with No Regrets

Shortly before she passed away, I asked my Grandma Bach if she had any regrets in life. She said the only ones she had involved not things she did but the risks she didn't take. With that in mind, I'd like to suggest the following: If you believe you are going to be alive five years from now (and I hope you do), then there are really only two potential outcomes. You either will be five years older and have achieved your dreams (or at least be well on the way toward achieving them) because you have used the tools in this book and gone for it, or you will just be five years older.

The choice is yours. Take the tools in this book and start now to begin your personal journey to the new woman you want to be in five years—more financially secure than you are now, more successful in your career, happier, even healthier. And remember: If you encounter a few setbacks along the way, don't let them deter you. You're not suppose to get everything right the first time. (And think about this: Mistakes and failures are just market research for your future successes!)

As you grow and take greater control of your life, please know that my thoughts and prayers will be with you. This journey we call life is an incredible gift, and I hope that in some small way this book has touched you for the better. I want you to know that I both respect you and admire your desire to be smart and finish rich—and that I look forward to meeting you some day . . . along the journey.

WHERE DOES YOUR MONEY *REALLY* GO?

One of the most important parts of getting your financial life together is having a solid grasp on exactly what your current cash flow is. To do this, use the worksheet below.

First, determine how much you earn . . .

Your Income

Wages, salary, tips, commissions, self-employment income	$_____
Dividends from stocks, bonds, mutual funds, savings accounts, CDs, etc.	$_____
Income from rental property	$_____
Income from trust accounts (usually death benefits from an estate)	$_____
Alimony, child support, social security widows benefits	$_____
Social Security benefits	$_____
Other income	$_____

TOTAL MONTHLY INCOME $_____

Second, determine what you spend

Your Expenses

Taxes

Federal income taxes $\underline{\hspace{2cm}}$
State income taxes $\underline{\hspace{2cm}}$
FICA (Social Security Taxes) $\underline{\hspace{2cm}}$
Property taxes $\underline{\hspace{2cm}}$

TOTAL TAXES $\underline{\hspace{2cm}}$

Housing

Mortgage payments or rent on primary residence $\underline{\hspace{2cm}}$
Mortgage payment on rental or income property $\underline{\hspace{2cm}}$
Utilities $\underline{\hspace{2cm}}$
Homeowners or renter's insurance $\underline{\hspace{2cm}}$
Repairs or home maintenance $\underline{\hspace{2cm}}$
Cleaning service $\underline{\hspace{2cm}}$
Television cable $\underline{\hspace{2cm}}$
Home phone $\underline{\hspace{2cm}}$
Landscaping and pool service $\underline{\hspace{2cm}}$
Monthly Internet service $\underline{\hspace{2cm}}$
Condo or association dues $\underline{\hspace{2cm}}$

TOTAL HOUSING $\underline{\hspace{2cm}}$

Auto

Car loan or lease $\underline{\hspace{2cm}}$
Gas $\underline{\hspace{2cm}}$
Car Insurance $\underline{\hspace{2cm}}$
Car phone $\underline{\hspace{2cm}}$
Repairs or service $\underline{\hspace{2cm}}$
Parking $\underline{\hspace{2cm}}$
Bridge tolls $\underline{\hspace{2cm}}$

TOTAL AUTO $\underline{\hspace{2cm}}$

Insurance

Life insurance $_____

Disability insurance $_____

Long term care insurance $_____

Liability insurance (umbrella policy) $_____

TOTAL INSURANCE $_____

Food

Groceries $_____

Food outside of home $_____

TOTAL FOOD $_____

Personal Care

Clothing $_____

Cleaning/drycleaning $_____

Cosmetics $_____

Health club dues and/or personal trainer $_____

Entertainment $_____

Country club dues $_____

Association memberships $_____

Vacations $_____

Hobbies $_____

Education $_____

Magazines $_____

Gifts $_____

TOTAL PERSONAL CARE $_____

Medical

Health care insurance $_____

Prescriptions and monthly medicines $_____

Doctor or dentist expenses $_____

TOTAL MEDICAL $_____

Miscellaneous

Credit card expenses $_____

Loan payments $_____

Alimony or child support $_____

Anything you can think of that I missed! $_____

TOTAL MISCELLANEOUS EXPENSES $_____

TOTAL MONTHLY EXPENSES $_____

Murphy's Law Factor

Take the total expenses and increase by 10 percent $_____

Total Income

Minus total monthly expenses $_____

Net cash flow (available for savings or investments) $_____

Appendix 2

FINANCIAL INVENTORY WORKSHEET

DETERMINING YOUR NET WORTH

STEP ONE: FAMILY INFORMATION

Client Name _____ Date of Birth _____ Age ____

Nickname _____

Spouse's Name _____ Date of Birth _____ Age ____

Nickname _____

Mailing Address _____

City _____ State _____ Zip Code _____

Home Phone# _____

Work Phone# _____ Fax # _____

Spouse's Work # _____ Spouse's Fax # _____

E-mail_____ Spouse's E-mail_____

SS# _____ Spouse's SS# _____

Employer _____ Job Title _____

Spouse's Employer _____ Job Title _____

Are You Retired? Yes _____ Date Retired _____ No _____ Planned Retirement Date _____

Is Your Spouse Retired? Yes— Date Retired _____ No _____ Planned Retirement Date _____

Marital Status: Single ____ Married ____ Divorced ____ Separated ____ Widowed ____

Children   Date of Birth   SS#

Name 1) _____ _____ _____

2) _____ _____ _____

3) _____ _____ _____

4) _____ _____ _____

5) _____ _____ _____

Dependents

Do You Have Any Family Members That Are Financially Dependent Upon You or Could Be in the Future?

(i.e., Parents, Grandparents, Adult Children, etc.)

Yes ____ No ____

Name 1) _____ Age ____ Relationship _____

2) _____ Age ____ Relationship _____

3) _____ Age ____ Relationship _____

STEP TWO: PERSONAL INVESTMENTS
(DO NOT INCLUDE RETIREMENT ACCOUNTS HERE)

Cash Reserves

List Amount in Banks, Savings & Loans, and Credit Unions

Name of Bank Institution	Type of Account	Current Balance	Interest Rate
Example: Bank of America	Checking/Savings/Money Market	$10,000.00	2%
1.)			
2.)			
3.)			
4.)			
5.)			

Fixed Income

List Fixed Income Investments

Example: C.D., Treasury Bills, Notes, Bonds, Tax-Free Bonds, Series EE Savings Bonds	Dollar Amount	Current %	Maturity Date
.)			
.)			
.)			
.)			

Stocks

Name of Company	Number of Shares	Price Purchased	Approximate Market Value	Date Purchased
.)				
)				
.)				
)				
)				

Do You Have Stock Certificates in a Security Deposit Box? Yes _____ No _____

Mutual Funds and/or Brokerage Accounts

Name of Brokerage Firm/Mutual Fund	Number of Shares	Cost Basis	Approximate Market Value	Date Purchased
)				
)				
)				
)				
)				
)				

Annuities

Company	Annuitant/Owner	Interest Rate	Approximate Market Value	Date Purchased
•				
•				
•				

Other Assets (i.e., Business Ownership, etc.)   Approximate Market Value

•	$
	$
	$

STEP THREE: RETIREMENT ACCOUNTS

Are You Participating in an Employer Sponsored Retirement Plan? (These Include Tax-Deferred Retirement Plans Such As 401(k) Plans, 403 (b) Plans and 457 Plans) Yes _____ No _____

Name of Company Where Your Money Is	Type of Plan	Approximate Value	% You Contribute

You:

1.) _____ _____ _____ _____
2.) _____ _____ _____ _____
3.) _____ _____ _____ _____

Spouse:

1.) _____ _____ _____ _____
2.) _____ _____ _____ _____
3.) _____ _____ _____ _____

Do You Have Money Sitting in a Company Plan You No Longer Work For?

Yes _____ No _____ Balance _____ When Did You Leave The Company? _____

Spouse:

Yes _____ No _____ Balance _____ When Did He/She Leave the Company? _____

Self-Directed Retirement Plans

Are You Participating in a Retirement Plan? (These include IRAs, Roth IRAs, SEP-IRAs, SAR-SEP IRAs and SIMPLE PLANS)

Name of Institution Where Your Money Is	Type of Plan	Approximate Value

You:

1.) _____ _____ _____
2.) _____ _____ _____
3.) _____ _____ _____
4.) _____ _____ _____
5.) _____ _____ _____

Spouse:

1.) _____ _____ _____
2.) _____ _____ _____
3.) _____ _____ _____
4.) _____ _____ _____
5.) _____ _____ _____

STEP FOUR: REAL ESTATE

Do You Rent or Own Your Home?

Own _____ /Monthly Mortgage Is _____

Rent _____ /Monthly Rent Is _____

Approximate Value of Primary Home $ _____

Mortgage Balance $ _____

Equity in Home _____

Length of Loan _____

Interest Rate of Loan _____ Is Loan Fixed or Variable? _____

Do You Own A Second Home?

Approximate Value of Second Home $ _____

Mortgage Balance $ _____

Equity in Home _____

Length of Loan _ _____

Interest Rate of Loan _____ Is Loan Fixed or Variable? _____

Any Other Real Estate Owned?

Approximate Value $ _____

Mortgage Balance $ _____

Equity In Home _____

Length of Loan _____

Interest Rate of Loan _____ Is Loan Fixed or Variable? _____

STEP FIVE: ESTATE PLANNING

Do You Have a Will or Living Trust in Place? Yes _____ No _____

Date It Was Last Reviewed? _____

Who Helped You Create It? Attorney Name _____

Address _____

Phone Number _____ Fax _____

Is Your Home Held in The Trust or Is It Held in Joint or Community Property? _____

Risk Management/Insurance

Do You Have a Protection Plan In Place for Your Family? Yes _____ No _____

Insurance Company	Type of Insurance (i.e,. Whole Life, Term, Variable, etc.)	Death Benefit	Cash Value	Annual Premium
_____	_____	_____	_____	_____
_____	_____	_____	_____	_____
_____	_____	_____	_____	_____

Tax Planning

Do You Have Your Taxes Professionally Prepared? Yes _____ No _____

Name of Accountant/CPA _____

Address _____

Phone Number _____ Fax _____

What Was Your Last Year's Taxable Income? _____1

Estimated Tax Bracket? _____ %

STEP SIX: CASH FLOW

Income

Your Est. Monthly Income _____ Estimated Annual Income _____

Spouse's Estimated Monthly Income _____ Estimated Annual Income _____

Rental Property Income: Monthly _____ Annually _____

Other Income (Partnerships, Social Security, Pension, Dividend Checks, etc.)

Type of Income   Monthly   Annually

1.) _____   _____   _____

2.) _____   _____   _____

3.) _____   _____   _____

Expenses

Use the Where Does Your Money *Really* Go Form to Figure Your Estimate

Monthly Estimated Expenses _____ Annual Estimated Expenses _____

STEP SEVEN: NET CASH FLOW

What Do You Earn a Month After Taxes? $ _____

What Do You Estimate You Spend?   − $ _____

Net Cash Flow   = $ _____

STEP EIGHT: NET WORTH

Net Worth

Total Assets $ _____

− Total Liabilities   − $ _____

= Estimated Net Worth $ _____

STEP NINE: FINANCIAL OBJECTIVES

What Are Your Current Financial Goals and Objectives? _____

_____

_____

Is There Anything in Particular That You Are Currently Concerned With Regarding Your Financial Situation? _____

_____

_____

Are You Anticipating Any Major Life Style Changes That Could Require Money (i.e., Retirement, Divorce, Inheritance, Children Going to College, etc.)? _____

_____

_____

What Is the Best Financial Decision You Have Ever Made? _____

_____

_____

Have You Made Any Financial Decisions That You Regret? _____

_____

_____

Do You Own Any Investments or Real Estate That You Are Planning to Sell or Want to Sell in the Near Future? _____

_____

_____

If You Were to Hire a Financial Advisor, What Are the Three Most Important Things You Would Want Your Advisor to Do for You? _____

_____

_____

Any Additional Comments? _____

_____

_____

_____

I have read literally hundreds of books on motivation and investing. I believe no one person or company has the monopoly on good ideas, and I would like to share with you some of my favorite authors and coaches who have influenced me. I highly recommend the following authors' and speakers' books and programs.

ANTHONY ROBBINS: Tony Robbins today is regarded as one of the world's greatest motivational speakers and peak performance coaches. I have read all of his books, listened to all of his audio programs (more than once), and attended all of his seminar programs. I have also had the privilege of teaching at his Financial Mastery program three times. You have not experienced a motivational seminar until you've attended one of Tony's programs. They are awesome. I highly recommend his books and programs to anyone wanting to improve the quality of his or her life. To learn more about the programs, books, and audio products, you can reach Robbins Research directly by calling 800-445-8183.

DAN SULLIVAN: Dan Sullivan runs a three-year coaching program for entrepreneurs called Strategic Coach, which I attend every 90 days. This program is designed for entrepreneurs who want to clean out the messes in their lives and focus on what their unique abilities really are. This program teaches you how to increase your business while having more free time to appreciate and enjoy your life. The simplicity of his program and the focus it can give you is truly life changing. To learn more about the program and the products you can call Strategic Coach at 800-387-3206.

BILL BACHRACH: Bill Bachrach is one of the leading coaches to the financial advisor industry. His book *Values Based Selling* and his Trusted Advisor Program teach financial advisors how to help their clients tap into their values about money. I have attended his program and believe strongly that if you are a financial advisor you owe it to yourself and your clients to read his book and learn about his products and seminars. Bachrach & Associates can be reached toll-free at 800-347-3707.

I would also like to recommend the following books:

Awaken the Giant Within: How to Take Immediate Control of Your Mental, Emotional, Physical & Financial Destiny! Anthony Robbins, (Fireside, 1991)

Beating the Street: How to Use What You Already Know to Make Money in the Market, Peter Lynch and John Rothchild, (Fireside, 1993)

Chicken Soup for the Woman's Soul, Marci Shimoff and Jennifer Hawthorne, (Health Communications)

Don't Sweat the Small Stuff . . . and It's All Small Stuff: Simple Ways to Keep the Little Things from Taking Over Your Life, Richard Carlson, (Hyperion Press, 1997)

How to Win Friends & Influence People, Dale Carnegie, (Pocket Books, 1990)

Jesus CEO: Using Ancient Wisdom for Visionary Leadership, Laurie Beth Jones (Hyperion Press, 1995)

The Millionaire Next Door: The Surprising Secrets of America's Wealthy, Thomas J. Stanley and William S. Danko, (Longstreet Press, 1996)

The Money Club: How We Taught Ourselves the Secret to a Secure Financial Future and How You Can, Too, Marilyn Crockett, (Simon & Schuster, 1997)

9 Steps To Financial Freedom, Suze Orman, (Crown, 1998)

One Up on Wall Street, Peter Lynch and John Rothchild, (Penguin USA, 1990)

Prince Charming Isn't Coming: How Women Get Smart About Money, Barbara Stanny, (Viking Press, 1997)

Real Moments, Barbara DeAngelis, (DTP, 1995)

The Richest Man in Babylon, George S. Clason, (New American Library, 1988)

The Roaring 2000's: How to Achieve Personal and Financial Success in the Greatest Boom in History, Harry S. Dent, (Simon & Schuster, 1998)

Swim with the Sharks: Without Being Eaten Alive: Outsell, Outmanage, Outmotivate, and Outnegotiate Your Competition, Harvey Mackay, (Ballantine Books, 1988)

Think and Grow Rich, Napoleon Hill, (Ballantine Books, 1998)

The Truth About Money: Because Money Doesn't Come With Instructions, Ric Edelman and Cal Thomas, (Georgetown University Press, 1996)

Index

David L. Bach is widely recognized as one of the country's leading financial advisors and educators. A senior vice president of a major New York brokerage firm, David is a partner of The Bach Group in Orinda, California, which manages over a half-billion dollars for individual investors.

In addition to being a full-time financial advisor, David is the national bestselling author of *Smart Women Finish Rich*. He is nationally recognized as a crusader for women's financial empowerment and has hosted his own public television special on PBS called "Smart Women Finish Rich," which has aired nationally. His "Smart Women Finish Rich" seminars have received enormous praise and are currently being taught by hundreds of financial advisors around the country in over 100 cities. It is estimated that in 2000 alone, over 100,000 women will have attended "Smart Women Finish Rich" classes.

A nationally recognized keynote speaker, David speaks each year at over fifty major events, educating women and men on the importance of financial empowerment. David has appeared hundreds of times in the television, radio, and print media, most recently on CNBC, PBS, Women.com, IVillage, and CBS Marketwatch.com, and in print publications that include the *New York Times, Business Week,* the *Boston Globe,* the *San Francisco Chronicle,* the *Los Angeles Times, Individual Investor, Working Women, Family Circle,* and *Elegant Bride.*

He is the president of finishrich.com, whose mission is to help "Smart People Live and Finish Rich" . . . by educating men, women, and families about how to take charge of their finances. He is currently writing his second book, *Smart Couples Finish Rich,* which will be released in 2001.

David is married and lives with his wife, Michelle, in San Francisco, California.

How to Reach Us

If you would like more information about *Smart Women Finish Rich*, I have developed other products and services and can offer you information on:

- Keynote speaking
- "Smart Women Finish Rich" seminars
- "Smart Women Finish Rich" and "Finish Rich" products
- The Bach Group Retirement Planning Services

Please feel free to write to me and send an SASE to:

finishrich.com
David Bach
P.O. Box 996
Orinda, CA 94563
Phone: toll free at 1-877-ASK-BACH (1-877-275-2224)
Website: www.finishrich.com
E-mail: DavidLBach@aol.com

To everyone who has written and e-mailed me . . . THANK YOU from the bottom of my heart . . . I am incredibly grateful and humbled by the amount of letters and e-mails I have received thus far. If this book has made a significant impact on you, please know that I would like to hear about your successes!

Finally, due to legal liabilities, please understand that I cannot answer personal financial questions through e-mail or regular mail.